Rural urbanism

Manchester University Press

Rural urbanism

London landscapes
in the early nineteenth century

Dana Arnold

Manchester University Press

Manchester and New York

distributed exclusively in the USA by Palgrave

Published by Manchester University Press
Oxford Road, Manchester M13 9NR, UK
and Room 400, 175 Fifth Avenue, New York, NY 10010, USA
www.manchesteruniversitypress.co.uk

Distributed exclusively in the USA by
Palgrave, 175 Fifth Avenue, New York,
NY 10010, USA

Distributed exclusively in Canada by
UBC Press, University of British Columbia, 2029 West Mall,
Vancouver, BC, Canada V6T 1Z2

British Library Cataloguing-in-Publication Data
A catalogue record for this book is available from the British Library

Library of Congress Cataloging-in-Publication Data applied for

ISBN   0 7190 6820 7 *hardback*
EAN   978 0 7190 6820 1

First published 2005

14 13 12 11 10 09 08 07 06 05   10 9 8 7 6 5 4 3 2 1

Typeset
by Carnegie Publishing, Lancaster
Printed in Great Britain
by Biddles Ltd, King's Lynn

In memory of my father

Contents

List of tables

List of illustrations

Preface

This study aims to conceptualise our understanding of London as a city firmly rooted in land and the kinds of values associated with it. The principal focus is London landscapes in the early nineteenth century, which are shown to be the inheritors of sets of social and cultural relationships that evolved throughout the long eighteenth century. Some of the material presented in this book may be familiar: Bloomsbury, Regent's Park and Regent's Street have already been the subjects of historical investigation. Here their histories are recast within the investigative frame of this book. Moreover, a substantial amount of new archival information is presented throughout, which complements existing literature and opens up new fields of enquiry. The result is at times a forensic examination of the evidence in order to piece together the intricate economic processes that underpinned the development of London landscapes.

The relationship between the country and the city is not a new topic. But here urban and rural landscapes are compared according to their similarities rather than their differences, as has previously been the case. This enables us to think about urban landscapes as being like their rural counterparts. We can read them in terms of the process of improvement for the landowner whilst not forgetting that they are also cultural artefacts. My previous studies of the country house and its landscapes, and more recently urban experience and social life in London, have helped formulate the arguments presented in this book. In this work I attempt to move on from these geographically discrete enquiries to bridge the dominant country/ city divide in histories of the long eighteenth century.

This work has been supported by a Visiting Scholarship at the Getty Research Institute in Los Angeles and a Visiting Fellowship to CRASSH, University of Cambridge where I enjoyed the generous hospitality of King's College. I wish to thank these institutions for providing an extremely stimulating and collegial environment in which to work through my ideas for this book. My thanks also go to Dr Elizabeth McKellar, Professor M. H. Port and Professor Adrian Rifkin all of whom have shown great interest in the project. I am also indebted to the anonymous readers for Manchester University Press for their extremely helpful comments and observations. Any omissions and oversights remain my own. Finally, I wish to thank Dr Ken Haynes for being himself.

Dana Arnold, London

List of abbreviations

Notes on the text

Spelling and punctuation in quotations have been kept as in the original source. Units of measurement have not been modernised and are given in yards, feet and inches. Similarly, financial information remains in pounds, shillings and pence.

Introduction

This book examines an intensive period in the development of London, when in the opening decades of the nineteenth century a concerted attempt was made to transform the metropolis into a modern European capital. The re-imaging of London is considered for the first time in relation to attitudes towards land, landownership and use of landscapes. And it is argued that methods of land management and development, and the associative values of landscape usually connected with rural environments, were in fact portable between country and city and formed essential components in the re-imaging of the metropolis. The study begins with the eighteenth-century country house, which was an essential vehicle through which a patrician culture expressed individual and national identity through the complex interactions of architecture and landscape. The aesthetic vocabularies of antiquity and arcadia were appropriated and a new syntax formulated to create an effective national visual language with encoded meanings for the educated classes. Yet, during the long eighteenth century, society became increasingly urban and the uniformity and domestic scale of town planning might have stifled the use of this aesthetic language. Instead, however, we find this distinct set of intellectual systems and conventions are brought into the metropolis and used both in the furtherance of the social and cultural hegemony of the ruling elite and conversely in the creation of a modern metropolitan infrastructure which represented new sets of social and political values. Here, London's landscapes, whether a set piece of urban planning, as at Hyde Park Corner, or a royal park, could be 'read' by a viewing public whose senses were already trained to understand the meanings of self-consciously constructed rural spaces which explored the resonance between nature and antiquity.[1] This sensibility to landscape moved from country to city and London became an evocative arena for the public display of taste, wealth and status, social intercourse and the economic systems of urban life. As such, London represented at once notions of national identity and modernity, as well as nostalgia and reminiscence, which were understood and interpreted by its foreign and British publics.

House building and estate development were a core part of architectural production in England, if not the British Isles, in the long eighteenth century. Together they encapsulated the social, economic and political system where land ownership was an essential part of the definition of social class. Central to this was the country house, surrounded by its garden or parkland, and set within the working farmland of the estate.[2] These different kinds of land-scapes functioned as signifiers of the social and cultural pre-eminence of the ruling elite through their layout, function and size.[3] This was achieved partly through the design and symbolism of the landscape garden, and the feelings of admiration and nostalgia evoked by the use of classical architecture, antique remains and imitation ruins in the decoration of these landscapes. Here, the representation of Aeneas's journey at Stourhead, or the varied archi-tectural features of the landscape at Stowe, ranging from gothic through to classical, spring to mind as pertinent examples.[4] Additionally, the productivity, profitability and acreage of the working land was a status symbol in itself and generated the wealth necessary to adequately effect the necessary aesthetic. There is no doubt the new farming techniques employed on large estates such as Woburn in the latter part of the eighteenth century were admired for their ingenuity, efficacy and yield.[5] Moreover, picturesque systems of viewing landscape, including an appreciation of the romantic sublime, were based on working landscapes such as those at Richard Payne Knight's Downton and Uvedale Price's Foxley.[6]

The originality of country house architecture shows how imagi-native and various the reconfigurations of antique and Italianate architectural formulae could be. As such the country house, arguably the most important building type of the long eighteenth century, was an essential vehicle through which a patrician culture could express its values. This gave the ruling elite the freedom to express individual and national identity through the complex interaction of forms underpinned by a distinct set of intellectual systems and conven-tions. This was not merely trying to look like Rome. Instead, the aesthetic vocabulary of antiquity, including the orders and the temple portico, was appropriated and a new syntax formulated to create an effective national visual language with encoded meanings for the educated classes. Alongside this, the creation of country house landscapes with distinct ideological and political meanings helped create and augment the status of the ruling elite. But for the formula to work, the viewing public had to want to engage with the aesthetic. To this end picturesque systems of viewing disseminated through touristic literature, and the desirability of adequate educa-tion and *ergo* 'class' to appreciate references to antique architecture were powerful forces in the shaping of an appreciation of the country house and its estate. These attitudes towards the landed estates of the elite helped engender the illusion of inclusion into an exclusionary society that bound together different classes through a feeling of unity.[7]

Mapped against this is the emergence of London as an increasingly important metropolitan centre and core part of the evolving notion of nationalism and national consciousness. And there is a strong relationship between country house building and the urban development of London. At the beginning of the eighteenth century country house building ran far ahead of the development of London, but as this peaked towards the end of the century the pace of growth in London caught up and overtook it.[8] Yet there were similar players involved: the landed classes, who had consolidated their power through land ownership during the eighteenth century, now made their imprint on the capital.[9] The 'Great Estates', owned by the landed elite, became the subject of the same intensive development as their country house landscapes. Just as antiquity was vital for the aesthetics of country houses and landscape theory so it became a driving force in the shaping of the modern metropolis and the visual expression the importance of London as a centre for national government.

There is no doubt that, like the country, the city was exposed to an ever-expanding public during the long eighteenth century. This metropolitan symbol of the cultural and political hegemony of the ruling elite was consumed in a range of ways each adding a further layer of meaning to it. Moreover, the increase in home tourism coupled with a growing interest in architecture meant the urban environment was of interest to many levels of society and became a bench mark of class difference, social aspirations and architectural criticism. In this way, the metropolis embodied aspects of national identity that were recognised and decoded by its various publics.

Rather like a country house and its landscape the city can, then, be seen as a signifier of the complex social cultural and political forces that had shaped it, and as an emblem of the shift in focus from rural to urban environments in the latter part of the long eighteenth century. This had begun with the development of Bath, York and spa towns like Buxton, as well as the distinctive improvements made to the architecture and planning of the capital cities of Dublin and Edinburgh. Here antiquity was used as a mask for the intricate web of forces involved in the production of these distinctive urban environments. The uniformity – at least in aesthetic terms – lent by antique architectural forms acted as a kind of aesthetic palliative, in the same way as the picturesque in country house landscape design had smoothed and levelled the social and economic iniquities of landownership, enclosure and sharp farming practices.[10] Just as an appreciation of the picturesque aesthetic, to which the middle- and upper-class eye was trained, reflected the social status and taste of the viewer, so an appreciation of the new urban aesthetic, which borrowed from antiquity, did the same. In both cases aesthetics represented a new kind of modernity and progress and helped to formulate an identity.[11] This raises questions about how London can be seen as a self-consciously constructed artefact and that its re-imaging at this time was part of the process which transformed it from what John Summerson has described as 'a huddle of bricks with a steepled skyline' into a world-class city and first city of empire. This re-imaging of London can be traced in the move from the domestic landscape of the garden square to the public landscape of the royal urban park, and from the anonymous, functional Georgian terrace house to the Regency villa.

As the aristocracy and the nobility deserted their increasingly grand and opulent country estates for their relatively modest town accommodation, their landed estates in London were subject to

0.1 J. Wallis, *Plan of the Cities of London and Westminster*, 1802

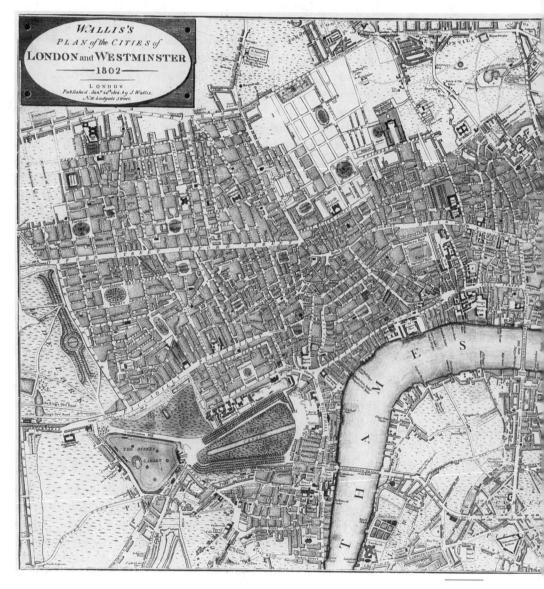

considerable social, economic and topographical change. This demographic shift in the favoured location of the ruling elite precipitated a
huge expansion of London in the period and the fabrication of a new
urban domestic environment to meet the need of these residents in
the previously undeveloped or greenfield site of the West End of
London. (figures 0.1 and 0.2) The westward growth of London
refocused the metropolis around the court and parliament, which
were becoming increasingly important aspects of the social and political map of the country as a whole. In the same way as the interests of
the landed aristocracy had refashioned the rural landscape, so they
also impacted on the fabric of the capital city. Garden squares, usually
built on land that formed part of a family estate in London, are the

predominant feature of these new metropolitan environments. The
careful economic management of these lands through the building of
leasehold terraces of houses by speculative developers, and the
aesthetic management of this dense urban living areas through the
enclosure of land to form garden squares can be seen as drawing on
the principles of country house estate development.[12] Moreover the
stripped-down aesthetic of the Georgian terrace houses ranged
around a square are often associated with rationality. By contrast, the
garden squares were often landscaped providing a picturesque
feature, indeed the well-known country house landscape designer
Humphry Repton laid out Russell Square. The cachet of a metropolitan palace or grand town house belonging to the family could also
help to lift the aesthetic qualities of a garden square, where the traditional interplay of architecture and landscape underpinned the whole
development, albeit in a new configuration.[13]

The Regent's Park project (*c*. 1812–30) was the first substantial
intervention in the existing urban fabric. It can also be seen as the
start of the deliberate creation of urban environments by the state
rather than aristocratic landowners to shape residents' and visitors'
experience of the metropolis. The Regent's Park took the idea of ideal
communities beyond the urban frame of reference to include
elements of country house estate planning. Of specific interest here
is the creation of distinctive villa residences in a 'picturesque setting'.

0.2 United Kingdom
Newspaper, *Plan of London
from Actual Survey, 1832*

Previously, the villa had been a suburban dwelling of the upper echelons of society, now it became an urban species. The Regent's Park villas, the inheritors of both this tradition and the great mansions of the Restoration period – large freestanding town houses set in their own grounds, were all'antica confections equal to their rural cousins. The vast terraces that girdled the Regent's Park were grandiose versions of the urban terrace but this time dressed up with the aesthetic trappings of the authority of antiquity. The construction of park and street – the aesthetic upgrading of the metropolis and its social infrastructure – was produced by the same building process of speculative leasehold development established for garden squares. The difference here is that the crown was landlord, or acquired land through compulsory purchase, in this first attempt to upgrade London and give coherence in terms of its planning and design.

The New Street, later Regent Street, was the vision of George IV and his officers – most notably his principal architect John Nash. It was designed to provide an essential link between the new development of the Regent's Park on the northern edge of London and the city centre and to add majesty and grandeur to the urban landscape. Regent Street was imposed over a pre-existing street pattern, forging a line north–south through the centre of London and carving through the existing urban plan to redefine access, circulation and vista through the metropolis. But beyond this, it also established a new sewerage system, which was vital to the development of the metropolis and redefined trading areas and trading thoroughfares, and affected the economic life of the city. It also intentionally separated the affluent society of the West End from its poorer neighbours to the east of the New Street. It is here that the re-imaging of London can be seen be seen to represent the social and political context of the city. The open agenda behind Regent Street to create a class divide through London shows the fissure between the rich west and the poor east. Indeed, Regent Street itself was intended to offer protection to the elite, not only as a barrier but also to facilitate troop movement across the city in case of civil unrest, as in the opening decades of the nineteenth century the French Revolution and its bloody aftermath were still fresh in the minds of many. Moreover, the friction within the British class system was becoming increasingly apparent as the demands for wider enfranchisement became more vigorous.

The rebuilding of London Bridge reveals how complex social and political relationships could be within a metropolitan context. The landed elite formed the core of the patrician governmental system, whilst the middle and merchant classes operated within the financial heart of the metropolis the City of London. The continued disenfranchisement of those who provided much of the capital that drove both London and the country as whole was a cause of growing discontent. The conflict between classes, in this case rich and poor, had already found architectural expression in Regent Street. Here the social and political context of the rebuilding of London Bridge provides an interesting counterpoint to the elite's domination of the metropolis.

The relationship between urban and rural landscapes comes full circle in the improvements carried out in the royal parks in west London in the opening decades of the nineteenth century: Hyde, St James's and Green Parks were an important part of the project to re-image London. These were not new parks, but the spread of the city westwards and increasing awareness of the social and political importance of landscape raised new design questions and addressed significant ideological issues concerning these urban spaces. The shaping and codifying of London's landscapes had begun almost unconsciously with the formation of garden squares as part of the eighteenth-century building boom. Moreover, the positive reactions to Regent's Park as a public open space show the general appreciation of this caesura in the terraces of houses which were spreading all over London. The royal parks follow on from this. Hyde Park and Green Park bordered, and halted, the development of fashionable west London, but they were not part of any speculative development.

Hyde, St James's and Green Parks surrounded Buckingham Palace, the new royal residence, and formed part of its grounds. As such they collectively constituted the kind of landscape similar to those that surrounded country houses. The landscape of country houses had already been identified as containing a variety of meanings. And although these parks were in an urban setting the landscaping issues surrounding their improvement had resonance with the wider debates about landscape in the early nineteenth century. The use of these design principles to shape urban space offered a subtler reading of the cityscape than that presented by the abrupt class consciousness of developments like Regent Street. The parks were owned by the Crown and were laid out to enhance the image of the monarch and the state and to provide effective communication between important public buildings. A detailed examination of the accounts and Crown estate papers relating to these works presents for the first time a coherent picture of the plans and development of these urban landscapes. These aspects of the urban landscape were the concern of the Commission for Public Walks set up in 1833. The commissioners' report also commented on the philanthropic undertones in the concern to provide city dwellers of all classes with open spaces with fresh air and on the role played by the parks in the shaping of this sensory experience of the city. Indeed, the period covered in this book is a distinct moment in the history of London when the push towards modernity – to re-image London – harnessed methods developed by the elite for their country estates. But these urban developments are played out against a backdrop of political unrest and change. And by the 1830s the 1832 Reform Act, and the deaths of George IV in 1830 and William IV only seven years later, precipitated a seismic shift in the social, political and indeed physical landscape of the metropolis.

The importance of the principles of landscape design and all'antica architecture, together with patterns of landownership and building development, confirm the ongoing dialogue between country and city. Here, the urban landscape, whether it be a royal park, a set piece of urban planning or a garden square, could be 'read' by a viewing public whose senses were already trained to understand the meanings of these self-consciously constructed spaces. This analysis of the re-imaging of London offers a new reading of the metropolis as the aesthetic management of its landscapes charts the shift in control from landed elite to Crown and state, and a shift in emphasis from gated, enclosed private garden squares to the public open space, which like the country house landscape appeared to offer benefit for all.

The approach taken in this book differs from the existing literature on London as it focuses on the particularities of land. More traditional histories of the city have concentrated on the production and development of the urban environment as seen, for instance, in the work of John Summerson and Donald Olsen.[14] By contrast, recent studies have considered the nature of urban experience from a range of perspectives including gender and class and the city as a consumable object.[15] This volume attempts to reconceptualise our understanding of the city in the long eighteenth century as one rooted in land and landownership and their associated values. This may seem a very obvious point but, despite the large body of work on city spaces and concepts of urban space, the land – the essential element for urban spaciality – has been largely ignored.[16] This stands in distinct contrast to work on the country estate where discussions of management practices, development and aesthetics are all based on the land. This way of considering landscape is here brought into the city – as the concept of rural urbanism – to enable discussion of London landscapes in the early nineteenth century.

1 There is a large body of literature on this subject, including: M. Andrews, *The Search for the Picturesque*, Aldershot, Scolar Press, 1989; D. Arnold (ed.), *The Picturesque in Late Georgian England*, *Papers given at the Georgian Group Symposium 1994*, London, The Georgian Group, 1995; A. Ballantyne, *Architecture, Landscape and Liberty: Richard Payne Knight and the Picturesque*, Cambridge, Cambridge University Press, 1997; S. Daniels and P. Garside (eds), *The Politics of the Picturesque*, Cambridge, Cambridge University Press, 1994.

2 Discussed, for instance, in H. A. Clemenson, *English Country Houses and Landed Estates*, London, Croom Helm, 1982, and J. V. Beckett, *The Aristocracy in England 1660–1914*, Oxford, Clarendon Press, 1986.

3 S. Daniels and S. Seymour, 'Landscape Design and the Idea of Improvement 1730–1900', in R. A. Dodgson and R. A. Butlin (eds), *An Historical Geography of England and Wales*, London, Routledge, 1990, pp. 487–520.

4 Discussed for instance in J. Dixon Hunt, *William Kent, Landscape Garden Designer*, London, Zwemmer, 1987, and K. Rorchach, *Early Georgian Landscape Gardens*, New Haven and London, Yale University Press, 1983.

5 G. E. Mingay (ed.), *The Agrarian History of England and Wales*, vol. 6, *1750–1850*, Cambridge, Cambridge University Press, 1985.

6 Ballantyne, *Architecture, Landscape and Liberty*, and S. Daniels and D. Cosgrove, *The Iconography of Landscape*, Cambridge, Cambridge University Press, 1988.

7 A. Tinniswood, *A History of Country House Visiting*, Oxford and London, Blackwell and National Trust, 1989, and D. Arnold, 'The Country House and its Publics', in D. Arnold, *The Georgian Country House: Architecture, Landscape and Society*, 2nd edn, Stroud, Sutton, 2003, pp. 20–42.

8 G. E. Mingay, *English Landed Society in the Eighteenth Century*, London, Routledge, 1963; F. M. L. Thompson, *English Landed Society in the Nineteenth Century*, London, Routledge, 1963.

9 H. A. Habakkuk, *Marriage, Debt and the Estate System: English Landownership 1650–1950*, Oxford, Clarendon Press, 1994.

10 This is discussed in A. Bermingham, *Landscape and Ideology: The English Rustic Tradition 1740–1860*, Berkeley, University of California Press, 1987.

11 T. Williamson, *Polite Landscapes: Gardens and Society in Eighteenth-Century England*, Stroud, Sutton, 1995.

12 D. Arnold, 'Living off the Land: Innovations in Farming Practices and Farm Design', in Arnold, *Georgian Country House*, pp. 152–66.

13 M. H. Port, 'Town House and Country House: Their Interaction', in Arnold, *Georgian Country House*, pp. 117–38.

14 Donald J. Olsen in *Town Planning in London: The Eighteenth and Nineteenth Centuries*, 2nd edn, New Haven and London, Yale University Press, 1964, and John Summerson, *Georgian London*, Harmondsworth, Peregrine, 1947.

15 See for instance E. Wilson, *The Sphinx in the City*, London, Virago, 1991, and although later than the purview of this book, J. Walkowitz, *The City of Dreadful Night*, New Haven and London, Yale University Press, 1990, is representative of a growing body of work on the latter half of the nineteenth century that looks at the city as a consumable artefact and questions of how

cities were experienced. My own study *Re-presenting the Metropolis: Architecture, Urban Experience and Social Life in London 1800–1840*, Aldershot, Ashgate, 2000, looks at these issues with regard to London in the earlier part of the nineteenth century. J. Rendell, *The Pursuit of Pleasure: Gender, Space and Architecture in Regency London*, London, Athlone, 2002 offers a feminist reading of gendered spaces.

16   There is some consideration of the land in G. Tindall, *The Fields Beneath*, London, Weidenfeld & Nicolson, 2002.

Rus in Urbe

The landscape design principles used in the aesthetic enhancement of country estates, together with efficient farming techniques, remained the concern of improver landlords throughout the eighteenth and early nineteenth centuries. Here, attention is focused on how these also became driving imperatives in the development of the elite's urban land. Common to both enterprises is the shifting attitude of the elite to their involvement in commerce and the use of middlemen to execute these projects. The gentleman farmer became the overseer of country estates where model farming practices ensured that Britain became self-sufficient in food. Alongside this the new working landscape comprised a different topographical and demographic layout. Large fields and manure heaps were commonplace and new model villages were built for whole communities that had been displaced to allow for this kind of development. The economic imperatives behind these changes were masked by a civilising aesthetic. In the case of the land this took the form of the picturesque landscape either within the confines of a landscaped garden or as part of a larger scheme governing the estate as a whole. The architecture of the gentlemen farmers' houses and of the new model villages was intended to be exemplary – a fine example of modern style. These practices found their equivalents in the urban development of London. The great estates of the landed elite were built by speculative builders who produced uniform terraces of houses ranged around landscaped garden squares, which offered aesthetic delight and accessible open space for the would-be occupants.

By the beginning of the nineteenth century the growth of the middle class in terms of the population as a whole, and the rise of the social credentials of the speculative builder were essential factors in the development of the metropolis. The concerns of the landed elite to make money – sometimes only in the long term – from their urban and rural lands cohere around the development of Bloomsbury. Here the interests of an aristocratic landowner, a charitable trust and private individuals can be explored through the entrepreneurial activities of the speculator builder James Burton. The second case study, on Regent's Park, sets this kind of building activity in a broader historical and economic frame. Here the methods of estate development used by the elite are adopted by the Crown to produce a unique mix of speculatively built terrace houses and villas. Moreover, the use of landscape design to enhance the aesthetic consequences of this economic activity was also similar to that used by the aristocratic landlords. The Regent's Park terraces encircled the park itself as a kind of variation on the garden square, and the villas stood within the park itself, each seeming to be the sole occupant of a vast landscape garden.

1 Bloomsbury

The garden square remains one of the hallmarks of London's town planning and a key factor in the development and growth of the city. It encapsulates much of the aesthetic, social and economic impetus behind the growth of London between 1700 and 1840, and more specifically the design and execution of the re-imaging of the metropolis in our period. The almost extravagant use of real estate to create a quasi rural environment enclosed by town houses betrays the important relationship between the rural landscape – the country, and the urban landscape (the city). But beyond this the significance of land and attitudes towards landownership, and in particular its development for profit, can be seen to be an essential ingredient in the re-imaging of the London in the eighteenth and early nineteenth centuries. Moreover, this change in the nature of the urban environment echoed the substantial intervention being made in the countryside as a result of improved farming methods and enclosure.

Patterns of landownership in London have been considered in terms of the building of the great estates[1] and there is no doubt that the aristocratic landowners played an essential part in the evolution of the metropolis in the long eighteenth century. The new garden squares of the West End were built on land owned by the ruling elite, who also owned a large proportion of the countryside. But few parallels have been drawn between the building activities on the elite's great estates in London and their rural counterparts. The development of country estates by improver landowners to form more profitable farmland has been masked by the preoccupation with the picturesque. The landscape garden, in fact usually only a small fraction of the estate, continues to offer an attractive diversion from the economic and aesthetic realities of commercial farming. These are, however, evocatively described by Benjamin Silliman, an American visitor to Britain at the beginning of the nineteenth century. His description of the countryside presents an interesting and vivid counterpoint to the usual eulogies of the picturesque viewers: 'Nothing is more common, when one is travelling in England, than to see in the roads adjacent to the fields heaps of compost, consisting of turf, tops of vegetables ... dead animals, the offals of the yards and stables ... everything ... which is capable of being converted by putrification into vegetable mould.'[2] By contrast the hard-nosed commercial practices of the speculative developer on the London estates of the elite have been seen as laudable. But even here the landscape in the form of the garden square acts as a diversion from the intensive use of land for profit. Indeed a closer look at the development of the West End of London shows how the historical and historiographic disassociation of these urban and rural practices has obscured their similarities.[3] Most striking in this regard is the attitude towards land development for medium- to long-term profit and the use of middle-men to achieve these aims that can be found on both kinds of estate. And it is significant that the ruling elite becoming involved in commerce of one kind or another.

The alteration of this attitude towards the fundamental relationship between land and landed wealth and commerce ruptured the structure and fabric of British society. It has its roots not in the growth of the towns and cities in eighteenth-century Britain but in the collapse of the tertiary economy – a very different kind of speculation to real estate. When the South Sea Bubble burst in 1721 so did the conviction that the interests of commerce and land should remain separate.[4] Many of the high-ranking culprits were shown to be as money-orientated as their lower-rank counterparts and the Prime Minister Walpole's scandalous protection of those of high rank from prosecution turned public opinion against the unquestionable social hegemony of the ruling elite. Certainly by the mid eighteenth century there was a general acceptance that the best political system acknowledged the interdependence of land, trade and finance and by default an acceptable interaction – in the interests of profit – between the various social classes of the middle and upper ranks.

There is no doubt that the country house and its estate was central to these developments. But behind all this was the need for venture capital to implement changes and invest in new equipment, livestock and buildings. This realisation of the economic possibilities of land precipitated a change in the attitude of the aristocracy towards commerce. And this encouraged and enabled the development of the great estates in London, which is an important example of the relationship between land and wealth.[5] The social impact of this was far reaching and a powerful force behind the changes in the landscape of the country as a whole. Early in the eighteenth century Daniel Defoe recognised the relationship between land and wealth in his remark, 'Multitudes of People make Trade, Trade makes wealth, Wealth builds Cities, Cities enrich the Land around them, Land Enrich'd rises in Value, the Value of Lands Enriches the Government.'

But this correlation between land and trade touched a fundamental cord in the make-up of British society. The interests of the landed elite and their consequent social standing were seen as different and distinctive from those who practised commerce. But as Paul Langford has remarked:

> Agricultural improvement ... could complicate the old simple assumptions about the line of demarcation between land and commerce. The intermingling of the supposedly distinct worlds of finance, trade, and agriculture did much to promote the sense of a broad commercial consensus in the age of Walpole and Pelham ... The readiness of landowners to invest in paper securities, the anxiety of merchants to acquire a share in the land market, the rapid growth of credit and assurance facilities for all sections of propertied society, made the traditional notions of the specialised nature of commercial enterprize manifestly untenable.[6]

The same could be said for the development of the great estates in London by landowners, speculators and developers.

As the aristocracy and the nobility deserted their increasingly grand and opulent country estates for their relatively modest town accommodation,[7] their landed estates in London were subject to considerable social, economic and topographical change. This demographic shift in the favoured location of the ruling elite precipitated a huge expansion of London in the period 1700–1840 and the fabrication of a new urban domestic environment to meet the need of these residents in the previously undeveloped or greenfield site of the West End of London. The westward growth of London refocused the metropolis around the court and Parliament, which were becoming increasingly important aspects of the social and political map of the country as a whole. Just as the interests of the landed aristocracy refashioned the rural landscape, so they also impacted on the fabric of the capital city.

It is important to reflect on the question of who owned London and the influence this had on the evolution of the city. It is perhaps surprising that most of the capital belonged to members of the aristocracy – both old and new – rather than to the Crown. Lands and titles had been granted to many on the Restoration of the monarchy resulting in a rash of building activity and the appearance of great mansions in the open fields of the West End of London. In contrast to this new elite of the new Britain, the Crown owned relatively little land in London – virtually nothing in the City and little more in the West End. Instead Crown lands and properties were to be found on the periphery of the new social centre of the West End and on the outskirts of the capital including Richmond, Kew and Kensington. But the increase in court activity throughout the eighteenth century and into the nineteenth did influence the spread of London westwards and encourage the development of areas around the royal

residences most notably Pimlico and the area around Buckingham
Palace. But most importantly for this study, the royal parks, which
comprised most of the Crown lands, assumed greater significance in
the urban plan as London spread westwards. As a result their
meaning changed from peripheral, private royal demesnes to landscapes of national significance with a readily available viewing public.

URBAN PALACES

The emergence of the urban palace in the late seventeenth and early
eighteenth centuries was an important first step in the upgrading of
London's architecture and the development of distinct domestic
environments within the city. In this way the squares of the West
End represent the political and social history of the metropolis and
the country. Berkeley Square provides a typical example of a post-
Restoration landowner and the gradual development of the estate.
The square does not take its name from one of the great aristocratic
families but the 1st Lord Berkeley of Stratton, who was commander
of the Royalist forces in the Civil War. He acquired extensive lands
north of Piccadilly after the Restoration and erected a great mansion
there surrounded by substantial grounds laid out in the latest
fashion, providing a true sense of *rus in urbe*. John Evelyn remarked
of Berkeley House after a visit in 1672: '[the] new house, or rather the
Palace, for I am assured it stood him near 30,000 pounds, and truly
is very well built, and has many noble rooms in it ...!' The mansion
was destroyed by fire in 1733 but rebuilt by the architect William Kent
as Devonshire House. This upgrading of the architecture reflected
the new aristocratic occupant, the Duke of Devonshire, who had
purchased the property in 1696.

As the land in the West End of London became more valuable and
residential property more sought after, townhouses even for the
upper echelons of society became less grand, often being part of a
terrace, and the land surrounding these great mansions was leased to
developers for profit. Burlington House, a late seventeenth-century
mansion on Piccadilly, was the London home of the Boyle family,
who also owned country estates to the west of London and in
Ireland. The great house stood in ten acres of grounds which were
part of the open fields of the West End of London and were at least
equal in importance to the Boyles' rural estates. When Richard
Boyle, 3rd Earl of Burlington, married Dorothy Savile, daughter of the
Duke of Devonshire, the marriage contract stated that these ten acres
should stay in Burlington's and his heirs' possession (figure 1.1).[8] In
the early eighteenth century the house underwent substantial redevelopment and redesign in the early eighteenth century,
transforming it from a plain Charles II house into a classically styled

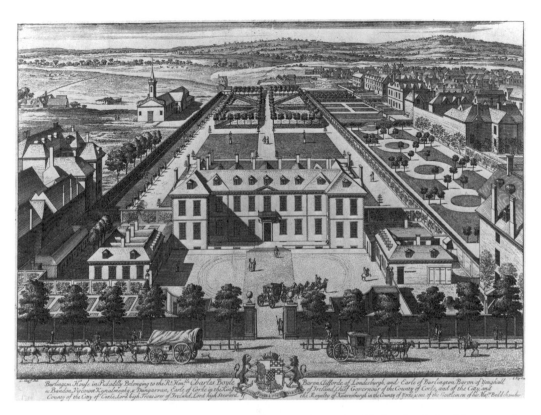

Burlington Houſe in Picadilly Belonging to the Rt Honble Charles Boyle Baron Clifforde of Londesburgh, and Earle of Burlington Baron of Youghall
& Bandon, Viscount Kynalmeaky & Dungarran, Earle of Corke in the Kingdome of Ireland, Chief Governour of the County of Corke, and of the City and
County of the City of Corke Lord high Treasurer of Ireland Lord high Steward of the Royalty of Knaresburgh in the County of Yorke one of the Gentlemen of his Maties Bedd chamber

1.1 J. Kip and L. Knyff, *Burlington House*, bird's-eye view from the south, *c.*1698–99

'neo-Palladian' mansion.[9] This in itself helped to helped improve the urban aesthetic and was part of the move to upgrade the cityscape by private landowners. But alongside his unusually keen interest in grand architectural projects,[10] Lord Burlington was closely involved with speculative development primarily as a way of raising money. The 'ten acres' at the back of Burlington House were developed by Burlington from the late 1710s (figure 1.2). Much of the speculative building work on the newly laid out streets was carried out by established architects such as William Kent, Colen Campbell and Henry Flitcroft; whilst Burlington himself designed General Wade's House on (Old) Burlington Street, which was based on a design by the sixteenth-century Italian architect Andrea Palladio. Adjacent to this, at no. 30, Burlington designed a house for his kinsman the 6th Earl of Montrath. These buildings (now demolished) are important evidence of the way estates were developed in the early eighteenth century, particularly as regards the upper end of the market and the self-conscious upgrading of metropolitan infrastructures by landowners in the interests of profit and the creation of discrete upmarket environments.[11] But beyond this we can see the same teams of architects and landowners who were redefining the English country house and its garden at work in the city. Burlington, Kent, Campbell and Flitcroft are associated with great houses such as

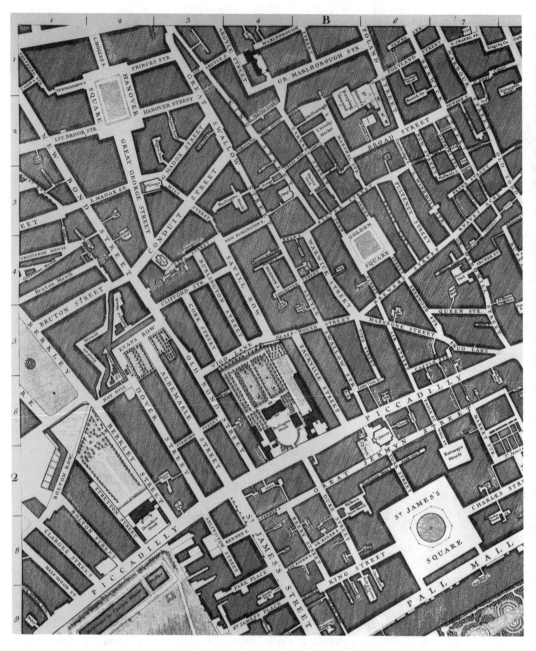

Chiswick House, Holkham and Mereworth, as well as landscape gardens such as Stowe and Stourhead. These geographically isolated examples are regarded as milestones on the development of architecture in Britain. That is not disputed here, but it is important to note that the same cast of characters were involved in the reshaping and re-imaging of the city as well as the country.

Despite the increasingly intensive development of city estates and open land owned by the aristocracy and the concomitant reduction

1.2 J. Rocque, *Plan of West End of London*, detail showing Burlington House and the 'ten acres', including the new Cork Street, Burlington Street and Saville Row, 1737–46

in the gardens and grounds of these urban palaces, the tradition of the splendid London mansion endured into the nineteenth century. Many of the nobility did, however, abandon their palaces for town houses to move further west as the geographical location of their own lands and residence fell behind the fashion. Lord Hertford's London villa in Regent's Park and town house in Manchester Square provide excellent examples of the magnificence of the private palaces of some members of the aristocracy, which equalled if not eclipsed their country seats. For instance, Devonshire House on Piccadilly was the more than adequate urban counterpart of Chatsworth in Derbyshire. It was designed by William Kent *circa* 1734–40 and underwent major alterations by James Wyatt between 1776 and 1790 and then by Decimus Burton in 1843.[12] The sums spent on the many grand re-furbishment schemes by the likes of the Earl of Grosvenor and the 6th Duke of Devonshire ran into tens of thousands of pounds, whereas the 3rd Duke of Northumberland established himself as the most serious rival to the extravagant George IV when he refurbished his town house on the Strand from 1818 to 1824.[13] The developing importance of the town house in terms of its form and function can be mapped against the increasing importance of London as a nexus of social and political systems. As such these metropolitan dwellings functioned like their country counterparts as symbols of the ruling elite where the status and breeding of the occupiers of town houses was evident in their innate taste. But unlike their rural cousins these urban palaces were usually only on show to their occupants' social equals, rather than the opportunistic country house visitor. Nevertheless, their presence in the metropolis upgraded the otherwise domestic and modestly scaled building stock.

NEW COMMUNITIES

The upmarket town house was an important feature of the re-imaging of London, but as the pace of building increased so the nature of the housing stock became more uniform and building plans more large-scale. Instead of discrete environments of luxurious town houses acting as satellites to an urban palace – or indeed a cluster of town palaces as seen, for instance, in the development of the land to the north of Piccadilly discussed in this chapter – there was a more wholesale imposition of a new community through the urban infrastructure and building stock. Once again events in the town ran parallel to those in the country where rural landowners had established a tradition of resiting and rebuilding communities for aesthetic and/or economic reasons, and whole villages were moved as part of the improvement of the estate or grounds.[14] Sometimes this kind of housing had philanthropic undertones and these new model villages were forerunners of the garden city.[15] One of the earliest schemes was implemented at Castle Howard in 1699. Others were New Houghton in Norfolk (1729) and Milton Abbas in Dorset (1774–80) for the first Lord Milton.

Perhaps one of the most brutal social consequence of these changes in the country house landscape was the demolition of cottages of the rural poor to force them to move on, resulting in a huge displaced population. In this way parish poor law rates could be kept low, which was of direct benefit to the farmers as the rates were payable by the tenant rather than the landowner. Ultimately the responsibility for these impoverished social groups must lie with the landowners as long as any remnants of a patriarchal system of government remained. And it was their negligence and absenteeism that allowed this middle-ranking group of tenant farmers to continue their activities.[16] As the aristocracy became an urban species the physical and social distance from the rural communities left this group vulnerable to the solely profit-orientated activities of the gentleman farmer. These ideas and influences on planning impacted on the development of the great estates. However city estates were the sites of less social upheaval than their country counterparts as there were fewer dependants or indeed residents to be disrupted by building developments. And, importantly, the systems of charity and succour in the city were outwith the neo-feudal customs and arrangements which operated in the country. But the great estates did establish distinct environments which helped to zone classes and this had significant consequences for the re-imaging of London, not least in the opening years of the nine-teenth century.[17] The aristocracy certainly led the way in these changes to the cityscape and the countryside. In country matters they were encouraged by George III who gave the agricultural improve-ments the stamp of royal approval and seal of social respectability, not only through his own farming endeavours, but also through his contributions, under the name Ralph Robinson, to Arthur Young's *Annals of Agriculture*, first published in 1784. Furthermore, the Board of Agriculture, established in 1793, had the King as its patron and 500 honorary members drawn from the nobility. Conversely, it was almost the absent presence of monarchy in eighteenth-century London that enabled the aristocracy to set the fashion and pace of urban development. The opulence of their town houses surpassed royal residences and not only did the ever-increasing pace of specu-lative building on their estates establish the domestic image of London but the street patterns formed on their land also created the road infrastructure of the West End that remains today.

Alongside the changes to the physical layout of estates there were also technical and scientific improvements. The reclamation of land,

improved drainage and irrigation techniques, as well as the introduction of more effective methods of cultivation, dominated the
opening decades of the eighteenth century. These innovations were
essential for the successful implementation of new scientific farming
techniques and land management which came at the latter end of the
eighteenth century. But these developments also changed attitudes
towards the land and the communities that existed on it. It was no
longer just the landscape garden that underwent a complete
makeover to satisfy the aesthetic whim and wish to display the wealth
of the landowner. Now whole landscapes including farmland could
be reshaped and aesthetic theory could be mapped against this wish
for profit.[18] In this way, for instance, managed woodland planted for
profit became the subject of praise for its aesthetic qualities.[19] The
improver landlords were at the forefront of these changes, although
the gentry farmers were the mainstay of the implementation of agricultural improvements. Of the aristocracy those most noted for their
farming techniques and successes were Thomas Coke of Norfolk
(later ennobled), the 1st Marquess of Rockingham, the 5th and 6th
Dukes of Bedford, the 3rd Earl of Egremont and the 2nd Marquess
of Stafford. The list also includes the Duke of Portland of whom the
American traveller and writer Henry Colman remarked that on his
estate at Welbeck '[he] has drained ... and now irrigates three and
four hundred acres of land ... yielding three crops a year'. Colman
also remarked that the Duke had built 'several hundred miles of
drains'.[20] Colman, a qualified and experienced commentator on
agricultural matters, was clearly impressed by the improvements
carried out by the Duke of Portland and had no less admiration for
the work of the Duke of Bedford at Woburn. In his opinion: 'The
Duke of Bedford next to the Duke of Portland is the largest improver
in England; his estate at Woburn Abbey being no less than 20,000
acres ... and his reclaimed land exceeds 18,000 [acres] ... His farm
establishment at Woburn Abbey is deemed the most extensive and
complete of any in the kingdom.'[21] Indeed by the mid nineteenth
century Henry Colman remarked, 'farming here is a profession, and
one of the highest that can be pursued'.[22] These substantial interventions in the landscape were made in the pursuit of long-term
profit and economic stability for the estate and the family who
owned it.

Evidence of the view that land was a commodity to be reshaped
and reappropriated for efficiency and profit can also be found in the
city. Aesthetic considerations followed on as the educated eye of the
elite was tutored as to how to appreciate these fabricated views and
environments just as the visitors to the country estate had their
template for viewing. Likewise in the city the landed elite were able to
carve up land and create neighbourhoods of a distinct social identity.

Moreover, in the metropolis the aristocracy were free from the social
and moral responsibilities for the poor to which they had at least to
pay nominal lip service in their country estates. The building regulations and economic contingencies of the speculative developers
restricted the architectural scope of these building projects, but this
policing of the building process also ensured a uniformity and social
homogeneity that reinforced and promoted the status quo of the
country as a whole. In this way the great estates of the ruling elite
both shaped the capital in terms of its urban plan and laid out its
demographic pattern. And many of the improver landlords in the
country turned their attention to the city estates where similar
processes of draining, levelling and the creation of distinct environments could lead to long-term profits – just like planting a forest.
This work was usually delegated to speculative builders who replaced
the gentry farmer as middleman. But there were often considerable
financial inducements from the landowner – not least the granting of
peppercorn rents for a period of years (usually two) whilst the land
was being developed and loans of money to the developers to allow
them the capital necessary to get started. And as more land was developed so the value or use of the land as anything other than housing
diminished. Open fields used for grazing or market gardening
became squeezed between new estates which made them too small to
be profitable, or inaccessible. As a result the eighteenth-century
landscape of the city changed due to speculative development as
drastically as that of the countryside was reconfigured by enclosure.
Behind both phenomena were the landed elite.

The country house and its estate was an important representation
of national identity throughout the long eighteenth century. The
ways in which this identity was created developed and changed. The
pictorial iconography of the landscape garden gave way to a more
general way of seeing and appreciating the landscape. Some aspects
of this were imported into urban architecture and design – most
notably here the garden square and the royal park. Both these traditions established the symbolic nature of land and provided a cloak of
respectability with which to dress the new farming practices or the
rapaciousness behind the development of London. The importance
of farming to Britain's social structures cannot be underestimated,
and the identification of social and political systems with farming is
widely manifested. Arthur Young affectionately described the population as 'turnips' and George III was known as 'farmer George'.
These factors together with a productive landscape and efficient
model farms made the country house a potent symbol of a progres-
sive nation. The same can be said of the urban terrace and its
importance for the re-imaging of London. One of the key strands of
this new national identity to survive into the early nineteenth

century was the continuing development of a class consciousness as part of an evolving national consciousness. This had already been encoded into the most fundamental component of the city: the town house. Numerous bulding acts regulating the materials and design of town houses followed the Great Fire of 1666. The 1774 Building Act identified four different rates of houses by size and grade of materials.[23] Commensurate with this was the association of the different rates of houses with various classes of occupants as first-rate houses commanded higher rents than those of a lower rating. This made zoning possible as the building of houses of a certain rate would, in theory, ensure a certain class of occupier. In this way the decisions made by landlord and builder had a distinct impact on the demography of an area and patterns of population and class across London. The Acts did, in effect, enable the identification of housing stock for different social classes. This identification is not foolproof – larger houses could provide lodgings for several families and the desirability of areas could change. But the rate system did facilitate the creation of areas with distinctive social aspirations. Late eighteenth- and early nineteenth-century Bloomsbury is an interesting case study in this context. Much of the building work was carried out during a time when the relationship of the area to the centre of London was going through changes – the area was now to the east of the centre but had the benefit of the New Road, begun in the 1750s which ran east–west along the northern edge of London.

BLOOMSBURY, OR EAST MEETS WEST

The area referred to as Bloomsbury in this chapter is spread across the parishes of St Giles in the Fields, St George Bloomsbury and St Pancras. The whole area was bounded on the west by Russell Square, to the north and east by Speldhurst Street (later Hastings Street) that crossed Judd Street where it terminated in Tonbridge Street which ran on a north–south axis. The southern edge was bordered by Bloomsbury Square (figure 1.3). The land was owned by four very different kinds of owners. The Foundling Estate, where work began in the area, was owned by the Coram Foundation and situated to the west of Southampton Row. This adjoined the three other estates that were developed at this time. The Bedford Estate, owned by the 5th Duke of Bedford was situated to the south-west of the Foundling Estate. These two estates comprised the western half of the whole area under discussion. The remainder of the land belonged to the Skinners' Company Estate (a City livery company), which was to the north of the Foundling Estate, and to Mr Edward Lucas a private landowner, whose estate was also to the north. Moreover, the land was in one of the less fashionable areas of early

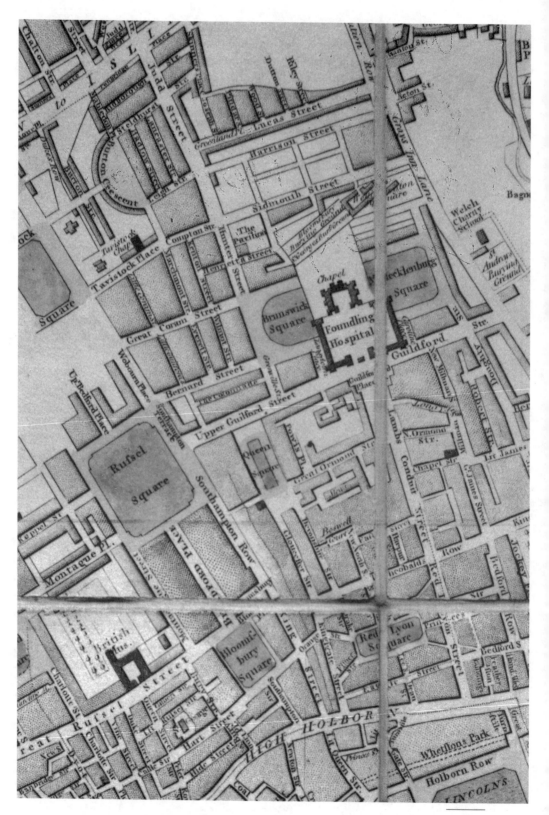

26

nineteenth-century London as the thrust of the city's growth was now westwards. Not only was Bloomsbury an isolated pocket to the north-east of the city centre but, counter to popular trends, it was developed in a west–east direction, pushing the edge of Bloomsbury toward the unfashionable East End. As such Bloomsbury provides us with an example of an area of London that was being developed in the wake of the fashionable move westwards. But neverthelesss it has the essential ingredients of an aristocratic landlord whose commercial interests were more than adequately catered for by a speculative developer. Morever, James Burton's vision for Bloomsbury, which transcended the different boundaries of landownership, shows us how these building practices faciltiated the rise of the middleman – the middle-class builder rather than the architect as a key player in the development of London at this time.[24]

In the early eighteenth century Bloomsbury was considered one of the healthiest areas in London. Situated on the northern rim of the city, it afforded fine prospects of the hills of Highgate and Hampstead. There were three noble houses in the area: Southampton House (later known as as Bedford House), Montague House (later to house the first British Museum) and Thanet House (home of the Earl of Thanet) which was situated opposite Dyot Street (now George Street). The focal point of the area was the emergent Bloomsbury Square which was first called Southampton Square (figure 1.3). Southampton House formed the northern portion of this square and Montague House was situated slightly to the west of it. The residents of Bloomsbury Square were from the higher classes, demonstrating that in the earlier part of the century this was an extremely fashionable area of town. The added kudos of an aristocratic town house forming part of the layout only enhanced the square's desirability – residents included the likes of the Earl of Chesterfield. According to the early nineteenth-century commentator Rowland Dobie, Southampton House occupied 'one of the finest situations in Europe for a palace! ... [its] great situation and approach and gardens and view to the country at the back making a country retreat almost unnecessary'.[25]

The Duke of Bedford, as the principal aristocratic landowner, is an appropriate case study for the exploration of this complex web of issues. His estate in Bloomsbury underwent several stages of development starting with one of the first speculative developments: Covent Garden. Moreover the Dukes of Bedford, as we have seen, were renowned for innovatory farming techniques and land reclamation at their country estate at Woburn. Here the city estate became the focus of attention. We can also chart how a member of the aristocracy was prepared to lease property from a fellow peer in order to live in the fashionable West End and give his great London

1.3 *A Pocket Plan of London*, 1812, detail of plan of Bloomsbury; Tonbridge Street is not shown

mansion over to speculative development – a true barometer of the impact of fashion and place on the re-imaging of London in this period. In this way Bloomsbury offers a microcosm of the social and economic life of London and the rising importance of speculative development in the evolution of the metropolis, and the way some of the building practices of the country were absorbed and adopted into the city. This is evident in the interaction between an aristocratic landlord, a charitable institution, private landowners and one of the most successful speculative developers of the early nineteenth century, James Burton. Despite the variety of landowners, the coherent vision of the urban plan of Bloomsbury may well relate to contemporary ideas about town planning as seen in the balance between buildings and landscaped areas, and the successful integration of the two, and the use of a variety of forms of open space. These elements were important not only in the building of the great estates but also in the re-imaging of the metropolis at this time, which encouraged the viewing public to read the urban landscape as they would a country house landscape. But beyond this Bloomsbury provides a specific instance of the processes and practices of speculative building. This also became an essential part of the re-imaging of London by George IV and his officers, without which their grand schemes could not have been implemented.

THE BUILDER

James Burton provides the link between these different landowners and shows how a middleman was essential to the process of upgrading London's architecture and infrastructure. His first speculative venture was in Southwark where there had been considerable building activity since the construction of Blackfriars Bridge in 1769. Between 1785 and 1792 Burton built seventy houses of all four ratings near the southern end of the bridge and carried out developments at other locations in east and north London (table 1.1). The next twenty-two years of his life were spent on his work in Bloomsbury. Between 1792 and 1814 he built or enabled the building of 1,756 houses – nearly two per week (table 1.2). By 1814, when Burton left Bloomsbury to begin work on the Regent's Park and Regent Street, his wealth and social status had increased substantially as had his reputation as an architect/builder. Alongside this Burton had forged an important working relationship with S. P. Cockerell, surveyor to the Foundling Hospital, and it is this successful team of speculative builder and surveyor which began work on the Regent Street project in 1814.

Although not unique in London's building history, Burton's sustained and substantial building activities in Bloomsbury show his

Table 1.1 *Town houses of all rates constructed by James Burton, 1785–1823*

Estate	1st-rate houses	2nd-rate houses	3rd-rate houses	4th-rate houses	Total	Estimated rental including ground rent (£)	Estimated gross value (£)
Stanford, Bennett and Brunswick Street, Albion Street, Newgate and Giltspur Streets, Eastcheap, Tyndale Place, Crescent Place, New Bridge Street, Water Lane, Old Broad Street and Clapham Common 1785–1792	17	24	15	14	70	7,420	90,300
Foundling Estate 1792–1802	29	159	172	226	586	36,240	296,700
Bedford Estate 1798–1803	132	43	8	153	336	32,240	299,400
Skinners Estate 1807–1816	4	146	284	189	623	21,190	309,600
Lucas Estate 1808–1814	1	0	143	67	211	10,120	78,800
Kent 1803–1807	3	0	4	20	27	1,500	25,000
Regent Street etc. 1815–1823	39	104	38	10	191	29,170	338,400
Regent's Park 1815–1823	76	21	14	78	189	25,060	317,100
Colonel Eyre's Estate 1818–1823	10	3	116	4	133	9,060	93,600
Totals					2366	172,300	1,848,900

Source: R. Dobie, *The History of the United Parishes of St Giles in the Fields and St George Bloomsbury*, London, 1829. 'Abstract Statement of Buildings erected by or for a Individual, from 1785 to 1823, both inclusive; exclusively of Buildings erected for others under his superintendence.'

Table 1.2 *James Burton's building activities in Bloomsbury*

Name of estate and when work carried out	1st-rate houses	2nd-rate houses	3rd-rate houses	4th-rate houses	Total no. of houses
Foundling Estate 1792–1802	29	159	172	226	586
Bedford Estate 1798–1803	132	43	8	153	336
Skinners Company Estate 1807–1816	4	146	284	189	623
Lucas Estate 1808–1814	1	0	143	67	211
Total no. of houses	166	348	607	635	1,756

Source: Based on the figures in table 1.1.

commitment to the area. The unity of his work implies an overall vision for the area which was a necessary part of a successful speculative development. A near-contemporary account of Burton's work, Rowland Dobie's *The History of the United Parishes of St Giles in the Fields and St George Bloomsbury* (1829) presents a broad sweeping history of the area from the earliest known records to the time of publication. Dobie identifies James Burton as a prime mover in the

Table 1.3 *A complete list of the Houses and Tenements built on the Foundling Hospital Estate since 1792, and on that of his Grace the Duke of Bedford since 1798, within the Parish of St George, Bloomsbury*

Name of street	No. of houses	Name of street	No. of houses
Abbey Place	17	Keppel Mews, South	35
Bloomsbury Square	10	Keppel Mews, North	42
Brunswick Square	12	Montague Place	35
Bedford Place	40	Montague Street	36
Bedford Place, Upper	50	Montague Mews	13
Bernard Street	40	Marchmont Street	40
Brunswick Mews	21	Marchmont Place	20
Coram Street, Great	59	Rhodes Mews	9
Compton Street	9	Torrington Square	70
Coram Street, Little	33	Torrington Street	5
Coram Place	16	Torrington Street, Little	6
Chapel Place	16	Tavistock Mews	21
Colonnade	26	Russell Square	65
Everett Street	29	Russell Place	16
Guilford Street	14	Wilmot Street	27
Guilford Street, Little	33	Russell Mews	7
Hunter Street	37	Woburn Place	51
Hunter Mews	7	Woburn Mews	21
Henrietta Street	29	Woburn Mews, West	13
Henrietta Mews	23	Southampton Row, West	20
Kenton Street	41	Southampton Mews, West	39
Keppel Street	40		

Notes: Total number of houses and tenements built: 1,198.
Number built by James Burton 1792–1803: 663.
Number built by James Burton in St Pancras parish: 259.

Source: R. Dobie, *The History of the United Parishes of St Giles in the Fields and St George Bloomsbury*, London, 1829.

development of the area who had had a fundamental impact from his initial involvement in 1792. This is quantified in a list compiled by Dobie in his *History* of 'Houses and Tenements built on the Foundling Hospital Estate since 1792 and on that of his Grace the Duke of Bedford since 1798, within the Parish of St George Bloomsbury' (table 1.3). Burton's significant role is corroborated, in the case of the Foundling Estate, by S. P. Cockerell in his *Report to the Governors* of 1807:

> Mr Burton is the one individual (under the attention of the five gentlemen who compose the original building committee, and I hope

I may add my own labours and exertions) to whom your excellent charity is indebted for the improvement which has taken place on the estate. All that has been done by the other builders is comparatively trifling and insignificant. Without such a man, possessed of very considerable talents, unwearied industry, and a capital of his own, the extraordinary success of the improvement of the Foundling Estate could not have taken place.

Mr Burton has expended above £400,000 for the permanent benefit of the property of the Hospital. Great part of this he has done personally; the other part he has done by builders engaged under him, whom he has supplied with money and materials, secured by mortgage, or receiving his compensation in what are called carcass or profit rents, and has still heavy mortgages subsisting on unfinished buildings. By his own peculiar resources of mind, he has succeeded in disposing of his buildings and rents, under all the disadvantages of the war, and of an unjust clamour which has been repeatedly raised against him; and at the same time those gentlemen who have speculated in purchases upon the estate with any degree of prudence, as many have done, have not had cause to repeat their speculations.

The measure of letting a large portion of land to such a man as Mr Burton was, I conceive, founded in prudence, and is justified by the event. Where several builders are all original contractors, the delay or insolvency of one thwarts the efforts of the whole; and builders with small capital never proceed with the same confidence and spirit as where they act under the guidance, and with the aid of such a man as Mr Burton, who while he watched over and was interested in the success of the whole, was ready to come forward (and he has done it in a great variety of instances, and in some with considerable inconvenience and loss) with money and personal assistance, to relieve and help forward those builders who were unable to proceed in their contracts; and in some instances he has been obliged to resume the undertaking, and to complete himself what had been weakly and imperfectly proceeded in.

Weighing these circumstances liberally and candidly, if gentlemen will now reflect how impossible it is that all the parts of the buildings which cover the Foundling Estate should have been equally free from defects, and if they will consider the magnitude and extent of what Mr Burton has done, and appreciate correctly its deficiencies, and then examine the variety and situation of the persons he has been obliged to employ, they will rather be surprised that the whole has been completed so perfectly and unexceptionably as it now is, than complain of a few trifling imperfections.'[26]

Furthermore, the revised plan for improvements on the Bedford Estate drawn up in 1800 cites Burton as the person from whom further particulars may be obtained so confirming his growing involvement with the area. This led the author of a contemporary history of London to identify Burton as the 'eminent' builder responsible for most of the speculative building in the north of the metropolis.[27]

THE EXTENT OF THE WORK IN BLOOMSBURY

The work in Bloomsbury between 1792 and 1814 was extensive and rapidly executed. During this time an array of speculative builders and their sublessees helped create Southampton Row (extending into Woburn Place) which acted as the spine of the building work. Dobie's estimate of houses built in the parish of St George's Blooms-bury between 1623 and 1829 is a useful indicator of the increasing pace of development (table 1.4). To the east of the southern end the parallel streets which formed the western edge of the Foundling Estate were constructed; whilst further to the south and west of Southampton Row, Russell Square was laid out. This development is perhaps the most traditional in terms of London's planning as the houses were ranged around a landscaped *square* square. Further to the south, part of the former gardens of Bedford House (demolished 1800) were built over to create the gardens and mews of Montague Street, Bedford Place and Southampton Row which run parallel from the south end of Russell Square. These rectangular spaces created a subsidiary spaces to Russell Square. To the east of the north end of Southampton Row on the Skinners' and Lucas Estates, James Burton was the sole developer and here he was able to explore different spatial possibilities and uses of enclosed landscape. Burton Crescent, in an echo of the Royal Crescent in Bath, curved away from Southampton Row to form the head of a distinct, hierarchical unit which stands out in the urban plan of London. The arms of Burton

Table 1.4   *Number of houses in Bloomsbury in the years 1623, 1732, 1734, 1799 and 1829*

Year	No. of houses
1623	136
1732	900
1734	954
1799	916*
1829	1,976

Note: * Dobie contests this figure, stating that there are no records of houses being demolished. He does not claim that there was any significant increase over the 1739 figure.

Source: R. Dobie's calculations for the total number of houses built in Bloomsbury over a 200-year period (R. Dobie, *The History of the United Parishes of St Giles in the Fields and St George Bloomsbury*, London, 1829).

Crescent extend into Speldhurst (later Hastings) Street and Leigh Street, with Hadlow and Lancaster Streets (later Sandwich and Thanet Streets) running parallel between them (figure 1.3).

FINANCE

The information in tables 1.1 to 1.5 gives some indication of the intense level of financial activity based on the land in Bloomsbury. And it must be remembered that the money invested and made here is only a fraction of the building economy of London as a whole. The mutual benefits for landowners and developer/builders were not dissimilar to the business practices on country estates. Indeed, speculative developers were given considerable assistance in their business endeavours by landowners. Alongside the system of peppercorn rents, loans were made at preferential rates to ensure that developers had the necessary capital. The willingness on the part of landowners to help developers build on their land can be viewed as shrewd long-term financial planning. There would be income from ground rents during the term of the lease. But the real money came once the leases expired on the property and reverted to the landowner so ensuring assets and an income from the resale of leases and ground rent for future generations. This long-term financial planning is comparable to the practices of land managment on country estates. Moreover, despite the sweeteners offered by landowners the financial risk was the builder's own. The only loss the landowner faced was rent on the land whilst it was being developed but time limits were written into leases so minimising this risk. Perhaps most importantly, the landowner need not become directly involved with the building work which was too much like trade. His or her wishes could be conveyed by the estate office or included in contractual agreements. But speculative development was not always successful and this was warned against in *An Appeal*[28] and *A Further Appeal* which imply that the figures and profitability of the proposed development of the Foundling Hospital lands were falsely inflated. The author, John Holliday, identifies a practice which explains how ordinary speculative developers could perhaps afford to work on estates:

> But builders are supplied with large savings during long minorities witness the many hundreds of leases granted by the Dowager Duchess of Portland, the Honourable Mr Harley, and the other Trustees, before the present Duke of Portland came of age ... witness the immense sums lent by the late Mr Palmer to those who built Bedford Sq, and Gower Street without which (as he frequently owned) the Buildings would never have been finished.[29]

The author goes on to suggest, rather facetiously, that all the £70,000 assets of the Foundation should be lent directly to the builders.

Burton's success was not wholly due to the willingness of landowners to support him financially. His own astute business practice was an essential ingredient. This is seen in his ability to think about the area as a whole, instead of the estates of individual landowners, which enabled the creation of a coherent infrastructure. Furthermore, Burton made the most of financial incentives from landowners, and kept a close watch on the activities of those to whom he subcontracted. This interaction of landowner and speculative developer is an important part of the building history of Bloomsbury and gives a flavour of how estates were developed in London. Table 1.2 indicates the volume and value of Burton's building activities. Even if the speed with which houses were built and the concession of peppercorn ground rents during the building period (these were sometimes extended until the building was let) are taken into account, speculative development required substantial financial outlay and was risky. How then did Burton afford to take on so much, so soon after his modest beginnings in London?

The impressive pace of acquiring land and building and the dexterous handling of financial matters is charted by Burton in a diary which reveals the complex social and economic web behind the process of building London. In December 1791 Burton commenced the foundations for the building to the east of the Foundling Hospital.[30] Yet less than two years later in October 1793 he sold this estate to Charles Connolly Esq. for 3,000 guineas.[31] In February of the same year Burton had commenced the foundations of the buildings to the west of the Foundling Hospital. The impetus of the proposed speculative development had made the land more desirable but Burton realised the paucity of access to the eastern part of the Foundling Estate would be problematical. This was also the opinion of S. P. Cockerell who in 1802 stated that the Foundling lands to the west had been developed rapidly and successfully partly because of the good access and connections between roads, whereas the development of land on the eastern portion 'is manifestly owing to the want of general communications extending from respectable quarters to that side, and nothing can so strongly point out the necessity of opening the intended communication north of the hospital'.[32] In March 1793 Burton made more of his capital available for speculative development as he quit the distillery business he had entered into with a Mr Howell. This provided a further £8,000 in capital which would be paid by Howell over a period of seven years.[33] On 10 May Burton began to build at the corner of Lansdown Place and Guilford Street and made a further agreement to take on more land on Guilford Street itself. In December of the same year he took all the remainder of the ground north of Guilford Street which was 210 ft deep at 17s. per foot and the vacant ground at the north end of Queen Square (this was at a peppercorn but the land had to be enclosed at Burton's own expense). In the following year Burton consolidated his development of this specific area. On 4 March 1794 he purchased Mr Newenham's estate on Queen Square for £4,000, and only weeks later on 26 March took up leases on ground to the north of this estate to the line of Guilford Street at a cost of £25 a year (?per foot). Work began soon after. On 30 June Burton commenced building the houses opposite Queen Square. His plans were hampered by the problem of access or rather Burton's proposed solution to it. Mr Stephenson (presumably a local resident) obtained an injunction from Chancery to prevent Burton making a way from Queen Square to Guilford Street.[34] In 1795 work began a little further north and in April of the same year building commenced on the south side of Brunswick Square. The following year he contracted for the remaining ground of Brunswick Square and land north of Bernard Street at £500 per annum (see figure 1.3).[35] By 1798 work on the Foundling and Bedford Estates was in full flow. The fluctuations in the London speculative building trade do not appear to have affected Burton as badly as other builders and a diary entry for 1799 gives a summary of his achievements in Bloomsbury. He remarked that at this time all the houses in Guilford Street, Southampton Terrace (now Russell Square east side) were disposed of and all those on the south side of Brunswick Square were occupied. Fifteen of eighteen houses on the west side of Brunswick Square were still being built. All of Burton's nine houses in Guilford Square were occupied. In nearby Bernard Street Burton had disposed of five houses and was in the process of finishing a further six on the south side, whilst on the north side of street he was building a further twenty houses. Burton's keenness to consolidate his landholding is demonstrated here as he remarks that Mr Scrimshaw was building two houses on the south side of Bernard Street from whom he purchased the improved ground rents. He was also building seven houses on the east side of Little Guilford Street.[36] The diary not only gives valuable insight into the pace and volume of building in London at this time but also reveals the complexities of the financial arrangements. The building programme in Bloomsbury, like many others on the great estates, benefitted from support in terms of loans and mortgages at favourable rates from the landowners. There was financial help from the Duke of Bedford who lent Burton £7,000 on mortgage (stated in the building agreement for the east side of Tavistock Square and Woburn Place, 21 November 1800), and paid him £5,000 for demolishing Bedford House and allowed him to sell the materials. Only two years later the Bedford Estate 'was lending sums of £150–£600 for three years, to such persons as chose to accept them'.[37] In January 1802 Burton received £7,000 in return for security of seven houses on the south side of Russell Square.[38] And Burton's diary entry for 1800 includes a table showing an 'arrangement of leases issued early in 1800 and was endeavoured to be acted upon' which gives further information about these (table 1.5). Burton explains that the leases

Table 1.5   *Excerpt from James Burton's notebook and diary: entry for year 1800 showing the arrangement of leases*

Situations	Rent per foot	Do. for redemption of land tax	Average fronts	Do. depths of houses	Whole depth	?Sewer may be added on mortgage (£)
Bloomsbury Sq N	21/–	6/–	21.6	36	80	400
Montague St W	20/–	5/6	25	40	110	350
Do E	16/–	4/6	21	35	65	
Bedford Pl	21/–	6/–	25	40	110	450
South(ampton) row W	16/–	4/6	21	36	65	300
Russell Sq S	21/–	6/–	27	40	90	450
Do W	25/–	6/–	27	40	110	350
Bernard St N	15/6	4/–	21	33	70	350
Do S	12/9	3/6	20	30	53	300
Wilmot St E	12/6	2/6	17	28	60	150
Do W	12/6	2/6	17	28	60	150
Brunswick Sq W	21/–	3/6	19	45	100	400
Grt Coram St N	12/6		20	30	65	250
Do W	8/6		15	24	40	100
Tavistock Sq E	21/–	3/6	24	38	60	350
Mews	5/–	1/–	25	25		
South[ampton] Terr E	15/–		22	37	65	300

ran for between ninety-three and ninety-eight years with the period of peppercorn rent determined according to quantity. The funds to carry out the work were advanced progressively, except where security was given or a mortgage raised. Mortgages ran for a term of three years unless the building was completed within that time period. Developers were usually also responsible for laying in services to buildings and these could be costly. Here the sewers were priced at 7s. 6d. per foot on the frontage of the house and the cost of vaults – if built – at £10 per rod. The table gives a clear picture of the different kinds of costing and rents charged. This brief insight into the activities of just one speculative developer reveals at once the pace and complexity of the building not only of Bloomsbury but also of other great estates in the capital and the range of interested parties involved in these schemes.

MOTIVATION FOR THE DEVELOPMENTS

The motivation for each tranche of the building project was different on the part of each of the landowners. The late eighteenth- and early nineteenth-century schemes were part of an ongoing dynamic of the development of the area which had begun in the early seventeenth century. The development of Bloomsbury was quite patchy, one of the main problems being access to the estates without which they were not viable residential or commercial areas. This is demonstrated by Dobie who identifies the trend in development in the area by listing the number of houses sited there over a period of 200 years (table 1.4). These figures indicate a stagnation in building during the last three-quarters of the eighteenth century and the boost at the end of this period.

The development of the Bedford, Skinners' and Lucas Estates can be seen as part of a major trend in the London estates where long-term investment and return was the main objective of the landowner. The ground rents were small beer compared to the bounty at the end of the term of the lease when the property would revert to the landowner for resale or redevelopment. This microcosm of the economic climate of the building industry in eighteenth-century London did not, however, represent the motives of the Foundling Hospital. This institution was run by Governors who faced day-to-day problems of funding as well as trying to secure the long-term financial future of the charity.

In 1740 the patrons of the Foundling Hospital purchased 56 acres of land in Bloomsbury from the Earl of Salisbury (figure 1.4) The patrons had originally wanted to purchase a smaller plot of some 34 acres but it was deemed that the amount they did not wish to buy was the least attractive and would be made less so once unattached from the rest of the estate. The aim was to create two great fields of 34 acres with the hospital situated in the middle. An arrangement not unlike the great London houses of the elite, only here the land was intended as a breathing space considered essential for the children's well-being, and was part of the attraction of the plot. The Earl of Salisbury was sympathetic to the cause and donated £500 of the £7,000 sale price to the hospital – much to the anger of other prospective purchasers who would have paid more for the land. The condition of purchase was that the land should not be developed but used solely as a site for the hospital. The hospital's motives for wanting to develop the land were financial but a quick profit was needed rather than long-term financial investment. There was a financial crisis in the 1780 and the rampant speculative building trade was seen as a solution to the problems. Many considered this a short-sighted, if not erroneous assumption. These views were expressed in

two pamphlets: *An Appeal to Governors of the Foundling Hospital and the probable consequences of covering hospital lands with buildings* and *A Further Appeal to the Governors of the Foundling Hospital and justification of their conduct in not having covered the hospital lands with buildings since the institution of the charity,* cited above. It was argued that internal financial reforms would relieve the institution's problems[39] and the likely returns on the proposed speculative venture were called into question as rents were not much higher on lands given over to building rather than farming:

> Within a few hundred yards of the Hospital on the margin of the New Road, I have been well informed that the builder has contracted for three or four acres (to be extended to many more acres, if sub-contractors can be found) at a price which produces to the land-owner the *immense* sum of *twenty shillings per* acre annually.[40]

This was in fact little more than would be received from land used for agricultural purposes.[41] But objectors to the scheme felt that the land surrounding the Hospital would, if developed, produce a better market than this, perhaps partly because of the attraction of being sited near such an institution.[42]

Moreover, it was felt that the turning over of the fields to housing would severely impinge on the health of the children, 'that by building round the Hospital, it will *by degrees*, bring it into the town, and thus render it much less healthy for the purposes for which it was erected'.[43] More children, it was argued, might die from the

1.4 Thomas Shepherd, *London in the Nineteenth Century*, London, 1829, view of the Foundling Hospital

effects of living in a polluted atmosphere than from any financial stringency during any period when administrative reforms were implemented.[44] It must be remembered that one of the motives for building the hospital in the middle of fields was the benefit of the fresh air to the occupants.

The Bedford Estate was developed under different circumstances. A rapid change took place in the Duke's view as to how the land should be developed in the period 1787–1800. The change was probably motivated by the fact that London's fashionable quarters were moving ever westward, making Bloomsbury and in particular the Duke's residence, Bedford House, increasingly unfashionable. In 1787 the Duke was adamant that no building work should take place to the north of Bedford House as this would spoil the views to the north unbroken to the Hampstead and Highgate hills (figure 1.5).[45] The Duke's attitude had changed by 1795 as the Foundling Estate needed to make roads opening into the Duke's private road. At the same time the Duke decided to begin to develop the area north of Bedford House known as the Long Fields. The fields were to be landscaped and turned into an ornamental pleasure ground and the roads bordering the fields to east and west were to be laid out. These became Southampton and Bedford Terraces respectively. A covenant was added to the agreement with the developers of this land:

the area or lawn extending northwards from the garden belonging to Bedford House to the estate of Lord Southampton, and also extending

1.5 Sutton Nickells, *Bloomsbury Square and Southampton, later Bedford House with the Hampstead and Highgate Hills in the distance*, 1746

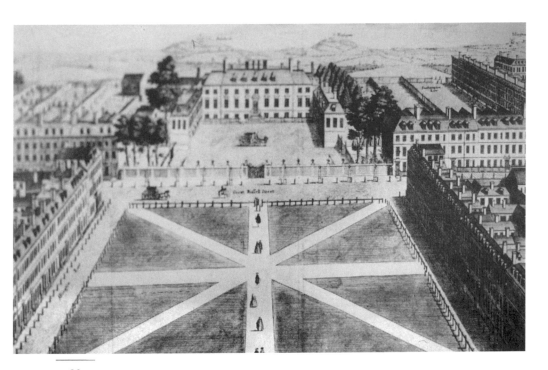

from the said intended [Southampton Terrace] westward to another intended terrace to be called Bedford terrace shall not be let or granted for building, nor shall the said Duke of Bedford ... permit any buildings to be erected thereon, except ornamental or other buildings for use of the ground, during the said term of ninety-nine years.[46]

Despite these conditions, the 5th Duke wanted houses to be built on the new roads. He entered into an agreement with the speculative developer James Burton who was working on the Foundling Estate for the development of his estate in 1798. Two years later Burton produced a plan 'for the intended improvements on the estate of his Grace the Duke of Bedford'.

In the same year the Duke obtained two Acts of Parliament to allow him to develop his estate. Burton's plan was engraved for the benefit of prospective speculators in 1800 and again in 1806 when Burton included Woburn and Torrington Squares. Some of the plots were let to subcontracting masons, joiners and ironworkers acting as small scale speculative developers. But Burton ensured stylistic uniformity even more rigorously than he had during the work on the Foundling Estate. Indeed Burton's design for one of the terraces on the Bedford Estate was exhibited at the Royal Academy in 1800.[47] The Bedford Estate was a risky venture as over half of the houses were first-rate and by this time fashionable London was further west and the better class of tenant wanted to live there. Even the Duke of Bedford vacated Bedford House in 1800 giving it over to demolition and went to live on another estate in a leasehold house in the West End. This raises the questions of whether the Bloomsbury estates met public demand for housing stock or whether market forces were ignored in favour of an imposed, ideal demographic make-up which ran counter to actual trends.

The Skinners' and Lucas Estates were developed at Burton's instigation. During the years 1803–7 he negotiated with both parties and convinced them that such a venture would be profitable for all concerned. Of all of Bloomsbury this has Burton's most individual stamp as he emulated the aristocracy in using place names of personal significance. Burton Street and Crescent on the Skinners' Estate had an obvious connection with the builder whereas Mabledon Place and Tonbridge Street on the Lucas Estate referred to Burton's country residence, Mabledon, near Tonbridge in Kent. Perhaps appropriately, although the architecture was similar to that on the Bedford Estate, the bulk of the housing stock was third- and fourth-rate.

INFRASTRUCTURES

The poor access to Bloomsbury appears to have been a powerful force in holding back the development of this area earlier in the century. Burton worked hard to establish good communications to his developments and it is possible to see how the overall road pattern in Bloomsbury was established at least in part through his endeavours. He concentrated his efforts on the borders of the Foundling/Bedford Estates. The development of Southampton Terrace was the backbone of Burton's plan. It was anchored by Russell Square which Burton developed almost completely and the gardens were landscaped using Repton as the designer. A near-finished square made access to the east easier and the whole area more desirable. From Russell Square Burton pushed north developing land on both the Foundling and Bedford Estates. This move northwards might appear curious at first but perhaps Burton had his eye on the Skinners' Company's fields which lay to the east of the north end of Southampton Terrace and, of course, the New Road.

The lack of infrastructure was not necessarily seen as negative by landowners. The Duke of Bedford had actively discouraged the building of new access roads to his estate and the objectors to the development of the Foundling Estate admitted that although there were buildings to the east, west and south at some distance to the hospital these could encroach on it very easily. 'Have we all not observed, that building about this metropolis is like wildfire; it catches from field to field, and goes on *ad infinitum*?' This isolation is confirmed in *A Further Appeal*: '[There is] No road or way to west or north out of the land into the Metropolis or to the New Road. The late noble owner had no carriageway into it except from the Great North Road.'[48] The author does concede that access to the area from Lamb's Conduit Street is currently under consideration.[49]

Speculative development was risky at the best of times, so it is hard to imagine why Burton, still at an early stage in his career, would be attracted to such an isolated site. The answer lies in part in the construction of the New Road which ran east–west across the northern edge of the city. Indeed the author of *A Further Appeal* identifies this as having greatly enhanced the rents on the Portland and Bedford Estates to the west of the hospital. There rent of between £50 and £100 per acre was charged as the estates could be accessed from the east, west and south and in many cases from the New Road which was still under construction. The positive effect of the New Road on the development of the Bloomsbury estates is recognised by Dobie, who also acknowledged that access was a vital element for a successful speculative venture.[50]

The situation was more complicated than just one of being able to reach the Bloomsbury estates. Firstly, access should be from and to the fashionable end of town. Roads serving the unfashionable East End were not as useful or attractive to prospective purchasers as those leading westwards. Secondly, the road system was interdependent.

The successful development of the Foundling Estate required the construction of roads across the Bedford Estate. Moreover, the later development of the Skinners' and Lucas Estates would have been less viable without the important new road building of the major estates in the area.

The Foundling Estate needed new roads to be built across the Bedford Estate to allow access from the west. This clashed, however, with the wishes of the Duke of Bedford who, as we have seen, stated in 1787 that he wanted to keep the area to the north of Bedford House perfectly clear with an uninterrupted view to the hills beyond. But by 1795 this opinion had changed as two parallel roads were built running north from the house on either side of the gardens. The gardens were to become ornamental pleasure grounds serving the houses to be constructed on each of the roads. The easternmost of these two roads was to be known as Southampton Terrace, and James Burton and Henry Scrimshaw took up a building contract with the Bedford Estate on 6 July 1795 with the covenant that the fields were not to be built on. The Duke changed his mind in 1800, the year he vacated Bedford House and moved further west, and Burton and Scrimshaw released him from the covenant. It was in their interests to do so as the prospects for and profitability of Southampton Terrace improved considerably. Previously the ornamental fields had served only to isolate the terrace from fashionable west London as there was no direct route across them. This change impacted on the neighbouring Foundling Estate as the lands which abutted the eastern edge of the Bedford Estate became more attractive, and Burton took up building leases on them.[52]

Access across estates was not always granted free of charge. In 1795 the Foundling Hospital had granted land worth £1,800 to the Duke of Bedford in return for the four openings into his estate. Twelve years later the Skinners' Company (or rather Burton) negotiated two openings into the Foundling Estate on 15 November 1807 at a cost of £1,500. These openings were continuations of Hunter and Marchmont Streets. An agreement was also made that neither landowner would build houses of less than second-rate for at least 200 feet north and south of the boundary.[52] Burton had contracted with the Skinners' Company for land at Sandhills,[53] the name given to the estate he developed, on 28 July of that year, at £2,500 per annum.[54] Access was essential for the success of the project but it is likely that Burton was confident of a successful outcome as he had worked with the Foundling Hospital. The agreement of the rate of house that could be built is perhaps the result of previous experience where houses of lower rates usually fringed the edges of estates. These downmarket dwellings usually had more of a detrimental effect on neighbouring areas than the estates on which they were built. Although sums paid for access rights might seem large, good connections greatly enhanced land values and the saleability of property.

DEMOGRAPHIC TRENDS

As we have seen, between 1792 and 1814 Burton built 1,756 houses in Bloomsbury (table 1.2). No figures have yet come to light quantifying the whole building process in Bloomsbury during this time. Some assumptions can be made. Dobie's chart of 'Houses and Tenements built on the Foundling Hospital Estate since 1792, and on that of his Grace the Duke of Bedford since 1798, within the Parish of St George, Bloomsbury' (table 1.3) identifies 663 of the 1,198 houses constructed between 1792 and 1803 as being the work of James Burton. Dobie cites a further 259 as being by Burton in the neighbouring parish of St Pancras.[55] These figures correspond to the totals given for Burton's work on the Foundling and Bedford Estates in table 1.2. If it is assumed that the proportion of work by Burton was the same in each of these parishes for both estates it is clear Burton was responsible for building over half the housing stock. As Burton negotiated solely to develop the Skinners' and Lucas Estates it is likely that the rating of the houses built over the whole of Bloomsbury was heavily influenced by him. Landowners sometimes specified that houses should be of either first or second rate, but the final decision lay with the builder. Moreover, houses of lower rates were sometimes squeezed into estates to increase the developer's revenue, although the presence of downmarket dwellings detracted from the general quality of the area.

It is perhaps surprising that landowners did not always actively engage in decisions concerning the precise rates of houses to be built on their land even though this would influence their short- and long-term level of income. Burton did have restrictions imposed on him by landlords of the Foundling and Bedford Estates. For instance, on the Foundling Estate Cockerell's plan intended 'That there shall be such principal features of attraction in the Plan as shall not be too great for a ?due proportion of the whole but yet sufficient to draw Adventurers to the Subordinate parts.'[56] There were a considerable number of houses of lower rates, but it was clear that these should not interfere with or diminish the character of the houses of higher rates. The hierarchical plan made the Hospital the focal point. The square to the east was to be made up of only first-rate houses and enclosed gardens, the square to the west should have first- and second-rate houses on the principal streets. The areas to the north and south of the hospital should contain third-rate housing whereas the easternmost edge of the estate (Grays Inn Road) should be fourth-rate with a view to converting them to shops once the area became more frequented. The Bedford Estate also had restrictions. The houses on Montague Street and Southampton Row had to be first- or second-rate. Those in Bedford Place and Russell Square were all to be capital first-rate houses. But the remainder of the estate was unspecified and Burton built nearly as many fourth-rate houses on the eastern edge as he did first- and second-rate on the rest. The area east of Southampton Row bordered the Founding Estate and the class of housing created an undesirable downmarket barrier between the two. This lesson had been learnt by the Foundling Hospital when it granted access to the Skinners' Estate through the extension of Marchmont and Hunter Streets. In this instance both parties agreed to build houses of not less than second rate for 200 feet on either side of the boundary. This still gave Burton plenty of scope to develop the Skinners' and Lucas Estates with mostly third- and fourth-rate housing. Despite the sophisticated plan he imposed on this area Burton must have realised that fashionable London was further west. Instead, he aimed for the growing numbers of middle-class city dwellers who would benefit from and appreciate the landscaped surroundings and convenient access provided by the New Road.

Southampton Row acted as a kind of north–south axis through Bloomsbury dividing the two principal estates and indicating the difference in demographic make-up of the two halves. This phenomenon reappeared slightly further west in a very different context with the development of the New Street: Regent Street. Here Burton interacted with and made a significant contribution to the infrastructure and housing of this huge building project which had a distinctly political subtext.

The idea of community in terms of the social mix of the area and inclusion of commercial premises (mostly shops) and uniformity of design is present in Bloomsbury. The former was dictated to some extent by the number of houses of each rate built on the estates which was a form of social segregation. The long runs of terraces with more stylistic uniform houses and a logic to the street pattern across the estates shows a knowledge of contemporary approaches to town planning. This is complemented by the variety of forms of open space in the area: in his urban layouts, alongside traditional garden squares, were forms relatively new to London such as long thin spaces and the crescent. Here as elsewhere in London during the opening years of the nineteenth century the architectural dialogue between France and Britain comes to the fore. The sources for some of these planning features are probably the ideas on town planning discussed by eighteenth-century French theorists such as Jacques-François Blondel and Pierre Patte whose ideas were current.[57] Both Frenchmen stressed the importance of good connections and rationality in town planning. Patte's concerns were expressed in his *Memoires sur les objets les plus importants de l'architecture* (1769), where he argues for good connections in terms of roads and vistas between the various parts of a city, but warns against the uniform monotony which might follow from such planning principles. But there were important differences between these ideas and the design issues faced by James Burton in laying out the Bloomsbury estates. The French theorists were concerned mostly with improvements to existing cities – most notably Paris – whereas Burton's projects were all new build with the added advantage that once completed the New Road was to give improved access from other parts of the city. Moreover, Burton faced the practical and diplomatic problems of liaising with estate owners with different outlooks and interests.

Continental town planning theory had already been influential in Britain. Covent Garden was perhaps London's best-known example. It was designed by Inigo Jones for the 4th Earl of Bedford in the second quarter of the seventeenth century and drew on Italian town planning models. In the eighteenth century the urban design of cities outside London including Edinburgh, Buxton and Bath was influenced by developments in contemporary European theory and practice. Indeed, John Wood the Elder's (1704–54) work in Bath, which was continued by his son John Wood (1728–81), is of particular interest here. Wood drew on Bath's Roman origins for some of his ideas for the development of the city.[58] But it was also a highly successful marriage of the town planning ideas expressed by theorists like Blondel and Patte and a speculative development. The variety of forms used by Wood to punctuate this new urban environment: Queen's Square, the Circus and the Royal Crescent were connected by a coherent road system and gave variety and interest to the urban plan.[59] Even without their nomenclature the various shapes and associations of these open spaces added cachet to Wood's development. It is interesting to note the similarity between Wood's use of the crescent form and Burton's. In both cases the lie of the land is exploited through the use of an unusual curved layout of a terrace which gives a sense of grandeur to the composition. Notably whilst Wood called on associations with the monarchy to enhance his scheme further with names like the Royal Crescent, Burton used his own name for his scheme. Wood's exploitation of the town planning elements of his designs to enhance the profitability of his speculation may well have appealed to Burton. And James's overall vision for Bloomsbury also has resonance with the French town planning theories, but how far these were picked up in distilled form from the work of men like Wood is open to question.

Indeed, Burton's efforts in Bloomsbury had a striking effect on the London cityscape. Burton's uniformly facaded terraces ranged around his rational plan, which included elements like crescents, rectangular as well as square open spaces, provided a distinctive discrete environment within London. Certainly Russell Square, one of the area's finest, was frequently mentioned in guidebooks to London. *The Ambulator* (1811) described Russell Square as 'remarkable for the elegance of its houses, its ornamental area and the very fine bronze statue of the late Duke of Bedford'[60] (see figure 1.6). Bloomsbury was sometimes commented upon. *The Picture of London* (1815) describes Bloomsbury, beginning with Russell Square which had been landscaped by Humphry Repton at Burton's behest:

> Russell Square on a side of Bloomsbury is one of the largest and finest squares in London. Broad streets intersect it at the corner and middle which add to its beauty and remove general objection to squares by ventilation the air ... the extensive enclosure is a square containing oval shrubberies, a square lawn in the centre intersected with gravel walks ...[61]

The unified facades of the West End terraces and the introduction of vistas and a more coherent urban plan across the different estates was another way of codifying the urban landscape and expressing national identity. *The Picture of London* recognised the importance of garden squares to the image of the metropolis and included a new section devoted to them in the 1815 edition. The commentary

1.6 Thomas Shepherd, *London in the Nineteenth Century*, London, 1829, view of Bedford Square

covered a large number of the London squares of which Grosvenor was seen as the finest, with its equestrian statue of George II in the centre and the houses ranged around it being 'some of the most magnificent in the metropolis'. Next in terms of their beauty were Portman, Montague and Manchester Squares, the latter having 'a small house on the north side [Hertford House] which is one of the best in London'. These features helped to create a kind of upper- and middle-class identity through differentiations in housing rate, street width and landscape which helped these classes to connect with the city. Here again the interaction between social class and the reshaping of the metropolis presented a unified national image. Moreover, the names of the squares and streets were a reminder of who owned London, as the *Percy History* remarked: 'The names and titles of the country residences of our nobility are often perpetuated in our squares and streets, particularly those of the dukes of Bedford, Portland and Grafton.' This language of the city shows the close links between the aristocratic practice of the development of land for profit in both the country and the city. Arthur Young's description of the changes in the Norfolk landscape indicates the impact modern farming techniques were having on rural topography, as well as being emblematic of the kinds of changes taking place on the great estates:

All the county from Holkham to Houghton was a wild sheep-walk before the spirit of improvements seized the inhabitants ... and this spirit has wrought amazing effects; for instead of boundless wilds, and uncultivated wastes, inhabited by scarcely anything but sheep, the county is all cut into enclosures, cultivated in amost husband-like manner, richly manured, well peopled, and yielding an hundred times the produce it did in its former state.[62]

The impressive nature of the architecture and urban planning helped to reinforce the class structure which underpinned the concept of national identity. This pattern of development of grand facades and first- and second-rate housing continued in the Regent Street project which was a conscious attempt to zone the city according to class (this is developed further is chapter 3). And it is important to consider the wider implications of the work in Bloomsbury for the re-imaging of London in the early nineteenth century especially the coherent planning, the establishing of a team of speculative builder and architect in the personae of James Burton and S. P. Cockerell who were capable of executing large-scale projects and not least the coming together of country and city in the creation of urban landscapes and infrastructures.

1 Olsen, *Town Planning in London*, and Summerson, *Georgian London*, place emphasis on the importance of the great estate for the development of London. More recent studies, including Elizabeth McKellar, *The Birth of Modern London*, Manchester, Manchester University Press, 1999, and Linda Clarke, *Building Capitalism: Historical Change and the Labour Process in the Production of the Built Environment*, London, Routledge, 1991, have argued for a more mixed pattern of development across the metropolis in the long eighteenth century. These studies have provided important counter-examples to the estate model and the great landowner championed by Olsen and Summerson. The present study re-asserts the importance of the great estate but focuses on the adoption of practices of land development used on the elite's country estates, which also provides some connective tissue between the great landowners, developers and speculative builders.

2 Benjamin Silliman, *A Journal of Travels in England, Holland and Scotland and of two passages over the Atlantic in the years 1805–1806*, 3 vols., New Haven, The Trustees of Yale College, 1820, vol. iii, pp. 147–8.

3 See for instance Sir John Summerson's discussion of 'The Great Estates' in his seminal volume *Georgian London*, pp. 163–76, 191–7.

4 See *The Particulars and Inventories of the Estates of the Late … Directors of the South-Sea Company*, 1721.

5 See for instance D. Cannadine, 'The Landowner as Millionaire: The Finances of the Dukes of Devonshire, c. 1800–c. 1926', *Agricultural History Review* (1977), pp. 77–97.

6 P. Langford, *Public Life and the Propertied Englishman 1689–1798*, Oxford, Clarendon Press, 1991, p. 308.

7 See M. H. Port, 'Town House Country House: Their Interaction', in Arnold, *Georgian Country House*, pp. 117–38.

8 Marriage settlement between Richard Boyle, 3rd Earl of Burlington and 4th Earl of Cork, and Lady Dorothy Savile, 18 March 1720/1, Harvard Library, MS Eng. 218.20, f. 21.

9 See D. Arnold, 'It's a Wonderful Life', in *Belov'd by Ev'ry Muse: Richard Boyle 3rd Earl of Burlington and 4th Earl of Cork (1694–1753)*, London, Georgian Group, 1994, pp. 5–14.

10 This evoked criticism from his contemporaries who felt Burlington had become too close to trade in his close involvement with architectural design and practice.

11 See Pamela D. Kingsbury, *Lord Burlington's Town Architecture*, RIBA Exhibition Catalogue, London, 1995.

12 'Devonshire House', *Country Life*, 13–20 November 1981. Devonshire House was demolished in 1924–25.

13 *Survey of London*, vol. 18, p. 17. The works were carried out by Thomas Cundy. C. R. Cockerell drew up a survey and report in 1819 (Alnwick Castle MS 94 f 6).

14 See G. E. Fussell and C. Goodman, 'The Housing of the Rural Population in the Eighteenth Century', *Economic History Review*, 2 (1930–33), pp. 63–90; N. Cooper, 'The Myth of Cottage Life', *Country Life*, 141 (1967), pp. 1290–3.

15 See G. Darley, *Villages of Vision*, London, Architectural Press, 1975, and 'In

Keeping with the Mansion: The Making of a Model Village', *Country Life*, 153 (1975), pp. 1080–2.

16 This is fully explored in Langford, *Public Life and the Propertied Englishman*.

17 See chapter 3.

18 This is discussed more fully in S. Daniels and C. Watkins, 'Picturesque Landscaping and Estate Management: Uvedale Price and Nathaniel Kent at Foxley', in Daniels and Garside (eds), *The Politics of the Picturesque*, pp. 13–41 and C. Watkins, 'Picturesque Woodland Management: The Prices at Foxley', in D. Arnold (ed.), *The Picturesque in Late Georgian England: Papers Given at the Georgian Group Symposium 1994*, London, Georgian Group, 1995. See also Andrews, *The Search for the Picturesque*, M. Andrews, 'A Picturesque Template: The Tourists and their Guidebooks', in Arnold (ed.), *The Picturesque in Late Georgian England*, and Ballantyne, *Architecture, Landscape and Liberty*.

19 On this point see C. Watkins et al., 'The Prices at Foxley', in Arnold (ed.), *The Picturesque in Late Georgian England*, pp. 27–34.

20 Henry Colman, *European Life and Manners in Familiar Letters to Friends*, 2 vols., Boston and London, 1850, Letter XXXII, October 1843.

21 Ibid., Letter LXXXIX, 7 February 1845.

22 Ibid., Letter XXXII, October 1843.

23 Summerson, *Georgian London*, pp. 125–9, claims that the Act was drafted by Sir Robert Taylor and George Dance the Younger, but this cannot be substantiated. However, Taylor and James Adam did petition the House of Commons, on behalf of London builders, for new regulations, which indicates that these new controls were largely welcomed.

24 For instance, Sir John Soane made his name through successful speculative developments. See P. de la Ruffinière du Prey, *John Soane, the Making of an Architect*, Chicago and London, University of Chicago Press, 1982.

25 R. Dobie, *The History of the United Parishes of St Giles in the Fields and St George Bloomsbury*, London, 1829, p. 138.

26 This was a pamphlet written by S. P. Cockerell addressed *To the Governors and Guardians of the Hospital for the Maintenance and Education of Exposed and Deserted Young Children: Assembled in General Court*, London, 1807. Henceforth 1807 Report.

27 James Peller Malcolm, *Londinium Redivivum*, 1802, vol. 1, p. 5.

28 *An Appeal to the Governors of the Foundling Hospital and the probable consequences of covering hospital lands with buildings*, London, 1787, p. 34. Henceforth *An Appeal*.

29 *A Further Appeal to the Governors of the Foundling Hospital and justification of their conduct in not having covered the hospital lands with buildings since the institution of the charity*, by John Holliday, Esq., London, 1788, p. 17. Henceforth *A Further Appeal*.

30 Diary, 1791. James Burton's fragmentary diary, with some additional notes, is held in the Hastings Museum. It is inscribed with an affidavit from a Mr Gates (unknown), a commissioner for oaths, 'This is the manuscript book marked A referred to in the statutory declaration of Alfred Henry Burton. Made before me on the tenth day of December 1901'. It is referred to henceforth as 'Diary' followed by the year in which the entry was made.

31 Diary, 1793.

32   London County Record Office, Foundling Hospital Building Committee Minutes, 2, pp. 31–5, 27 March 1802.

33   Diary, 1793.

34   Diary, 1794.

35   Diary, 1796.

36   Diary, 1799.

37   Malcolm, *Londinium Redivivum*, vol. i, p. 7.

38   Mentioned in a letter dated 20 January 1802. Bedford Estate papers, Bedford Office, London.

39   *An Appeal*, p. 24.

40   Ibid., p. 23.

41   *A Further Appeal*, p. 12.

42   *An Appeal*, p. 24.

43   Ibid., p. 32.

44   Ibid., pp. 22–3.

45   Olsen, *Town Planning in London*, p 48.

46   Building contract between the Bedford Estate and James Burton and Henry Scrimshaw for Southampton Terrace, 6 July 1795, as quoted in Olsen, *Town Planning in London*, p. 50. See also p. 42 of this chapter.

47   This was exhibited as No. 1066: *West view of the houses erecting at the back of Bedford House on the south side of Russell Square*, J. Burton, Architect, Southampton Terrace.

48   *A Further Appeal*, p. 6.

49   Ibid., p. 7.

50   Dobie, *History of the United Parishes*, p. 149.

51   Olsen, *Town Planning in London*, p. 52, states that these were originally third- and fourth-rate houses perhaps because access was poor.

52   Foundling Hospital Building Committee Minutes, 3, pp. 84–5.

53   This reference is ambiguous. It could refer either to the land owned by the Skinners' Company in London known as Sandhills (see figure 1.3), which was developed by Burton or the company also owned land in Kent known by the same name. Burton also purchased this to build Mabledon. Both transactions were going through at about the same time.

54   Diary, 1807.

55   Dobie, *History of the United Parishes*, p 147.

56   1807 Report.

57   For a fuller discussion of both Blondel and Patte's contribution to town planning see A. Picon, *French Architects and Engineers in the Age of Enlightenment*, Cambridge, Cambridge University Press, 1992, esp. chapters 4 and 8.

58   The full range of possibilities of sources for Wood's designs are discussed in T. Mowl and B. Earnshaw, *John Wood: Architect of Obsession*, London, Millstream Books, 1988.

59   A full account of the development of Bath is given in W. Ison, *The Georgian Buildings of Bath*, Bath, Kingsmead, 1980, esp. pp. 22–5, 111–80.

60   *The Ambulator*, London, 1811, p. 23.

61   *The Picture of London*, 3rd edn, London, 1815, pp. 159–60.

62   A. Young, *A Six Weeks Tour through the Southern Counties of England and Wales*, London, 1768, pp. 3–4.

Regent's Park

2

The speculatively built villa was a new form of building development in London and a hallmark of the design of Regent's Park. The park was originally conceived as an adjunct to the city, but it became feasible only with the extension of the plan to include an umbilical link with the centre of London in the form of Regent Street. This created a new dynamic in the development of London and the evolution of the city's infrastructure. The development of Mary le bone or Marybone Park (as the Regent's Park was originally named) on the edge of the city created a satellite environment half in the country half in the city which was purposefully linked with London (see figure 3.1). Previous histories of this area have concentrated on some of the personalities involved, in particular John Nash.[1] There is no doubt that he was an important figure in the project. But if the sights are shifted and attention is focused on the relationship between the landowner, the architect/builder as well as Nash as the 'overseer' a different picture emerges. The point here is not to replace one personality with another to enable the telling of a city's history. Rather, it is to demonstrate that if less attention is placed on the necessity of leading figures or 'auteurs' in the construction of urban histories the evolution of cities can be shown to be more of an interactive process between landowners, architect/builders, patrons and broader social and cultural forces. And in particular here, Regent's Park demonstrates how the systems of land development used by the ruling elite on both their town and country estates were adopted and adapted by the Crown to facilitate a novel urban property venture which included speculatively built villas and terraces plus landscaping and the creation of social space. Of particular note in the latter regard are the designs and layout of both the Zoological and later the Botanical Gardens. In this way the distinctive urban landscape of the park evolves from the resonance between the speculative ventures of the builders of the park and the driving imperative of the ever-growing city.

THE PROJECT

The Regent's Park was the crowning glory of the north end of the New Street. It is significant in the context of the development of urban planning as it imposed for the first time an open space, to which the public had some access, on the cityscape. This shows a significant shift in attitudes towards the production of the urban environment. First, it contrasts markedly with the garden squares and terraces which were the established pattern of development. The fields and market gardens which comprised Marybone Park would have lent themselves well to such an intensive form of land development seen elsewhere in London. Secondly, the self-conscious making of parkland within the city demonstrates an awareness of the potential to use landscape to shape the urban environment and the individual's response to it.

It is easy to forget that the process of the development of Regent's Park, just like the great estates, was that of turning farmland into an urban environment. The huge expansion of the West End of London was built on land used for smallholdings and market gardens, Indeed, the area known as Marylebone supplied London with much of its hay and dairy produce. The leases on these farms had been renewed without much question since the time of Charles I and had provided the Crown with a stream of income, albeit a steadily declining one. But these leases were due to fall in in the opening decades of the nineteenth century and the area was now ripe for development as the north-westwards spread of the city had been capped by the New Road. The Marybone Park offered the possibility of London pushing past this boundary.

The potential of the area had been noticed at the end of the eighteenth century by the Duke of Portland who made an unsuccessful bid, together with his surveyor John White, to build a turnpike road across the land to link the two sides of the Portland estate.[2] This was stopped by John Fordyce, the Surveyor General, who understood the value of the 500 acres of land and saw that Portland's plan would have curtailed any future development of it by the Crown. Indeed, Fordyce was well aware of the substantial income the likes of Portland and his fellow peers Bedford and Grosvenor had made, and were still making, from their estates. Land revenues provided important income for the Crown and here was an opportunity to adopt the successful model of estate development used by the ruling elite. Before his death in 1809 Fordyce had set up a competition to develop the land that attracted three entrants: John White, the Duke of Portland's surveyor; John Nash; and the Surveyors to the Office of Woods and Land Revenues Thomas Leverton and Thomas Chawner. Fordyce also realised that the project needed to be linked with the West End so the plans for the New Street, later Regent Street, were drawn up (see chapter 3).

John White's plan respected the rural character of the park. The perimeter was fringed with villas whilst the central area was largely free of buildings and had tree-lined avenues running through it and a crescent-shaped road at the south linking the park to the West End (figure 2.1). The plan by Thomas Leverton and Thomas Chawner aimed to develop the park along the established lines of garden squares and terraces of housing. Leverton and Chawner envisaged extending the familiar grid system of the streets and squares of the West End to cover the whole the area of the park but with more open spaces and villas at the northern end. This would certainly have been the most intense and possibly also most profitable development. But Regent's Park offered new and different design options from the pockets of land in the West End owned by the ruling elite. Here a large, uncluttered (and literally greenfield) site was available to be laid out according to picturesque principles that masked the commercial nature of the speculatively built villas and terraces. This use of landscape as a disguise for commerce had already been seen on country estates; here this rural practice became urban.[3]

John Nash provided the third plan which by 1811 had became the blueprint for the project (figure 2.2). This included a decorative lake, and an inner and outer circle of road which were laid out almost immediately. A peripheral ring of terraces, a small royal palace facing a formal basin of water, a magnificent church to serve as a valhalla to the nation's heroes, a barracks, a service area and fifty-six villas each

2.1 John White, *Plan for Regent's Park*, 1809, from John White, *Some account of the proposed improvements of the western part of London, by the formation of the Regent's Park, the New Street, the new sewer, &c, &c; illustrated by a variety of plans and accompanied by explanatory and critical observations*, 2nd edn, London, Cadell and Davies, 1815

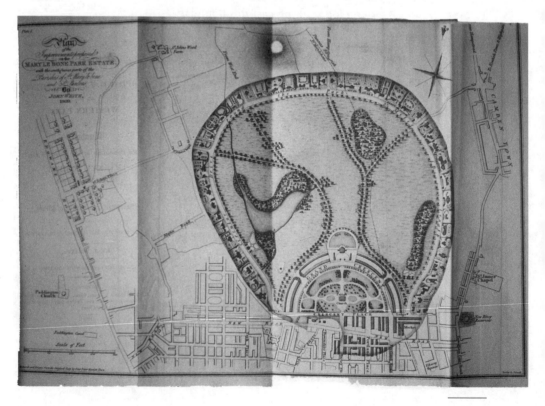

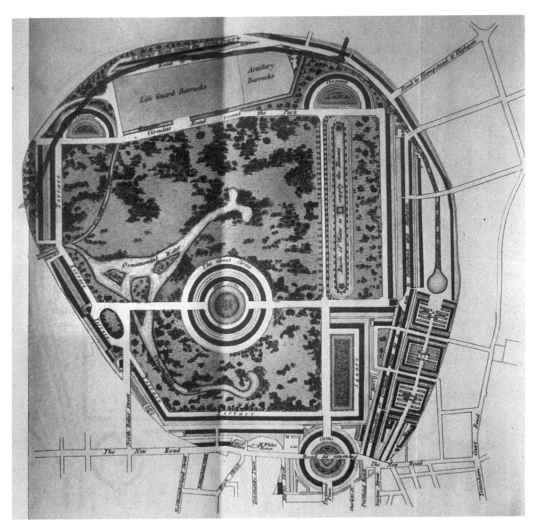

2.2 John Nash, *Plan for Regent's Park*, 1809–1811, from John White, *Some account of the proposed improvements of the western part of London, by the formation of the Regent's Park, the New Street, the new sewer, &c, &c; illustrated by a variety of plans and accompanied by explanatory and critical observations*, 2nd edn, London, Cadell and Davies, 1815

sited so as to be invisible to its neighbours and thus to appear to be in sole enjoyment of the whole estate. This scheme perhaps owed more to White than Nash cared to admit. White's rural informality here met with the set pieces of urban planning such as the circus and the crescent that had become the hallmarks of modern town planning. Like the Regent Street project the venture was to be principally financed by private individuals taking leases from the Crown and building under the watchful eye of Nash who had the right of veto on all plans. But in practice Nash seems to have been involved with discussions about design at only sporadic intervals, as revealed below.

The Napoleonic Wars hampered the development of the park as speculators were unwilling to risk their capital. Things picked up by 1818 and the Fifth Report of the Commissioners of Woods in 1826 pronounced the work almost complete (figure 2.3). There had, however, been sacrifices. The inner double ring of terraces, the two

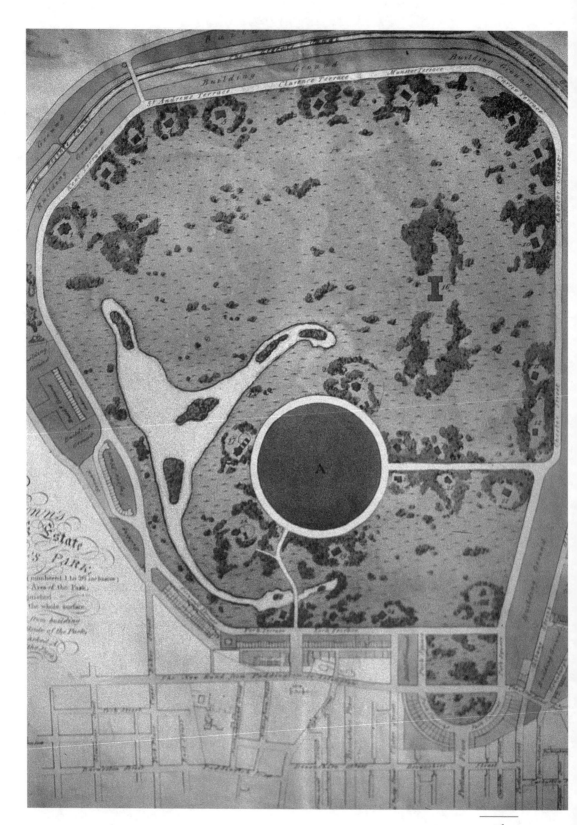

northernmost terraces, the royal palace and the handsome church had all been abandoned; the barracks were resited and the number of villas drastically reduced, first by over half to twenty-six and then to a meagre eight. The increasingly generous landscape setting of the villas and terraces was not necessarily part of Nash's original vision. This came about through economic circumstance. But the importance of the parkland and the relationship between the country and the city in Nash's plan were commented upon by contemporaries. In many ways this is reminiscent of the attitudes towards open spaces discussed in the preceding chapter on Bloomsbury:

> Mr Nash is a better layer out of grounds than architect, and the public have reason to thank him for what he has done for Regent's Park. Our gratitude on that point induces us to say as little as we can of the houses there, with their topolling statues, and other ornamental efforts to escape from the barrack style ...
>
> We have reason to be thankful that the Regent's Park has saved us from worse places in the same quarter; for it is at all events a park, and has trees and grass, and is breathtaking space between town and country. It has prevented Harley and Wimpole Streets from going further; has checked, in the last quarter at least, the monstrous brick cancer that was extending its arms in every direction.[4]

James Elmes in his *Metropolitan Improvements* (1827) rebuked some of the architectural impurities but made the observation that

> Trim gardens, lawns and shrubs; towering spires, ample domes, banks clothed with flowers, all elegancies of the town, and all the beauties of the country are co-mingled with happy art and blissful union. They surely must all be the abodes of nobles and princes! No, the majority are the retreats of the happy, free-born sons of commerce, of the wealthy commonality who thus enrich and bedeck the heart of their great empire.

Regent's Park and Regent Street gave a symmetrical, if curved, axis to the planning of London. This drew on the hierarchical planning of other European cities, for example Paris, and gave architectural expression to the developing relationship between monarch, populace and state. Regent Street linked the city and the park and the importance of this role was underlined by the impressive architectural termini at each end (see figure 3.1) The street culminated at the south in Carlton House, the residence of the Prince Regent.[5] The grand vision continued at the north end with the crescent, originally planned as a circus, and a ring of palace-like facade terraces which defined the outer perimeters of the park. The symmetrical nature of Regent Street and its terminations is amplified if the original plan for the park is recalled. The small royal palace or pavilion was to be in

2.3 *Plan of Regent's Park, 1826*

the park facing southwards towards the northern end of the street, echoing the royal palace at the other end.

The creation of a landscaped site at the edge of the city which provided upmarket housing of a variety of categories was an important development in London's urban plan. Moreover, the way essential parts of the plan were laid over the existing infrastructure, and the dominant role royal foci had in the planning, indicate a developing attitude towards the relationship between the monarch and the populace. As the whole composition of park, street and palace provided a possible processional route through to Westminster it redefined the relationship of the monarch, city and state. This was achieved through the medium of landscape – in terms both of approaches to design and of speculative building practices developed by the landed elite in town and country which here became a kind of rural urbanism. After all, Regent's Park like Regent Street was made possible by speculative developers; public funds could not have covered all the costs.

THE TERRACES

The Regent's Park terraces embellished the pattern of terrace house building common in London since the beginning of the eighteenth century. They provided a visual transition from the street to the park, expressing social status through the architectural vocabulary that articulated their grand, stuccoed facades. This enrichment and unifying of the London terrace to give the impression of a grand palace-style facade rather than a sequence of individual dwellings had been seen in the work of Robert Adam and, indeed, James Burton in Bloomsbury. But the effect in the Regent's Park was far more grandiose as each terrace was embellished on the exterior with columns, decorative sculpture and a stucco finish to give the effect of Bath stone. Yet the layout of the interior of each, and implicit social use of space, differed little from their West End counterparts.[6] And, perhaps most importantly, just as the terraces in the West End were ranged around a garden square so those in the Regent's Park looked out onto and bordered the landscaped parkland.

The construction of the terraces was slow to get going. Indeed building did not begin until 1821, three years after the first villa in the park. As with Regent Street and the villas in the Regent's Park James Burton was the first developer to take up a lease. And his role was such that the Commissioners of Woods described James as 'the architect of Regent's Park'.[7] Indeed where James led the way others certainly followed. In the case of the terraces these included William Mountford Nurse – the most significant contributor after Burton – J. M. Aitkins, William Smith and Richard Mott.

The building procedure for Regent's Park was similar to the later stages of the construction of Regent Street where architect/builders enjoyed more freedom as the street progressed northward (see chapter 3). There were no predetermined sites for the terraces – it was up to the individual developers to approach the Commissioners of Woods. They in turn consulted Nash who approved, if he did not supply, the design comprising an outline plan and main elevation. The Treasury then granted a warrant for a three-year lease at a peppercorn rent to cover the building period. Stipulations about the building quality and maintenance were outlined in the leases including the use of the uniform Bath stone coloured stucco common to both the terraces and the villas. The Burton terraces serve to exemplify the general building procedure and show how the working practices had interesting connections with those employed in Bloomsbury and Regent Street. This demonstrates how the template of effective management of speculative developments that had evolved in the building of the great estates could be applied to increasingly prestigious enterprises, which were just as risky financially.

Cornwall Terrace in the south-west corner of the park was the first to be built in 1821–23. The facade was designed by Decimus Burton, and exhibited at the Royal Academy in 1822, with at least some of the layout of the houses being devised by James.[8] The ground rent was set at £100 per acre but Nash intervened, claiming the sum was insufficient, resulting in it being doubled. Undeterred, the following year James took up a lease on Clarence Terrace and Mews from 1822 to 1824[9] (figure 2.4). Once again Decimus provided

2.4 Decimus Burton, *Clarence Terrace and Mews*, 1823–24, anonymous engraving

the design for the principal facade which was exhibited at the Royal
Academy in 1823. Here the methods for increasing profitability learnt
by James from his earlier building ventures came to the fore. Two
extra houses were squeezed in behind the Ionic screen, a practice also
seen in the Regent Street terraces. In the same year James also built
the western half of York Terrace, with W. M. Nurse constructing the
eastern portion. Both builders agreed to adhere strictly to Nash's
design in the interests of uniformity and to create an impressive
entrance way into the park via York Gate, which was situated
between the two terraces. This ability to follow instructions when
expedient contrasts with the Burtons' treatment of Chester Terrace
in 1824–25 where James's almost charmed ability to make money on
speculations cames into play. Here again the plan was Nash's,
comprising the longest terrace in the park at 925 feet screened by
fifty-two columns over which were to be statues on the theme of the
British worthies, a theme reminiscent of William Kent's design for
the gardens at Stowe a century earlier. The ends of the block were
to be brought towards the park. Burton deviated from this
monumental design which would rival Paris, as Nash commented
that the terrace 'was nearly as long as the Tuileries', as he saw a way
to make the development more profitable. Burton built additional
houses behind the forward blocks. The meant these had to be
detached from the main run to allow access to these dwellings. An
acrimonious dispute ensued and the removal of the forward wings
was called for by the Commissioners of Woods. The situation was
made more complicated by the fact that James Burton had quickly
sold on the leases to Mr James Landsdown who now also required
compensation for any demolition deemed necessary. The architect
William Wilkins was brought in to settle any compensation payable
by the Crown. In a private letter to Alexander Milne dated 6 May
1826 Nash stated his opinion about the dispute:

> It is [a] very painful circumstance to oppose or appear to oppose Mr
> Burton for whom I entertain considerable regard – but I feel that I
> ought not to stand by and see the Commissioners enter into a partial
> enquiry in which loss is assumed on one side without taking into
> consideration advantages which that side desire from a departure from
> their engagement, or from disposing of the ground in a manner unau-
> thorized by that engagement – I feel this sentiment still more strongly
> from entertaining a different opinion as to the necessity of taking down
> the Houses, convinced that the removal of them will produce a worse
> effect than by altering the screen so as to obscure the buildings which
> are behind.[10]

Nash had supplied a sketch plan showing how the extra houses
could be hidden from view and a visual link made between the end

blocks and the main terrace by means of a screen. He was convinced that the forward standing end blocks were essential for the 'beauty' of the facade and should not be demolished. The Commissioners differed in opinion from Nash but remained chiefly concerned with the overall attractive appearance of the terrace. Moreover, he realised Burton had already gained financially by increasing the volume of building on the plot and stood to gain again from the compensation he would receive if the extra buildings were demolished. The deciding factor for the retention of the blocks and houses was introduced by Nash as he continued:

> I tremble too for the amount of compensation which Mr Wilkins will be bound to award, if he is to consider only the question as put to him in the Queries – I enclose Queries which would lead to an investigation of the whole concern – I hope I have done my duty and no more than my duty in stating the whole of my opinion on the subjects which I do not wish to do as an official document, but to induce you against the measure about to be adopted.

Cornwall, Clarence and Chester Terraces show how the mechanics of speculative development informed the building process of Regent's Park. The Crown and the Commissioners of Woods remained a landlords and exercised governance over the project and took as lively interest in the quality of design. This level of engagement challenges the primacy usually ascribed to John Nash as overseer of the project. Moreover, the expertise and willingness to take risks (in more ways than one) of the speculative developers were essential to the successful execution of the park. And the aesthetic appearance of the terraces remained of crucial importance. Indeed, the idea of a stylistically harmonious purpose-built community was not unlike the new model farms that were fast becoming a feature of the rural landscape.

THE VILLAS

The villas were detached residences standing in compact private grounds which in turn comprised part of the larger public park. The Burtons were involved in the design and/or construction of all but one.[11] The Regent's Park villas, like the terraces, were Crown leasehold but their design was not prescribed or supplied by Nash although, in principle, he had the final veto over plans. There is no evidence, however, of Nash having had any influence over the designs. It was the individual occupants and architects who gave architectural expression to this new kind of urban building type. This raises the important question of who lived in Regent's Park? And what, if anything, did they have in common which made Regent's Park an attractive proposition for a house?[12]

2.5 Decimus Burton, *The Holme*, 1818, from T. Shepherd and J. Elmes, *Metropolitan Improvements*, London, 1828

The first resident in the park was James Burton who moved into The Holme in 1818, continuing his tradition of living on his own building developments (figure 2.5) If the fact that a speculative developer, although by now rich and socially established, was the first to occupy one of the villas caused no controversy, the design of the residence he built certainly did. The Commissioners of Woods remarked to Nash:

> In your observation that 'it is to be lamented, for the beauty of the Park, that Mr Burton was allowed to build the sort of House he has built', the Board (having recently inspected the Park and the Villa in question) command me to state to you that they entirely concur; but they cannot record this concurrence, without unequivocally stating to you, at the same time, that in their judgment the whole blame of having suffered such a building to be erected, as well as the consider-able expense to which it is their further mortification to find, by your Letter, the Crown has been put in planting out the deformities of this building, rest entirely with yourself; The Board consider it to be your special Duty to take care that any Building to be erected in Marylebone Park should be so constructed as not only to deform but to constitute a real ornament and a substantial and profitable improvement ... of the Crown's Estate.[13]

It is noteworthy that Nash took much of the blame for The Holme and that James Burton continued to work in Regent's Park. The concern over the stylistic appearance of The Holme perhaps indi-cates the integral relationship between the park and newly emerging cityscape. Moreover, their outrage did not stop the Commissioners employing Decimus Burton only few years later to carry out improvements in Hyde, St James's and Green Parks. Indeed their reason for choosing him to carry out work in the royal parks was the standard of his work in Regent's Park.[14] The Burtons stayed in the park until 1831 when they moved to a villa in their own speculative development of a small town in Sussex, St Leonards.[15] Little is known except the names of the subsequent residents of The Holme.

The lease on one of the few villas not to be designed by Decimus Burton was taken up by Charles Augustus Tulk MP, a philosopher and philanthropist of independent means. He moved into St John's Lodge, designed for him by John Raffield, also on the inner circle, shortly after the Burtons took up residence in the park. Tulk stayed only three years and his villa stood empty for a further five until 1826 when it was taken by John Maberley MP. In 1829 Maberley let it to an aristocratic tenant, the Marquis of Wellesley, the brother of the Duke of Wellington, who employed Decimus Burton to enlarge the villa. In 1833, when Wellesley began his second term as Lord Lieutenant of Ireland, Isaac Lyon Goldsmid moved in and also enlarged the villa.[16]

The remaining villas were all designed by Decimus Burton and some were built by James. South Villa was under construction by 1819. The lease was bought by David Lance of 40 Nottingham Place, only a short distance from the park; within one year Lance had sold his lease to William Henry Cooper who remained there until 1836 when he moved to Painshill, Surrey, where Decimus Burton carried out alterations. Albany Cottage, later known as North Villa, had been occupied by 1824 by the diarist Thomas Raikes. This was designed by C. R. Cockerell with some participation from Decimus Burton.[17] Hanover Lodge, designed by Decimus Burton for the Napoleonic veteran Sir Robert Arbuthnot, was occupied in 1827.

Three of the villas stand out through their design and occupants. Grove House was one of the most specular and well positioned villas, designed and built between 1822 and 1824 by Decimus Burton for George Bellas Greenough, an eminent natural scientist who lived there until his death in 1856 (figure 2.6). St Dunstan's was designed by Burton in 1825 for the Marquess of Hertford, one of George IV's closest associates, who held onto to the villa until his death in 1842 (figure 2.7). Holford House, the last of the eight, was owned by the wealthy city merchant James Holford who applied to the commissioners for land for a house in the north-west of the park in 1833 where he lived until his death in 1854. This too was designed by Burton. The two latter villas were much larger and more flamboyant than the others and used for lavish entertaining. The more personal nature of the planning of these villas perhaps partly explains why these were occupied by single tenants for substantial periods of time.

The leasehold nature of the villas, the rapid turnaround and variety of occupants, and their semi-urban location show the

departure the Regent Park dwellings made from the established villa tradition and the urban terraced house. They offered the idea of a landscaped villa through the fusion of private and common grounds: a kind of English picturesque in miniature. The intention had always been that each villa would be sited so that it appeared to stand alone in the whole park. The villas were not necessarily seen as long-term residences or any kind of permanent base; instead they were sold on for profit or convenience. In many ways they served as a glorified town house on the edge of the city with a link via the new Regent's Street to the centre.

2.6 Decimus Burton, *Grove House*, 1822–24, from T. Shepherd and J. Elmes, *Metropolitan Improvements*, London, 1828

2.7 Decimus Burton, *St Dunstan's*, 1825

James Burton was one of the first to take up leases on the villas. These give us some idea of the mechanics of the building procedure and the way in which it was financed. Nash's grand scheme for Regent's Park had languished after the initial landscaping works until Burton took up his first lease on 23 November 1816 for a plot of land, on which he built The Holme, of just over two acres including the ditch on the outside of the sunken fence around the premises. The ground rent was staggered into three stages, which was not unusual, and shows that the villas were to be built as rapidly as the terraces which were springing up all over London.[18] The building had to be kept the colour of Bath stone, this effect being achieved by painted stucco. Burton agreed to spend £5,000 on the construction of the villa, and its design was, as were all buildings in the park and Regent's Street, subject to the approval of John Nash.[19] These covenants were a means of quality assurance employed in several of the villa leases. In some ways this is reminiscent of the rate system of terrace house building where some standards could be assured through the specification of a certain rate of house. This sum appears in several of the villa leases regardless of the lessee as, for instance, the Marquis of Hertford faced the same stipulations when he took up his lease in 1825.[20]

Burton's second lease on a smaller plot of land was taken out two years later in 1818 in the south-west corner of the park.[21] Here, following the same conditions as their first lease the Burtons built South Villa (demolished in 1930).[22] It is interesting to note the discrepancy between the different plots in the park in terms of their final ground rents. The larger plots were not necessarily more expensive in real terms. This was perhaps due to their location. But even so the larger the plot the more substantial the contribution of the building and the gardens around it to the overall landscaping of the park.

DECIMUS' VILLAS

The leasehold nature of the villas and the building controls imposed on their designers and builders are new elements in the history of the villa. The mechanics of the leasehold and building process are distinct from the design problems faced in producing this novel kind of urban dwelling where the architectural language of the country estate was brought into the city.

The first question to be raised with reference to Regent's Park is the use of the term 'villa', as Burton's houses were distinct from their eighteenth-century predecessors.[23] Decimus Burton certainly drew on the neo-classical adaptations of Palladian formulae seen in the work of Adam, Holland and Soane. Robert Adam's studies of the Pantheon, Roman Tholoi and Thermae also introduced planning ideas which were readily adapted to small villa design giving the grandeur of antiquity to an otherwise modest dwelling in a different way from Palladio. This is seen chiefly in the imaginative treatment of space as well as the applied antiquity of elements like the Palladian temple portico entrance. But Burton's villas are not merely derivative, as he introduced into the designs many new and influential ideas which responded to the changing social climate and the urban context of these buildings. He commented on his work when providing material for J. Britton and A. Pugin's *Public Buildings of London* (1825–28): '[I have] aimed only at imbibing the spirit of [my] great models, and have fearlessly deviated from them when rigid adherence would have been incompatible with [my] design.'

The description of Albany Cottage in James Elmes's *Metropolitan Improvements* demonstrates some contemporary problems with architectural terminology: 'As a specimen [Albany Cottage] of the English cottage ornee, it is scarcely to be surpassed, even in this region of architectural and picturesque beauty.' But the design is as dignified as the others in Regent's Park – despite the Burtons' interference with Cockerell's plans. A single-storey three-bay central block punctuated by four Doric pilasters was flanked by a pair of slightly higher two-storey wings. A terrace with a metal awning fronted the central block with curved steps leading to the grounds. One possible suggestion for this terminology is that Elmes 'was simply desperate to use a different word'.[24] But it must be remembered that architectural vocabulary and criticism was not necessarily as precise at this time as it is today.

Decimus Burton's villas in Regent's Park differ from each other considerably in form and function. The larger houses, usually with a flamboyant owner, were used principally for entertaining and contrast with the small, compact but prestigious residences which perhaps had more in common with the casinos which had proved so popular at the end of the eighteenth century. The Holme, The Grove and St Dunstan's provide ideal case studies through which to explore the differences in approach to design of father and son and to compare the way in which both Burtons produced architecture to meet specific social needs.

The Holme (figure 2.5) shows the influence of Decimus' training at the Royal Academy Schools. It also contains many features that were to recur throughout his work in the park. Geometry is the overriding design principle. The house is a rectangular block surmounted by a triangular roof intersected on the garden side by a semi-cylindrical bay topped by a dome, part of which is a sphere. The transverse axis is established further by the portico on the entrance front. This type of small-scale house had been popular in England and France since about 1750. Well-known precedents of which Burton was well aware include Robert Adam's Ranger's Lodge 1768 in Green Park and the river front of Rousseau's Hotel de Salm, Paris (1782–86). Sir John Soane, Burton's mentor at the Royal Academy Schools had occasionally used the semi-cylindrical form of the bay as seen at his Letton Hall plans dating from 1785–88. Nash had also used these ideas in his Casino at Dulwich Kent for R. Shawe in 1797 and at Rockingham, Co. Roscommon (*circa* 1810).

A spinal corridor ran through the house, creating an enfilade effect terminating with a polygonal conservatory on the eating-room side of the house. This transition between interior space, conservatory and landscape was frequently used by Burton in many of his country house and villa designs. The loggia or portico was not well suited for the English climate. The conservatory, of which Burton was a pioneer designer, offered landscape views with the option of central heating.

Grove House (figure 2.6) was one of Decimus Burton's first major buildings and the occupant, George Bellas Greenough, became a close associate who did much to further Burton's career. The designs were exhibited at the Royal Academy in 1822 along with his view of Cornwall Terrace.[25] The plan and exterior expressed the contemporary fashion for Greek Revival design but, in contrast to the severity of the temple-like appearance of William Wilkins's The Grange (1812), Grove House displays a fluidity that provides a less pedantic link between Greek religious architecture and a building type whose sources are essentially Roman, Italianate and domestic. The classical language of architecture is invoked in the screen of Greek Doric columns around the semi-circular bay of the east facade to signal the gender of the sole occupant of the villa. Elsewhere, specific reference is made to the Erechtheum, which is itself a break with the rigidity of Greek temple design. This is seen, for instance, in the variation of levels and elevations and in the direct quotation of the north porch of the Erechtheum in the principal elevation of the house on its south side. The interior also reflected both the identity of Greenough as a natural scientist and the fashion for things Greek. In the library a plaster-cast frieze of the Panathenaic procession from the Parthenon ran around the top of the bookcases and mahogany cabinets that held his collection of specimens.[26] As a bachelor Greenough did not require the usual suite of family accommodations. Thus the first floor is smaller in area than the ground floor and the arrangement of bedrooms in a cruciform pattern gave each chamber direct access to a terrace which is the flat roof of the room beneath. These private terraces afforded attractive vistas of the surrounding area.

Indeed, the design of the grounds surrounding Grove House were of almost equal importance to that of the villa itself, and the architecture at times elides with the landscape. For instance, the three rooms on the garden front of the house ran efilade, giving a sense of openness. The grounds were some of the most splendid not only in terms of their location within the park but also through Greenough's enthusiasm for gardening. A screen brick wall cut off the view to the north of the house (away from the park) so directing the viewer's gaze towards the villa's grounds and the park itself. Towards the end of the run of the screen wall facing south was a small glass and iron conservatory semi-elliptical in plan and elevation and ¼ elliptical in section. This is an early style of Burton conservatory which used a brick wall as part of its structure rather than being freestanding, and made entirely of iron and glass.

Grove House became one of the most famous of the Regent's Park villas and images of it were widely published in Europe and America. The American architect Ithiel Town built a close copy of the villa in New Haven in 1830. In common with many architects he had seen Grove House on a visit to Europe which had included a visit to Regent's Park. And it was soon re-interpreted outside London near James Burton's adopted home territory of the area around Tonbridge, Kent. At nearby Keston, Decimus revised his design for Grove House in his scheme for Holwood House (1823–25) for John Ward MP.[27] Ward had been involved with some minor speculative developments on the New Street and had bought the estate which had once belonged to William Pitt. The old house was demolished and the design of the new villa had to fit into an established Repton landscape.

Designs for the Marquis of Hertford's villa were exhibited at the Royal Academy in 1823 (see figure 2.7) and the villa completed by 1825.[28] It was known as St Dunstan's villa, as the clock of Old St Dunstan's in the West was purchased by the Marquis and sat in the grounds from 1832 onwards. The villa was situated in the north-west corner of the park with the garden facade overlooking the serpentine lake rather like Grove House and The Holme. The occupant was a colourful figure who was the basis of the Marquis of Steyne in Thackeray's *Vanity Fair* and Disraeli's Marquis of Monmouth in *Coningsby*. The design is more complicated than Burton's previous villas but still shows a synthesis of his favourite elements. The entrance is through a single-storey porch with two rows of columns one behind the other in the same order as the Tower of the Winds. This leads into the elliptical saloon. There are three rooms on the garden front which are enfilade; the centre room has a semi-cylindrical bay. Externally, on the entrance side the main two-storey block is interrupted by another at right angles to it. The interior of the building was expensively decorated and presents a procession of rooms suitable for the whole purpose of the villa: the lavish entertaining of the Marquis's friends.

The villas can be seen as the beginning of a trend in speculative suburban middle-class housing that still exists today. Indeed, the Burtons learnt much from their work in Regent's Park. They went on to produce designs for large-scale developments of small villas and terraces set in landscaped grounds at St Leonards,[29] Calverley[30] and Cobh.[31] The villa designs for these were microcosms of their larger predecessors in Regent's Park. The layout of the estates made them saleable, offering the middle class a sense of grandeur and the all important feeling of communality with the landscape.

Decimus continued to work in Regent's Park for several decades where he produced two distinct landscaped spaces: the Zoological Society Gardens (1826–41) and the Royal Botanical Society Gardens (1840–59). Alongside this he designed the Colosseum (1823–27), a novel building for public entertainment. All three enterprises made a substantial contribution to the urban landscape and the social environment of the park for residents and visitors. The purpose here is not to retell their development and building procedure (this has been done elsewhere),[32] but to underline the various ways in which the London landscape was developed in the opening decades of the nineteenth century.

The choice of Decimus Burton as architect to the Zoological Society and the Royal Botanical Society might seem surprising at first in the context of his other work in Regent's Park. But by the mid 1820s Decimus was working in other royal parks in London and in the early 1830s he was entrusted with the complete remodelling of the Phoenix Park in Dublin. Decimus was by this time an established practitioner whose skill at laying out grounds and landscaping was recognised by the Commissioners of Woods as he was their principal executant architect – although no such formal position existed, unlike the attached architects of the Office of Works.

The work in the London and Dublin parks made a substantial contribution to the re-imaging of both cities and demonstrates how the principles of landscapes design used in rural environments were easily imported into a metropolitan context. Hyde, St James's and Green Parks in London provided a landscape setting for a series of monuments celebrating monarch, state and the nation's heroes, the Duke of Wellington and Admiral Lord Nelson. In addition, the residences of both the King and the Duke of Wellington were located adjacent to the parks.

Similarly, the Phoenix Park was the backdrop for governmental buildings and monuments including the Vice Regal Lodge and Sir Robert Smirke's Wellington Testimonial (1817–22). The expression of triumphalism and the assertion of authority encoded in the design of these urban spaces owed its grammar and syntax to the language of landscape design of country estates which had been developed to embellish the reputation of the ruling elite. The invitation of the public into these urban landscapes helped to engender a feeling of inclusivity and ownership in the populace which served the political ends of monarch and state. These issues are discussed further with reference to London in the final two chapters of this book and have been discussed elsewhere in relation to the Phoenix Park.[33]

Burton's work for private clients in Regent's Park runs parallel to his substantial interventions in the royal parks. Nevertheless, the principles of landscape design used not only to embellish the natural topography, but also for didactic purposes, have resonance with the remodelling of the royal parks. The Zoological Gardens and those belonging to the Royal Botanic Society were learning environments, albeit less subtle than those found in the royal parks. Moreover, in all these projects the public perception and reception of the landscape design is an important aspect of the work.

The Royal Zoological Society was founded by Sir Stamford Raffles in July 1824. It comprised 151 members including residents of Regent's Park, of whom the Marquess of Hertford was one. Although the Society had premises in Bruton Street an open-air menagerie was required. The park was the obvious spot but the preferred site of the Inner Circle had been let to the nurseryman Mr Jenkins. Instead Burton was engaged to landscape an irregular, triangular-shaped site of five acres in the north-east corner of the park. The Society lease stated a ground rent of £18 per annum for the first three years which would rise to £400 per annum thereafter. Burton's plans were only partly realised, but demonstrate an interesting landscape arrangement.[34] He faced the additional problem of the plot being bisected by the Outer Circle. Burton's use of a tunnel to link the two features is still in use today, and his innovative designs for animal houses, including a clock tower which was part of the camel house and the giraffe house, show an imaginative approach to these design problems.

The Royal Botanical Society was founded in 1838 with J. D. C. Sowerbey as Secretary. It took over the grounds in the Inner Circle of the park, originally let to Mr Jenkins, at a rent of £102 per annum until 1899 and £285 per annum thereafter. Burton was appointed architect in 1840 and, with the help of Mr Marnock, the curator of the plant collection, laid out the grounds on a Linnaean arrangement, included medical, agricultural and manufacturing gardens, at the considerable cost of £12,000.[35] Burton's final design including high turfed mounds along the paths with appropriate breaks to allow views through the whole layout.[36] The high banks were to be made possible in part by the materials removed in the excavation of a lake. Both these elements were 'to render the Inner Circle more pleasing to the Public who are likely in consequence of the alterations in the Park to be more frequent visitors to the Inner Circle'.[37] The gardens proved a popular attraction as, unlike the Zoological Gardens, they were open to the general public.

RUS IN URBE

The production of town housing by speculative developers was not new. The terraces of west London, Bath and Edinburgh were a common feature of the eighteenth-century city and had done much to form the urban streetscape, but the Regent's Park project introduced a new type of housing into London: the urban villa. This is quite distinctive from both the freestanding, usually aristocratic, town house, of which there were many scattered across London, and its rural namesake. Up to the end of the eighteenth century the villa had provided a balanced contrast between the city and retreat. Here the villa was brought into the city, albeit on the perimeter, providing retreat, fresh air and a barrier between the Georgian street plan and the fields beyond. What is more, these villas were not aristocratic playthings which remained in the family long after the novelty had worn off. They were, instead, saleable commodities which frequently changed hands and, unlike their predecessors, were leasehold. Like their predecessors, the Regent's Park villas were set in the landscape but this was part private garden and part public park.[38] The landscaping of the villas' grounds and approaches were the responsibility of the architect and/or speculative builder and had an important effect on the overall appearance of the park. The villas and their gardens were integrated into the whole rather than being defined as separate precincts through the use of walls or tall hedges and fences. This relationship between buildings and landscape and subtle definition of their distinctiveness whilst they appear part of the whole was one of the most significant aspects of the park. It is perhaps appropriate that, partly on the basis of his work in Regent's Park, Decimus Burton went on to remodel the royal parks, which were to form another important phase in the shaping of London, and the aesthetic, social and political potential of landscape was used to the full.

1   See for instance J. Summerson, *The Life and Work of John Nash, Architect*, London and Cambridge, Mass., MIT Press 1980, pp. 114–29, and A. Saunders, *Regent's Park from 1086 to the Present Day*, 2nd edn, London, Bedford College, 1981, chs. 4 and 5.

2   See Saunders, *Regent's Park*, pp. 51–2.

3   This is discussed in chapter 1.

4   Leigh Hunt, *The Townsman*, nos. 2, 3 and 4, reprinted in L. and C. Houchans (eds), *Political and Occasional Essays*, London and New York, Columbia University Press, 1963, pp. 289–90.

5   See D. Arnold, 'The Arch at Constitution Hill: A New Axis for London', *Apollo*, 138 (379) (Sept. 1993), pp. 129–33.

6   See Summerson, *The Life and Work of John Nash*, and Saunders, *Regent's Park*.

7   Cres 2/774.

8   Cres 2/767.

9   Cres 2/772 and a groundplan of the proposed development is held in the National Archives, MPI 583 (1–6) 1823.

10 Cres 2/781.

11 See my essay, 'A Family Affair: Decimus Burton's Designs for the Regent's Park Villas', in D. Arnold (ed.), *The Georgian Villa*, Stroud, Sutton, 1996 (repr. 1998), pp. 105–17. My discussion of the villas in this book draws on material I published in this essay.

12 For a fuller discussion see E. C. Samuel, *The Villas in Regent's Park and their Residents*, London, Bedford College, 1959.

13 Letter from Alexander Milne, Secretary to the Commissioners of the Office of Woods and Forests, to John Nash, quoted in Saunders, *Regent's Park*, p. 94.

14 In 1823 Charles Arbuthnot, the Chief Commissioner of Woods, recommended Decimus Burton for the work in the royal parks on the basis that his 'plans for the other improvements of the parks [i.e. Regent's] had met with so much approbation' (Cres 8/16 f. 3).

15 See J Manwaring Baines, *Burton's St Leonards*, Hastings, Hastings Museum, 1990.

16 See J. Mordaunt Crook, 'The Villas in Regent's Park', pts 1 and 2, *Country Life*, 143 (1968), pp. 22–5, 84–7.

17 There appears to have been an unhappy collaboration between C. R. Cockerell and Decimus Burton. This is outlined in A. Saunders, *The Regent's Park Villas*, London, Bedford College (University of London), 1981, pp. 23–4.

18 Cres 6/122 ff 90–1. The lease was for ninety-nine years: the first year's rent was £14 13s. 6d., the second year £64 13s. 9d., rising to £129 7s. 6d. from the third year onward and was backdated to 10 October 1815.

19 Cres 6/131 f 47.

20 Cres 19/5 f 111, 13 September 1825. At least £5,000 was to be spent on the villa; the design had been approved and the layout of the ground was to be

approved by the Commissioners.

21 Cres 6/122 f 170. The rent payable for the first and second years was £15 13s. From the third year onwards it rose to £107 10s. per annum.

22 Saunders, *The Villas of Regent's Park*, p. 16, states that this villa can be attributed only to the Burtons but the Cres papers cited above clearly state that James Burton took up the lease in 1818. Moreover, the application by Decimus Burton to add an Ionic portico so soon after the start of the project infers he was the architect.

23 For a discussion of the term 'villa' see du Prey, *Sir John Soane*, pp. 265–95, and Arnold, *The Georgian Villa*, pp. ix–xii.

24 This is suggested by Saunders, *The Regent's Park Villas*, p. 24.

25 Drawings for Grove House, 1822–24, are held in the collection at the Victoria and Albert Museum, D1310–1907.

26 This was executed by John Henning, a member of Decimus Burton's regular workforce. Henning had made casts of the Elgin Marbles when they were housed in the courtyard of the Royal Academy on their arrival in London. See J. Malden, *John Henning*, Paisley, Renfrew District Council Museum and Art Galleries, 1977.

27 Drawings for Holwood House are held at the Victoria and Albert Museum D1894–1907. Ward also employed Decimus Burton to design the Calverley Estate in Tunbridge Wells, Kent from 1828 onwards.

28 A folio volume containing the ten drawings Burton exhibited at the Royal Academy are in the collection of the Architectural Association.

29 See Manwaring Baines, *Burton's St Leonards*.

30 This estate in Tunbridge Wells was designed by Decimus for John Maberley MP. Burton also designed a splendid villa for Maberley, Holwood House, Keston, Kent in 1825.

31 This work was carried out for Lord Midleton. Papers and designs relating to the project are held at the Surrey County Record Office.

32 For the Zoological Gardens see P. Chalmers Mitchell, *Centenary History*, London, 1929, and H. Scherren, *The Zoological Society of London*, London, 1905. For the Royal Botanic Society see Guy Meynell, 'The Royal Botanic Society's Gardens, Regent's Park', *The London Journal*, 6:2 (1980). For the Colosseum see Hugh Honour, 'The Regent's Park Colosseum', *Country Life*, 2 Jan. 1953. See also Cres 2/771 and Cres 2/777.

33 The Phoenix Park is discussed in my chapter 'Transplanting National Cultures: The Phoenix Park Dublin (1832–49), an Urban Heterotopia?' in D. Arnold (ed.), *Cultural Identities and the Aesthetics of Britishness*, Manchester, Manchester University Press, 2004, pp. 67–86. Burton's successful design for the Zoological Gardens in London and his growing reputation as a landscape designer led to his also being commissioned to design the Zoological Gardens in Dublin, situated in the Phoenix Park. A transcript of his plan and report, dated 27 October 1832, exists in Trinity College, Dublin Library (Zoological Society Minute Book, May 1830–July 1840, 10608/2/1 TCD).

34 The original plan is held in the National Archives, MPE 906.

35 Correspondence regarding the design of the society's buildings and grounds in the Regent's Park can be found in Cres 2/754. Burton's report on the laying out of the grounds was printed in the *Gardener's Magazine*, 16 (1840),

pp. 514–16.

36 Thomas Chawner and James Pennethorne of the Office of Woods had made several objections to Burton's original scheme of 1840 (Cres 2/754).

37 Letter from J. D. C. Sowerby to the Commissioners of Woods transmitting Burton's plans, 13 December 1841, Cres 2/754. Plans in the National Archives, MPI 574 (2).

38 For a fuller discussion of the notion of the picturesque in the creation of the royal parks in London during the early part of the nineteenth century see D. Arnold, 'Decimus Burton and the Urban Picturesque', in Arnold (ed.), *The Picturesque in Late Georgian England*, pp. 51–6.

11 Class and conflict

The developments in London's infrastructures are indexical of the issues of class and conflict that come to the fore in the period covered in this book. The road network expanded along with the prodigious growth of the capital in terms of its physical size and population. And the river remained an important mode of transport whilst the increased number of river crossings provided improved traffic circulation and access. These developments in the urban infra-structure made the city both more knowable and more controllable and in turn its populace became more manageable. The improve-ments to the London landscape were carried out against a backdrop of social and political unrest where one of the main areas of friction was the issue of social caste in relation to individual liberty and empowerment.

The construction of the New Street from 1815, or Regent Street as it was later named, carved a north–south axis through the centre of the metropolis. Imposed on the pre-existing street pattern, it formed the first grand route through London between the new upmarket speculative development of Regent's Park at its north end and the ever-grander royal residence, Carlton House, where it terminated at the south. The street was the vision of George IV and his officers – most notably his principal architect John Nash – and it was intended to add majesty and grandeur to the urban landscape. Regent Street just like the garden squares of the great estates, was realised through the endeavours of speculative developers, but this grand project also facilitated social segregation, placing the rich to the west and the poor to the east. Perhaps more importantly, the street also met the need for easier access across the city – not least for troops who might be called upon to deal with rebellious uprisings.

On the other side of London the rebuilding of London Bridge in the early 1820s can be considered within the framework of the emerging early nineteenth-century metropolis. Improvements in planning, the definition of the city's perimeters and entrance points and the erection of monuments to nation and state were all part of the re-imaging of the metropolis in which London Bridge played a significant and distinctive role. The balance of power between a national government interested in urban development and an estab-lished authority within the City of London creates a dialectic around the issues of civic and national pride. The discrete identity of London Bridge as the entrance-way into the City was appropriated and revised to help create an image of a modern metropolis which encompassed not just the City but also the City of Westminster and the Borough of Southwark. London Bridge became the prestigious eastern entrance into the city whereas Westminster Bridge defined the approach from the west. As such London Bridge became part of the infrastructure of the metropolitan improvements which attempted to give coherence to the fractured street plan of the capital. The disinterest shown in these projects by the authorities of the City of London demonstrate their feeling of dislocation from and disinterest in the creation of a new and vital identity for the metropolis.

3 Regent Street

Developments in the planning of London during the long eighteenth century were carried out during a period of continued political turbulence across Europe. It is possible to set the Metroplitan Improvements and specifically the creation of Regent Street within this context of conflict which was based largely on class difference.[1] Known initially as the New Street, Regent Street and the area then known as Charing Cross can be seen as a wish on the part of George IV and his ministers to reinforce the position of the Crown and enhance the authority of the state. These measures were also intended to protect the upper class residents of the West End of London, yet, paradoxically, their resistance to the Metropolitan Improvements – especially the New Street – was considerable.

The construction of Regent Street forged a line north–south through the centre of London and carved through the existing urban plan to redefine access, circulation and vista through the metropolis (figure 3.1). The street was the vision of George IV[2] and his officers – most notably his principal architect John Nash. It was designed to provide an essential link between the new development of Marylebone Park on the northern edge of London (see chapter 2) and the city centre and to add majesty and grandeur to the urban landscape. But Regent Street had its origins as much in the existing urban fabric as the drawing boards of the Office of Works. Previous studies have shown how the possibilities for social segregation, the need for access and a spirit of competition with France were essential components in the evolution and instigation of the Regent Street project.[3] This chapter explores different aspects of the building history of Regent Street which centre on two main issues. First, the contribution made to its development by the team of James Burton and S. P. Cockerell: this essential ingredient in the execution of the project was formed during Burton's work in Bloomsbury and it underlines Regent Street's genesis in the established pattern of building in London. Secondly the significance of the construction of a street rather than of an area is considered as a barometer of the relationship between class and conflict at this time – especially as this new thoroughfare was laid over the existing urban fabric.

The complicated building history of Regent Street has been told elsewhere, but this has been treated principally as part of the

3.1 *Map of Regent Street and Regent Park*, from J. Summerson, *Architecture in Britain, 1530 to 1830* (1953), 9th edn, New Haven and London, Yale University Press, 1993

biography of John Nash.[4] The need to attribute such a scheme to an individual architect has coloured the way in which the Regent Street project has been viewed, understood and interpreted. Other studies have presented the street as an isolated but homogeneous development in London,[5] but these approaches give less attention to the social and cultural significance of the first major urban planning project undertaken by the state which was, after all, carried out by private individuals. If the sights are re-aligned, and Regent Street is considered in terms of the impact on the planning and demography of London, its role in the shaping of the metropolis can be more easily assessed. Moreover, these factors can be mapped against established patterns of urban development, particularly the great estates and the interaction between housing and infrastructure. An examination of the role of James Burton in the development of the street reveals that, rather than being solely the grand vision of Nash, the project was more the result of an interaction between an active and experienced team of architects, surveyors and builders and the Crown as landlord. Most importantly, the same team of James Burton as architect/builder and S. P. Cockerell as surveyor emerges as a driving force in the project – doubtless benefiting from the experience of Bloomsbury. But the purpose here is not to re-attribute or ascribe authorship to other architect/builders than Nash. Instead, the street is discussed here as being partly the result of a team that had worked successfully in Bloomsbury taking on new ideas about town planning in London to create a distinctive urban environment. The Crown's involvement is also important as it is the beginning of significant state intervention in the urban landscape which had a social and political subtext. Regent Street can also be seen as the start of the deliberate creation of urban environments to shape residents' and visitors' experience of the metropolis. These emerge as important themes in the later chapters of this study.

The vision of a new plan for London held by George IV and his officers was to be realised in the same way as the landed aristocracy had developed their lands through the use of speculative builders. There are similarities between the Regent Street and Bloomsbury developments. It has already been seen how Burton's use of the full range of rates of houses in Bloomsbury established this kind of separation of the classes in the area. Indeed, the notion of social segregation is an explicit part of the new plan for the area outlined by Nash which was presented under three main headings: 'Utility to the Public', 'Beauty of the Metropolis' and 'Practicability'.[6] The New Street was to create for the first time a strong north–south axis through the city, and with it came a division of the classes. In cruder terms, the upper echelons lived to the west of the new street in the smart new squares, while shopkeepers, craftsmen and the very poor

lived to the east. Nash made no secret of his objective to 'provide a
boundary and complete separation between the Streets and Squares
occupied by the nobility and gentry, and the narrow streets and
meaner Houses occupied by the mechanics and the trading parts of
the community.'[7] On completion of the new street Nash wrote: 'my
purpose was that the new street should cross the eastern entrance to
all the streets occupied by the higher classes and to leave out to the
east all the bad streets, and as a sailor would express himself to hug
all the avenues that went to good streets.'[8]

The importance of infrastructure must not be forgotten, as the
question of access was as important to the development of Regent
Street as it was for the work in Bloomsbury. The New Road enhanced
the desirability and viability of Bloomsbury and the New Street
helped to do the same for the area between Marylebone and St James
and Regent's Park. John Fordyce, the Surveyor General of Land
Revenues, made an essential contribution without which the plan
would either have languished or had a much reduced impact on the
urban plan of London. Fordyce saw the chief obstacle to the development of Regent's Park as its isolation. He argued that a road
linking it to the Houses of Parliament was essential. This was recog-
nized as early as 1809 when he remarked:

> Distance is best computed by time; and if means could be found to
> lessen the time of going from Marybone to the Houses of Parliament,
> the value of the ground for building would be thereby proportionately
> increased.
>
> The best and probably upon the whole, the most advantageous way
> of doing that, would be by opening a great street from Charing-Cross
> towards a central part of Marylebone Park.[9]

The new road from the park to Charing Cross would reduce travelling time by one-third. Fordyce's understanding of the need to
rationalise the street plan and his recognition of the significance of
the area known as Charing Cross are important here. His fusion of
the two as part of a new vision for London is a cathartic moment in
the history of the city which created a distinct caesura on the urban
map. These ideas were taken up by John Nash[10] and became, in June
1813, 'An act for a more convenient communication from Mary le
Bone Park and the Northernmost Parts of the Metropolis ... to
Charing Cross ... and for the making of a more convenient sewage
for the same'.[11] Unlike Regent's Park, Regent Street was not
constructed on new land ripe for development. Instead, the compulsory purchase and demolition of property ruptured the existing
urban pattern. Nor did the street follow an obvious line across the
shape of London as the New Road had, which formed an east–west
axis across the northern edge of the city. Rather it was a response to

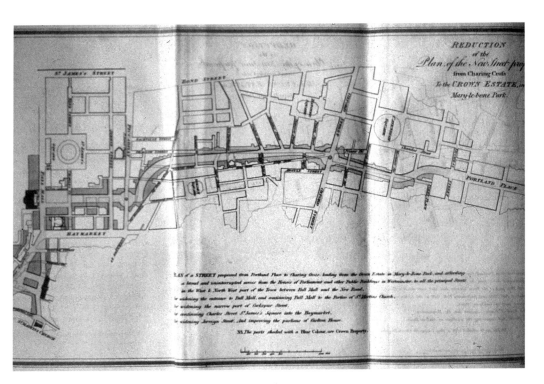

3.2 *Plan of a street proposed from Portland Place to Charing Cross ... The parts shaded in Blue Colour are Crown Property*, from John White, *Some account of the proposed improvements of the western part of London, by the formation of the Regent's Park, the New Street, the new sewer, &c, &c; illustrated by a variety of plans and accompanied by explanatory and critical observations*, 2nd edn, London, Cadell and Davies, 1815

this movement in the growth of the city and an attempt by the state to impose a uniform plan on it by creating a north–south axis that bisected the metropolis. It was a critical moment in the evolution of the city. Here the renewal of the metropolis as a response to changing social and cultural circumstance came to the fore.

The New Street changed the map of London and the city's social and demographic make-up. The area between Regent's Park and St James's posed problems if the Crown wanted to take part in any speculative developments, as many low class and therefore low-rent dwellings already existed on these Crown lands. The Crown stood to gain a great deal from the street's construction in terms of increased land values and rents as well as the enhancement of Carlton House, the residence of George IV, through its position as the southern focal point of the design. The aristocratic landowners whose lands covered or adjoined the line of the New Street were not wholly enthusiastic and their objection to the scheme was quite considerable (figure 3.2). The system of compulsory purchase of land on which to build the street affected the landowners in two ways. First it deprived them of one of their prime assets, land, and the potential for income from the property on it. Secondly, the landowners were denied the chance to participate in the newly created environment which was ripe for potentially profitable speculative development. Well-to-do occupants of houses bordering the New Street also objected to the scheme. This is exemplified in the attitude of the residents of the east

side of Cavendish Square. They objected in the strongest terms to the
New Street as it would drastically reduce the amount of land and
outbuildings to the rear of their properties. As a consequence Nash
had to reroute the New Street about 100 yards to the east and the
street had to make a sharp turn to the north-west to meet up with
Portland Place. But this did not diminish its role as an effective route
through the centre of London.

The Regent Street project was very attractive to the speculative
builders who, it was envisaged, would realize the plan. Most
obviously, the New Street made the speculative development that
flanked it accessible: it was a more directly effective piece of infrastructure than the New Road in Bloomsbury. Moreover, like
Bloomsbury, Regent Street offered the potential for mixed development of commercial and residential premises. But most importantly,
Regent Street made available land for development in a prime
location. The westward shift of the city's growth increased the status
of the area and its redevelopment through the New Street enabled a
redefinition of its demographic make-up. These elements were
distilled from the pattern of development of London's squares, but
here the aristocratic landowner was cut out of the sequence: the
urban form was produced through the interaction of Crown and
speculative builder.

REGENT STREET AND TRADITIONS OF TOWN PLANNING

An important factor behind George IV's wish to elevate the status of
London's architecture and urban planning was the example set by
other cities. Alongside other European capitals there were also towns
and cities within the British Isles with which George IV felt the need
to compete. Describing his grand scheme for London, Nash stated:

> Every length of street would be terminated by a facade of beautiful
> architecture ... and to add to the beauty of approach from
> Westminster to Charing Cross, a square or crescent, open to and
> looking down Parliament Street might be built around the Equestrian
> Statue at Charing Cross which at the same time that it would enlarge
> that space from whence as before observed the greatest part of the
> population of the Metropolis meet and diverge, it could afford a
> magnificent and beautiful termination of the street from Westminster.
> The lofty situation of Charing Cross and gradual assent to it are pecu-
> liarly calculated to produce a grand and striking effect. Such a building
> might be appropriated to additional offices for the Government or
> Royal Academy or Antiquarian Society might be placed there.[12]

Paris was seen as the immediate competitor and George IV is
reported as declaring that 'the splendours of Napoleon's Paris would

be eclipsed by what he planned for London'.[13] On his visits to Paris in 1814 and 1815 John Nash was certainly impressed by Napoleon I's creation of the straight rue du Rivoli with its classical arcades and mixture of shops and housing. This must have confirmed the decision he had made only a few years earlier to base the Regent Street development on the Continental model of a mixture of commercial and residential premises.[14]

The domestic character of London comes into sharp focus when comparisons are made to other capital cities in the British Isles. The aesthetic attractions of Edinburgh New Town provided a more than adequate spur to George IV's ambition, but in many ways Dublin was a more relevant precedent. The Wide Street Commission of 1756 sought to improve the circulation of traffic through Dublin by creating straight wide streets lined with substantial middle and upper class terrace housing. Furthermore, Dublin was the second city of Empire and had begun to outshine London through its streets and public buildings, most notably James Gandon's Custom House and the Four Courts (1776–96) and Edward Lovett Pearce's Parliament House (Bank of Ireland) (1728–39).

These comparisons are not to suggest that early nineteenth-century London lacked quality or character. Indeed, S. E. Rasmussen described London as a 'unique city':

> The English square or crescent ... is a restricted whole as complete as the courtyard of a convent. They form fine geometrical figures in the town plan, they are regular and completely uniform on all sides, and a series of such squares may be linked together in any order ... It is as if the traditions of the Middle Ages had been handed down to the present day in the squares in these domestic quarters. But the narrow courts of the old town have been transformed into the open squares of the newer quarters.[15]

But it is what Rasmussen does *not* say which is important here. The squares did not always fit neatly together – pockets of wasteland often lay in between them. Connections between the squares was not always commodious. And, most importantly, the nature of the new quarters was essentially *domestic*. As we have seen, John Wood's work in Bath must have set an example of rational town planning and design. This is seen, for instance, in the articulation of the facades of the houses on the Circus which draws its inspiration from the Colosseum in Rome. The aesthetic attraction of Bath is seen in Nash's insistence on the use of Bath stone coloured stucco on all the buildings erected as part of the Regent's Park and Regent Street project.[16] Indeed, James Burton's efforts in Bloomsbury must have had a striking effect on the London cityscape. Russell Square was frequently mentioned in guidebooks to London. *The Ambulator*

(1811) describes Russell Square as 'remarkable for the elegance of its houses, its ornamental area and the very fine bronze statue of the late Duke of Bedford'.[17] Burton's uniformly facaded terraces ranged around his rational plan which included elements like crescents; rectangles as well as square open spaces must have provided a distinctive discrete environment within London; and the whole area of Bloomsbury was sometimes commented upon. *The Picture of London* (1815) describes Bloomsbury, beginning with Russell Square, thus:

> Russell Square on a side of Bloomsbury is one of the largest and finest squares in London. Broad streets intersect it at the corner and middle which add to its beauty and remove general objection to squares by ventilating the air ... the extensive enclosure is a square containing oval shrubberies, a square lawn in the centre intersected with gravel walks.[18]

The commentary continues, noting that although Tavistock and Euston Squares are not finished Tavistock Square 'is in the best style of modern building' and praising James Burton's work in the whole area. This recognition of the contribution Bloomsbury made to the metropolis is followed by the eager anticipation of the construction of Regent Street and its 'ornamental' effect on London.

THE BUILDING PROCEDURE

Both the building procedure and the method of funding the construction of the buildings on Regent Street were similar to those used on the great estates. But, unlike the great estates the road, pavement and sewers were paid for out of public funds. Also, in many cases the land had to be acquired as it was not owned by the Crown. Only the ground at the very southern end of the New Street belonged to the Crown; the rest had to be compulsorily purchased. Not surprisingly, shortly after Nash's report passed into statute, receiving royal assent in 1813[19] the recently appointed New Street Commissioners met to discuss finance. They were Lord Glenbervie, W. Dacres Adams and Henry Dawkins, all Commissioners of the Office of Woods and Forests – the department overseeing the Regent's Park project (see chapter 2). The act had empowered them to borrow £500,000 for the construction of the New Street and a further £100,000 for the sewers and tributaries.[20] Nash felt private speculators would be unwilling to invest such sums and a loan of £300,000 was secured from the Royal Exchange at 5 per cent per annum.[21]

The building plots were initially put out to tender in 1815 when work was ready to begin. But this practice was soon abandoned as even Nash realised that some disreputable builders were offering the lowest price but were likely to produce very shoddy work. One of the few sites to be offered by tender was 106–54 Regent Street, which James Burton won. After this Nash fixed the price of the plot according to the footage onto the New Street and builders then made informal enquiries. This procedure became more of a bargaining process as the project progressed into the 1820s (see below).[22] James Burton was the principal builder, whilst Samuel Baxter, who built most of Oxford Circus, was the only other large-scale developer of note. The only part of the plan executed by Nash was the Quadrant, as no one else would take it on, which he subcontracted to builders operating on a more modest scale then the likes of Burton and Baxter.

It proved expedient to build the street in a south–north direction. For George IV this offered the attraction of ridding him, at the earliest possible moment, of his tradesmen neighbours who lived in the immediate proximity of Carlton House. The bang and clatter of the construction work might have been seen as a disincentive for this decision from the monarch's point of view, but for several years workmen had been almost permanently employed inside the royal residence, as its internal appearance was subject to an ongoing programme of redesign. For the King, the noise within would either drown or be drowned out by the din and commotion of the work outside his London home. And there was the added attraction of the project getting off to a prestigious start right outside the King's own front door, which would greatly enhance the status of Carlton House within the urban plan of the metropolis. There were, of course, more practical reasons for the decision to build south–north. Regent's Park, which stood at the northern end of the street, was under construction; work there was progressing more slowly than intended, and the plans for the layout of the park were subject to change. As such there was no immediate need for the link between the park and the centre of the city, which the street was intended to provide. In addition, the New Street finished at its north end in Robert Adam's majestic Portland Place, which acted as a kind of grand terminus until the design of the junction with the park was resolved. Perhaps the most fundamental reason for building south–north was the question of landownership. The line of the New Street ran across the estates of several members of the aristocracy from whom it was necessary to purchase the ground compulsorily. Given the vested interest the elite had in land, this was rightly not anticipated to be a simple task. In addition, once purchase was complete, a total of 741 houses required demolition to enable the construction of the street. Only 386 of these belonged to the Crown and they were concentrated on the southern half of the street (see figure 3.2). The huge task of negotiating the compulsory purchase of the necessary land was given to Nash but S. P. Cockerell, who was now relieved of his duties in Bloomsbury, was brought in to carry out the valuations.[23]

JAMES BURTON'S ROLE

Although James Burton's role in the building of Regent Street was far smaller than in Bloomsbury he still provides a valuable case study of how this distinctive kind of speculative development worked. The planning elements of accessibility and rationality, which Burton did much to develop in Bloomsbury, were already assured in the Regent Street project. In Bloomsbury Burton had had to persuade landowners to develop their land to enable his vision of the area to be realised. Here, the Crown owned or was compulsorily purchasing the land necessary for the street. Burton built fewer houses but the scheme was far more prestigious and the returns higher than in the less fashionably situated Bloomsbury as seen in table 1.1. Moreover, without Burton the project would have got off the ground far more slowly and probably not have been brought so near to completion.

It is usually assumed that Burton was introduced to Nash through their mutual acquaintance Humphry Repton. Repton had landscaped Russell Square for Burton and stayed at Mabledon, Burton's house in Kent, but this did not necessarily imply he would have any influence over the recommendation of builders for such an important project. Moreover, the assumption that Burton was brought in as Nash's man helps to reduce his role in the realization of the project.[24] Certainly Nash excercised some control over the aesthetic of the project as he provided designs for the buildings or was supposed to approve those submitted by speculative developers. However, if it is remembered that S. P. Cockerell was employed as Nash's assistant valuer,[25] a different view is possible. Cockerell was ideally qualified for his role in the New Street as he had been Surveyor to the Foundling Estate where he had worked with James Burton whom he had spoken most highly of.[26] Cockerell must have recognised that Burton had the skills, experience and means necessary for the successful execution of the project. Moreover, it is important not to discount Burton's own ability to recognize a good opportunity and capitalise on it – as he had done in Bloomsbury. Here the ingredients were right – a new street providing access and a unified architectural vision of the whole scheme. These had been the hallmarks of Burton's success in Bloomsbury. In terms of their experience and expertise, the combination of Cockerell as surveyor and Burton as architect/builder, which had proved so successful in Bloomsbury, was an essential element in this important development in London's urban plan.

Burton was responsible for the first portion of the New Street to be built: Waterloo Place (1815–16). The Place was the ultimate speculative development and, given Burton's experience in Bloomsbury, he was the ideal developer. It comprised a square of private houses whose facades, decorated with the classical orders, echoed the Place Vendôme in Paris. At the southern end of the square was the screen of Carlton House, against which the kudos of Bedford House, or the Foundling Hospital as a focal point for a speculative development, paled considerably. The houses flanked the east and west sides of the square and its north end was open to the beginning of Regent Street.

The next portion of the street was built between 1817 and 1820. Already the homogeneity of the plan was beginning to disintegrate. The building stock was a mixture of private dwellings and public/commercial buildings. Moreover, the plots of land were let either singly or in twos or threes, unlike Waterloo Place. Burton also made a contribution to this part of the street, taking up leases on nos. 4–12 Regent Street – plots designated to be for residential or commercial use. Burton constructed a huge multi-use block called Carlton Chambers where his son Decimus set up his first office. This decision about the type of edifice to be constructed is indicative of the impact developers had on the building stock of the New Street. The surrounding buildings were Nash's Warren Hotel (no. 1) and Robert Smirke's United Service Club (no. 2), G. S. Repton's Hopkinson's Bank and three houses[27] and St Philip's Church. The latter's site was granted by the Crown as part of the 1818 Church Building Act. Nash positioned the church directly opposite Carlton Street so that it closed the vista from Haymarket. Burton also built nos. 17–25 of this end of the street, now known as Lower Regent Street. From 1820 Burton took up leases on four blocks of land above the quadrant which made up nos. 106 to 128 and 132 to 154 on the east side, and 133 to 167 and 171 to 195 on the west. He also built numbers 295 to 319 near the north end of the street.

Burton's rental agreements were made on a regular basis. They show a steady approach to the building procedure of the New Street, which it was certainly in his interests to see completed to safeguard his investment in it and that in Regent's Park. A favourable interim ground rent was set for one or two years during the construction period. The full leases were granted once the building was nearing completion. These were backdated to the beginning of the lease agreement. This retrospective system of leases helped shorten the overall life of the lease, and the finite period of reduced rent was an incentive to build.

By November 1820 Burton had completed building on the ground between Leicester Street and 129 Swallow Street.[28] In March the following year he took up leases on three plots of ground on the east side of the New Street.[29] Work progressed steadily; in April 1822 he erected houses on several parts of the ground on the west side of the New Street between the Quadrant and Oxford Street and was now entitled to leases. In September Burton was granted a ninety-nine year lease for the erection of houses north of Burlington Street.[30] Only a month later he took up a lease on land to build a house and premises on the east side of the street between Chapel Court and the entrance to the King Street Chapel.

Burton built fewer houses in Regent Street than in Bloomsbury – 191 in eight years compared to 1,756 in twenty-two (table 1.1). If the houses built by Burton which comprised the Regent's Park terraces are included, the number is almost doubled to 380 in the same eight-year period. But the returns were better than Bloomsbury (see table 1.1). The annual rents were higher and the estimated gross value of the property greater than Bloomsbury. As with Bloomsbury, Burton was actively involved in the whole project which helped ensure its success, but this time his contribution was part of a much larger and more ambitious plan. The breakdown of the rates of houses he built again shows how his work influenced the demographic make-up of London. The majority of houses were second-rate with nearly equal numbers of first- and third-rate houses. The first-rate houses were more than likely those closest to Carlton House. As Regent Street progressed it was not unusual for builders to squeeze in extra houses behind Nash's facades. By reducing the houses to second-rate ones, enough space could be gained to insert an additional dwelling in the run of the terrace. The third- and fourth-rate houses mentioned in the table were on subsidiary streets.

GRAND DESIGNS

It is tempting to see these improvements solely as a move on the part of George IV and his officers both to cash in on established methods of estate development and to make London more impressive architecturally, that it appeared like a capital instead of, according to John Summerson, 'a huddle of bricks with a steepled skyline'. The London street plan had long proved problematical and there had been several attempts to remedy it. Summerson describes the legacy of the seventeenth century:

> [it] can be imagined by anybody who walks through Soho today with the object of proceeding consistently and with reasonable expedition in a given direction. Hardly a street goes anywhere except into another street which crosses it and enforces a left or right turn. Only one street, Wardour Street (in origin a medieval field track), goes all

the way through from north to south; and no street goes through from east to west.[31]

Summerson attributed this pattern of building to small-scale building projects on tiny plots, that is enterprises which had no overall plan or direction.

The Great Fire of 1666 had offered the first obvious opportunity to rationalise the street plan.[32] Amongst the many proposals for the rebuilding of the city was Sir Christopher Wren's plan for a series of streets radiating from St Paul's Cathedral. Wren's contemporary, John Evelyn, also produced several plans for the rebuilding of London on more rational lines.[33] Significantly, none of these plans was realized and London continued to develop in a piecemeal fashion well into the eighteenth century. The first signs of any further wish to combat the traffic jams and general inconvenience of the London street pattern was seen in John Gwynn's map and critical text *London and Westminster Improved* (1766). He proposed an extension of Haymarket northward, forcing a way through Soho and Oxford Street, and the widening of Swallow Street. There was no possibility of these plans being realised but they demonstrate the need for better circulation through the city and the lack of political will to impose it.

The renewed impetus for change in the opening decades of the nineteenth century, although concerned with the improvement of the urban aesthetic, had other important predicates. First, the use of the well-established methods of speculative development employed by the great estates, coupled with the compulsory purchase of the additional land required, made the ambitious urban plan of the Metropolitan Improvements a feasible proposition. But if these works are viewed in the broader political context of the late eighteenth and early nineteenth century the re-imaging of this part of the urban landscape takes on new meaning. The volatility of the social and political situation at the close of the eighteenth century is manifest in a letter from George IV to his people about his divorce, written on 1 December 1820. He described the situation in Europe on his marriage in 1792:

> The French Revolution was at its height; the Royal family of France had been murdered, Holland had imbibed the Revolutionary mania, and the Stadtholder had fled to this protecting country; at home a traitorous spirit was actively at work; trials for high treason had served only to increase the insolence of faction, and foster Rebellion, Ireland was on the verge of open Revolt; and every political appearance threatened an attempt upon a constitution of these realms; a dreadful war was raging and yet in the face of all these evils, it was the wish of my Royal Father to strengthen the Succession to the throne of these realms.[34]

There is no doubt that the terror of the French Revolution and the libertarianism of the newly declared French Republic were seen as imminent threats. Moreover the growing impetus for electoral reform in Britain only added to the fears of the ruling elite. It is important to consider the role the urban environment played in the perception and experience of social unrest. Ironically, the prodigious growth of the city itself – the product of the rapacity of speculative development encouraged by the elite – created anxiety and a feeling that London and its inhabitants had become a monster. The was articulated as far back as the 1770s in, for instance, Smollett's last novel, *The Expedition of Humphry Clinker.*

> London is literally new to me; new in its streets, houses, and even in its situation; as the Irishman said, 'London is now gone out of town'. What I left open fields producing hay and corn, I now find covered with streets, and squares and palaces, and churches. I am credibly informed that in the space of seven years, eleven thousand new houses have been built in new quarter of Westminster.
>
> [...]
>
> [T]here is no distinction or subordination left – The different departments of life are jumbled together – The hod-carier, the low mechanic, the publican ... the citizen, the courtier. 'all tread upon the kibes of one another' ... [they] are seen everywhere.
>
> [...]
>
> The diversions of the times are not ill suited to the genius of this incongruous monster called 'the public'.[35]

Smollett evokes not only the rapid spread of London, but also the sense that this growth made the city uncontrollable. Moreover, his description shows that the rigid social divisions of space were begining to be eroded. The densely populated metropolis with its squares and subsidiary streets resulted in a melange of social classes in its public spaces and places – whether it be the coffee house or the Strand. The elite encountered the poor and the increasing number of middle-ranking tradesman and business people in a way that was unknown in the hierarchical arrangements of their country estates. The idea of a 'public' rather than upper and lower class occupants underscores this shift in demography and the wish on the part of some for the ever-growing east-west divide.

There were practical and physical steps that could be taken to make London a safer place – for the King and the upper classes. This could be achieved through urban planning and a change in the make-up of the building stock which would in turn affect the demographic pattern of London. This separation of the classes was seen as a way not only of maintaining law and order but also of protecting speculative investments in property. Moreover, as subsequent chapters in this study demonstrate, the introduction of monuments, public buildings and royal palaces and parks as the foci for this new rational street plan enabled the state to express its power in a new and significant way.

CLASS AND CONFLICT

The Metropolitan Improvements in which the New Street played a key role also included the renovation of Charing Cross which had traditionally been the site of sparring matches between the state and the people.[36] Directly to the north-west were some of the city's poorest areas including rookeries such as Porridge Island, Seven Dials and St Giles's. Their growing presence on the edge of St James's was seen as potentially troublesome and a threat to the King, the government and the aristocracy. These fears were heightened by the recent Gordon Riots of 1780 which had caused widespread anxiety across London's upper classes. Mob violence, the proximity of poor to government and the existence of a geographical focal point for the people's protest in Charing Cross were not a happy mix. The more recent 'Crimp' riots of 1794–95 were a vigorous reminder of the power of the mob and the vulnerability of the West End.[37] Although the focus was the activities of 'crimp' houses, the mob targeted property and pulled down buildings as well as starting numerous fires. Most disturbances took place in the City, but as the crowd was driven away from one area by the army it re-assembled somewhere else. The four-day-long riot which took place around Charing Cross received considerable press coverage as it was on the very threshold of the West End. Alongside these 'named' riots, more spontaneous and short-lived manifestations of discontent were frequently acted out on the streets across London. The war with France and the food shortages of the mid 1790s gave ample cause for demonstration: crowds marched through the streets of the West End and even attacked the royal coach, although the Regent had been safely delivered to Carlton House.[38]

The Metropolitan Improvements and associated developments sought to deal with the perceived threat in three main ways: first, in the imposition of physical barriers between the different classes, secondly, in the building of new barracks and the strategic placing of troops in the capital, and thirdly, and most importantly, in the assertion of the power of the state and through the landscape, urban planning and careful placing of monuments and public buildings in the metropolis whose purpose was to underline the military and intellectual achievements of the nation.

The New Street certainly created a physical barrier between the classes, displacing many tradespeople around Haymarket and

completely ruining many businesses.[39] It also halted the spread of the
rookeries which were impossible to police. Nash also tried to ensure
that the lower classes should not penetrate these new developments.
It was decreed that the New Street and park 'shall be open at all times
to all his Majesties Subjects to pass and repass along the same
(except … Waggons, Carts, Drays or the vehicles for the carriage of
goods, merchandise, manure soil or other articles, or Oxen Cows
Horses or Sheep in any drove or droves.)[40] This measure could be
interpreted simply as a wish to improve the traffic flow through the
West End of London, and it certainly gives a flavour of the diversity
of traffic in London. Nash's real motive is betrayed in his response
to a petition by traders in St James's market for the right of access to
the New Street: 'No – it would spoil the beauty of the plan entirely –
for people riding up and down might see offal or something of that
kind.'[41] These comments underline the fundamentally different
nature of a street and a square in the urban fabric. Squares were
discrete environments, with the service and trade elements tucked
away from view and they could be more exclusive and even gated off
to make them private precincts. A street was a more fundamental
part of the city's infrastructure from which exclusion was more
difficult or openly prejudicial – as was most certainly the case with
Regent Street. Moreover the heterogeneity of its building stock –
private dwellings, offices, shops and a church – reminiscent in themselves of the unsuccessful scheme for Covent Garden of nearly two
centuries earlier, ran contrary to the divisive role the street was to
play in the in the Metropolitan Improvements.[42]

Attempts to exclude certain sections of the population from areas
of London went beyond Regent Street to its immediate environs. In
1822 inhabitants of the parishes of St Martin's and St Anne's Soho
also petitioned against the closure of 'the passage through the Royal
Mews recently shut in the interests of public service'.[43] The closure
is significant here as it had provided a convenient link for traders
between Soho and Westminster – two areas of very different social
make-up. But this is more than another example of the wish to segre-
gate the classes as the passage went through the Royal Mews at
Charing Cross. Charing Cross had been the site of a temporary
barracks. These were adjacent to William Kent's Royal Stables (1732).
As part of the general improvements of the area many of the near-
derelict buildings which made up the area known as 'The Royal
Mews' were demolished to leave the Royal Stables standing as a
suitable terminus at the top of Whitehall.[44] The barracks were rebuilt
in 1825 providing accommodation for 800 troops on the site of the
old Green Mews, situated further to the north behind the Royal
Mews, as the Master of Fortification stated, 'it [the barracks] gave
free access from the back of the barracks to all the North Parts of the

town'.[45] Concern with the movement of troops in the city and the building of new and the repositioning of old barracks was an essential part of the Metropolitan Improvements[46] which continued with the inclusion of new barracks in the plan for Regent's Park. This attempt to make London safer underlined the need for good communications across the metropolis.[47]

The Metropolitan Improvements were also intended to engender a sense of nationalism in the population. This is nascent in the original plan for Regent's Park, and was partly achieved in the work in the royal parks (see chapters 5 and 6), and this was complemented by an unrealised new road leading from this area to link with Robert Smirke's British Museum, a symbol of the nation's prestige through its collection of antiquities, begun in 1823. In 1825 Nash was required by the Commissioners of Woods and Forests to develop this area into a square at the junction of Whitehall, St Martin's Lane, the Strand and Pall Mall East and to improve the communications through the west of the metropolis which included the widening of the western end of the Strand. Nash was also asked to devise a 'more commodious access from the Houses of Parliament ... to the British Museum and the numerous respectably occupied new buildings in the part of the Metropolis, in which that Great National Repository is now being permanently established'.[48] This road would also have connected Bloomsbury with Charing Cross and Regent Street.

CONCLUSION

The specifics of James Burton's activities show how Regent Street operated as a speculative development. In addition the declared intentions of John Nash reveal the New Street, along with the other Metropolitan Improvements, to be an important instrument in the shaping of the socio-political geography of the metropolis. In the broader context of the class conflict of the early nineteenth century the improvements can be seen as an attempt to impose a disciplinary regime on the capital.[49] The improved infrastructure made the city more knowable and so less threatening – it became less of a monster, fear being replaced by rationality. The new sewer that ran under the New Street and the strict rules that governed the kind of traffic that travelled on it established an order of hygiene. Together these elements combined to form a new urban aesthetic. This operated rather like the landscape garden of the country house which drew attention away from the dung heaps towards the manicured nature of its design that expressed the sovereignty of the ruling elite.

Although it was firmly based on established patterns of land development and social management used in the great estates, the scheme for the New Street was too ambitious and too costly, nor was it ever completed as planned. The rug was pulled from under the project when, in 1826, George IV vacated Carlton House, consigning it to demolition,[50] so moving the royal focal point of the city to Buckingham Palace.[51] But the significance of George IV's vision was recognised by the diarist Henry Crabb Robinson who delivered his verdict on Regent's Park and Regent's Street: 'This enclosure, with the New Street leading to it from Carlton House, will give a sort of glory to the Regent's government, which will be more felt by remote posterity than the victories of Trafalgar and Waterloo, glorious as these are.'[52] The aesthetic expression of this triumph of the state and governmental authority in the West End had an important counterpoint in the City, where the rebuilding of London Bridge provided a very different arena for the display of the power politics of class and conflict.

NOTES

1 This name was not given to the street until 1819. Up until this time it was referred to as the New Street. Both names are used in this chapter.

2 George IV's interest in the New Street and other architectural projects in London began when he was Prince Regent (1812–20). For simplicity he is referred to as George IV throughout this book. His reign ended in 1830.

3 Summerson, *The Life and Work of John Nash*, chs 6 and 10, and T. Davis, *John Nash: The Prince Regent's Architect*, London, Studio, 1966, ch. 5.

4 Summerson, *The Life and Work of John Nash*, and Davis, *John Nash*.

5 H. Hobhouse, *A History of Regent Street*, London, Macdonald and Jane's in association with Queen Anne Press, 1975. Regent's Park and Street are revisited in J. Anderson, 'Marylebone Park and the New Street. A Study of the Development of Regent's Park and the Building of Regent's Street, London, in the First Quarter of the Nineteenth Century', University of London, unpublished PhD thesis, 1999. The later nineteeth-century social history of the street has been discussed by E. D. Rappaport, *Shopping for Pleasure: Women in the Making of London's West End*, Princeton, Princeton University Press, 2000.

6 1812 Report.

7 1828 Report.

8 Ibid.

9 The Surveyor General's Triennial Report, no. 4, 1809.

10 1812 Report.

11 53 Geo. III, c. 121.

12 1812 Report.

13 Letter from T. Moore to J. Corry, 24 Oct. 1811, as quoted in J. Summerson, *John Nash: Architect to King George IV*, 2nd edn, London, Allen and Unwin, 1949, p 107.

14 This is clear from Nash's 1812 plan which is annotated 'the New Street with colonnades on the Shops'.

15   S. E. Rasmussen, *London, the Unique City*, Cambridge, Mass., MIT, 1982, pp. 198–200.

16   This is mentioned, for instance, in a lease taken out by James Burton on a plot of land in Regent's Park, Cres 6/131 f 47. The conditions laid down by Nash were typical for those of the whole Regent's Park and Regent Street project.

17   *The Ambulator*, London, 1811, p. 23.

18   *The Picture of London*, 3rd edn, London, 1815, pp. 159–60.

19   Cres 26/1 f 6.

20   Summerson, *The Life and Work of John Nash*, p 80.

21   Cres 26/1 f 119.

22   1829 Report, pp. 12–13.

23   Cres 26/1 f 22.

24   Summerson, *The Life and Work John Nash*, p. 85.

25   Cres 26/1 f 22.

26   See chapter 2 p. 31.

27   Probably also by Repton, according to Summerson, *John Nash*, p. 131.

28   T29/191.

29   T29/195.

30   T29/213.

31   Summerson, *The Life and Work of John Nash*, p. 75

32   The area now known as the City was the centre of London in the mid seventeenth century and much of the West End was open fields, with Soho and Covent Garden being the western edge of the capital.

33   Wren's plan and three plans drawn up by Evelyn are reproduced in *Vestuta Monumenta*, vol. 2, 1789. Evelyn's description of his plan for London is published in E. S. de Beer (ed.), *John Evelyn: London Revived*, Clarendon Press, Oxford, 1938.

34   Quoted in *The King's Visit to Dublin As discoursed by Andrew Walsh, Darby Morris and John Simpson*, printed by G. Bull, 3 Redmond Hill, 1st edn 1822.

35   Tobias Smollett, *The Expedition of Humphry Clinker*, London, 1771, pp. 97–100.

36   For a full discussion of the social and political significance of the area now known as Trafalgar Square see R. Mace, *Trafalgar Square: Emblem of Empire*, London, Lawrence and Wishart, 1976.

37   A Crimp House was a kind of brothel that duped young men into being press-ganged into the armed services. See John Stevenson, 'The London "Crimp" Riots of 1774', *International Review of Social History*, 16 (1971), pp. 40–58.

38   There were many instances of spontaneous demonstrations and numerous steps taken by the government to control the populace. Examples of each can be found in M. T. Davis (ed.), *The London Corresponding Society 1792–1799*, 6 vols, London, Pickering and Chatto, 2002.

39   As a result of complaints that it was a nuisance from the residents of Piccadilly and St James's, Haymarket was moved to Cumberland Market, Regent's Park.

40   53 Geo. III, c. 121.

41   Report from the Committee on the Petition of the Tradesmen and Inhabitants of Norris Street and Market Terrace, 1817 (79), iii. 83.

42   Alongside his plans for residential and commercial premises, Nash designed All Soul's Langham Place in 1822–25.

43   Cres 26/188.

44   New royal stables in Pimlico were planned as early as 1820. This prompted George IV to permit the demolition of the east and west parts of the old mews to allow the construction of a road to link Pall Mall to St Martin's which effectively created the area later called Trafalgar Square.

45   Cres 26/178.

46   From 1796 there had been great developments in the building of barracks in London. Prompted partly by the Gordon Riots in June 1780 and the situation in France, a magazine was built in Hyde Park and a new barracks constructed on Knightsbridge.

47   On this point see D. Arnold, 'Rationality, Safety and Power: The Street Planning of Later Georgian London', The Georgian Group Journal (1995), pp. 37–50, 132–3.

48   Fifth Report to His Majesty's Commissioners of Woods Forests and Land Revenues, London, 1826.

49   The idea of an increasingly bureaucratic discipline being imposed on cities through the urban infrastructure is a thesis developed by Michel Foucault. See M. Foucault, Discipline and Punish: The Birth of the Prison, trans. Alan Sheridan (1977), Harmondsworth, Penguin, 1991.

50   Decimus Burton later constructed the Athenaeum (1827–30) on part of this site. The design was meant to follow Nash's for the United Service Club on the opposite side of Waterloo Place. Burton was constantly frustrated by Nash's tardiness in producing designs and responding to queries. Although this episode tells us little about the urban planning of London, it does reinforce the notion that the working relationsip between Nash and the Burtons was not as harmonious as might previously have been suggested. Documentation concerning the quarrels between Burton and Nash and the design of the Athenaeum can be found at the Athenaeum, and in the Burton/Croker papers in The Royal Institute of British Architects Library (Croker was the founder of the club) and Cres 2/710. A history of the Athenaeum was published by the club, The Athenaeum Club and Social Life in London 1824–1974, London, 1974.

51   Napoleon III was so impressed with the Metropolitan Improvements that on his return to Paris from his exile in Britain he encouraged Philippe, later Baron, Haussman to develop the city using similar planning principles. See D. Arnold, 'Paris Haussman: Le Pari d'Haussman', The Architects' Journal, (13 Nov. 1991), pp. 58–60.

52   Henry Crabb Robinson, Diary, vol. 1, ed. T. Sadler, London, 1872, p. 310.

4 London Bridge

In the opening years of the nineteenth century several new bridges were planned and built to improve communications across the Thames, and in response to the westward growth of London and demographic changes north of the river.[1] The rebuilding of London Bridge has a special place in this sequence. Old London Bridge was one of a small number of buildings, monuments and institutions which encapsulated the identity of London. It had been the only link between the city and the south bank of the Thames for over 1,700 years. Its history as a focal point of the national road network, such as it was in the pre-modern era, had earned the bridge a certain fame and it was one of the sights of Britain, if not Europe. Its imposing presence to those arriving by road or river served to reinforce the centrality of London to the nation as a whole whilst it acted as a physical barrier to the city and a symbol of civic order and authority. The decision to rebuild London Bridge in the early nineteenth century brought with it all this historical baggage. The importance of London Bridge and its function as a potent symbol was not forgotten but the nature of the state and metropolis that it signified had changed considerably. This symbolic nature of the bridge is further vivified by the fusion of bridges and monuments in contemporary architectural practice. Taking a lead from Renaissance and antique models the monumental bridge design was a standard part of architectural training. This is brought in to sharp focus with the competition to redesign the bridge because the construction of another symbol of urban and national supremacy coincided with the general scheme of the Metropolitan Improvements. The new bridge endured as a symbol of the modern metropolis well into the twentieth century. Improvements to the bridge approaches in the 1890s prompted the complete erosion of the remains of Tudor London in the interests of the ever-expanding heart of the empire. And the image evoked by the very name London Bridge ensured its survival to the present day. The current pre-stressed concrete structure was built in the late 1960s[2] and the rather plain, functional Regency[3] bridge was re-erected in Lake Havasu City, Arizona, where it stands as an isolated icon of London.

The long and complex histories of London Bridge raise interesting questions about the relationship between the symbolic and functional roles of buildings. A bridge can be a monument, a signifier of social or political pre-eminence, a national symbol or just a stretch of road that happens to pass over water. A consideration of the London Bridge *c.* 1800–40 in these contexts establishes its symbolic identity in Regency London and presents the notion that this metropolitan river crossing can be viewed as a matrix through which fundamental aspects of urban identity can be explored. Of particular interest here is the definition and development of London's perimeters, entrances and infrastructure; the city as a site of celebration for nation, state and heroes; the balance of power between a national government interested in urban development of the capital and an established authority within the confines of the City of London.[4]

DEFINING PERIMETERS AND CHANGING
INFRASTRUCTURES

London Bridge was part of the physical apparatus that defined the city's perimeter; it was the first bridge across the Thames and the structure dated from medieval times. It also provided an important part of the urban infrastructure being, for most of the eighteenth century, one of the only three ways of accessing the northern bank of the Thames from the south side of the river. The nucleus of London – the Cities of London, Westminster and the Borough of Southwark – hugged the river and had London Bridge at its eastern edge and Westminster Bridge, begun in the late 1730s, at its western. The third bridge, Blackfriars, begun in 1760, was situated between the other two.

The prodigious growth of London in both physical size and population in the opening years of the nineteenth century changed the balance of the metropolis. And this is reflected in the construction of more bridges in the Regency period, including Vauxhall, Waterloo and Southwark Bridges, all of which were built between 1813 and 1819. The expansion of London not only stretched the shape and the perimeter of the city but also altered the relationship of the metropolis to the river. From the early eighteenth century London had gradually spread westwards. Initially this was the result of the demand for better quality housing by the merchant and middle classes. And as London grew in national importance as the capital city and the centre of government and court life, a house in the increasingly fashionable West End became essential for persons of *ton.*[5] As this westward move gathered pace, so the population began to increase. The first census in 1801 revealed that the population of London had reached 864,845. By 1811 this had grown to 1,099,104. In the next ten years it increased by nearly 20 per cent to 1,225,965. In contrast to the steady momentum of the increase in the overall population, the number of inhabitants of the City declined. According to *The Percy Histories*,[6] the population of the City fell during the eighteenth century from *c.* 140,000 in 1702 to *c.* 56,000 in 1821. This might imply a decline in importance for the City, but depopulation did not detract from its role as a trading centre. It remained a vital part of the economic life of London and London Bridge marked the entrance to it by road from Southwark and by river for ships arriving from the east coast. The westward growth of London was largely confined to the north bank of the Thames. But this did not necessarily diminish the role of the river as an important part of its infrastructure. It remained a vital link between the two ends of the metropolis and an effective means of transporting goods.

As London expanded its girth, so the south bank of the Thames was seen as an area with good development potential. Not least, the open land invited the building of the rational road system which eluded the north bank. This would not only provide good communications across Southwark but also connect with the bridges. This provided new entry points into London and a more effective way of moving across the city. For instance, traffic crossing over London Bridge into Southwark could travel westwards more quickly and access the West End via Westminster Bridge. In 1760 the decision to build Blackfriars Bridge was part of a larger scheme to provide such

4.1 Anonymous, *A Plan of the Streets, Roads, &c. between Black Fryers Bridge, London Bridge, Westminster Bridge, Lambeth, Newington Butts, and St Margarets Hill*, 1769, engraving

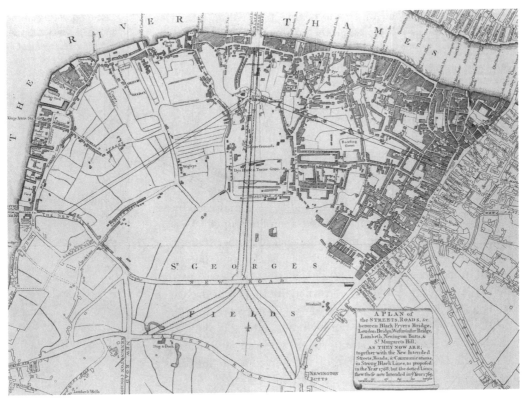

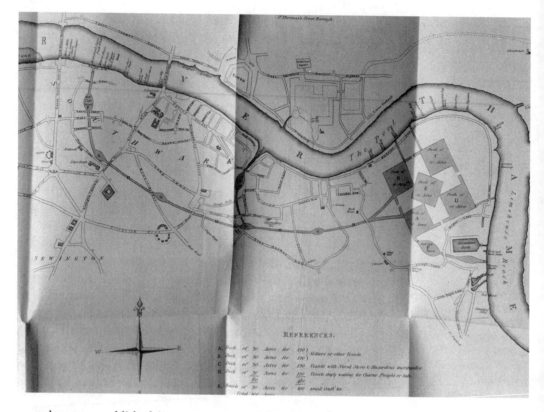

4.2 *Port of London Authority Reports*, vol. 1, A Plan for the development of the London Docks, 1799

a road system, published in an anonymous plan dating from 1769 which linked the three bridges and the north and south banks of the Thames (figure 4.1). These ideas remained current for the next fifty years and informed the ideas behind the rebuilding of London Bridge and its approaches. Traffic congestion was not, however, confined to the roads as the growing importance of London as a trading centre led to an increase in river traffic and the need for more docks. *The Port of London Report* of 1799[7] outlined unrealized plans for the improvement of the congested London docks which adds an interesting supplement to the east–west communications south of the river (figure 4.2). This idea is taken up in *Porto-Bello or a Plan for the improvement of the Port and City of London*, drawn up by Sir Frederick Morton Eden in 1798. Here the demolition of Old London Bridge is proposed to accommodate the coal or timber trade 'near the heart of the metropolis', which was seen as a far more important element in the city's infrastructure than 'a crumbling ancient structure'.[8] The author proposed the construction of a new bridge which would 'afford an opportunity for forming a Grand Street in a direct line from the wildest part of the Borough [of Southwark] to the Bank and the Royal Exchange'.[9] The Borough was seen as providing a mean entrance into the City with the area around London Bridge and Fish Street Hill being described as 'certainly very mean entrances into a large city; the latter, more particularly, from its narrowness and steep ascent'.[10]

The increased number of bridges diminished the river's role as a physical barrier between the north and south banks. By 1820 there were six main river crossings in the Cities of Westminster and London: Westminster, Waterloo, Vauxhall, Blackfriars, Southwark and London Bridges. The volume of traffic carried into the capital had grown substantially. A survey of 1810 carried out between 16 and 22 October of the use of Blackfriars and London Bridges gives a flavour of the volume and type of traffic flow.[11]

Table 4.1 *A survey of traffic across London and Blackfriars Bridges, 16–22 October 1810*

Type of traffic crossing	London Bridge	Blackfriars Bridge
People [means unspecified, presumably on foot]	56,000	37,000
Coaches	871	626
Carts and drays	2,576	1,269

Source: S. and R. Percy, *The Percy Histories or Interesting memories of the rise, progress and presentation of all the capitals of Europe*, 3 vols, London, 1823.

The figures relating to the number of carts and drays are perhaps the most significant as they reveal how the bridges, and especially London Bridge, supported the City as a trading centre even though the population of that area was declining. This role remained vital as any loss of income from the food and general supplies sold in the markets and revenue from import duties from goods delivered to the Port of London would have diminished the City's wealth and importance to the urban infrastructure and economy. The wealthy West End was mostly supplied by traders in the City. And this dependent relationship was jealously guarded, as seen, for instance, in the vigorous and successful opposition to the proposal for a fish market at Westminster in the 1750s for the greater convenience of local residents, for whom the journey to the fish market in the City was lengthy, inconvenient and where they paid substantially inflated prices.[12] Indeed, the primacy of the City was seen to be threatened by the completion of the much needed Westminster Bridge in 1750 as the symbolic identity of London Bridge as the capital's only river crossing and entrance from the south would be diminished. Moreover, the new bridge would divert traffic, or rather the trade, away from the City. Westminster Bridge did indeed signal the growing importance of Westminster as the centre of national government and the socially fashionable end of town. The public outcry over the use of a foreign architect to design the bridge, the Swiss Charles Labeyle, is indicative of how river crossings were seen to embody national identities and functioned as monuments in the metropolitan landscape.

THE CITY AS A SITE/SIGHT OF CELEBRATION FOR NATION STATE AND HEROES

During and immediately after the Napoleonic wars London became a site/sight of celebration of victories over, and the eventual defeat of, the French and functioned as a signifier of a distinctive national consciousness. This consciousness in turn shaped the urban land-scapes. Moreover, the city, as a site of sights, gave geographical place to the spectacles concerning victory which included mock battles – re-enactments of major military triumphs – in the royal parks. There were also exhibitions of series of tableaux which narrated the endeavours of heroes such as Nelson and Wellington.

The entrance points by road to the capital were identified as sites of commemoration. This is seen in the designs for Hyde Park Corner, which had become a significant gateway into west London.[13] Freestanding monuments were also proposed to embellish the cityscape.[14] The mood is captured by William Wood, who wrote in his 'Essay on National and Sepulchral Monuments' in 1808 of the need to build monuments to commemorate great national heroes: 'from the most remote antiquity, until the present moment, from savages of the southern hemisphere, to the polished nations of Europe, all mankind have agreed in erecting sepulchral monuments, to mark their admiration of the illustrious dead'. Street names were another way in which the city could become a site of commemora-tion. The nomenclature served as a reminder of civic and national virtue, rather than the landed elite of the West End whose estates were named in their honour. *The Percy Histories* identified eighteen places named after Nelson, eleven after Trafalgar, fourteen after Wellington and ten sites named after Waterloo. Bridges also played a role in this construction of a distinctive urban identity and were also sometimes appropriated or re-appropriated for commemorative purposes. The fickleness of fame also played a part here. For instance, Blackfriars Bridge in pre-Napoleonic times was originally called Pitt Bridge to celebrate William Pitt, Earl of Chatham, before the statesman's popularity waned. But Chatham Place stood and retained its name on the north side of the Thames. On the south bank the 'all-purpose' Albion Place punctuated this route in and out of London. To underline the responsiveness of urban nomenclature to the forces of history there was also a Nelson Square further south down the aptly titled St George's Road. Even royalty was not exempt from readings of the barometer of political and popular favour. The Regent's Bridge became simply Vauxhall Bridge, proving that even for George IV this was perhaps a bridge too far.

Attempts to acknowledge the Duke of Wellington's military achievement at Waterloo included the renaming of the Strand Bridge to Waterloo Bridge.[15] This is perhaps the most potent example of the symbolic identity of a bridge and its use as a site of commemoration within the metropolis. The plain Doric form of Waterloo Bridge was recognised by some critics as preferable to the fussy monumentality of 'foreign designs' or the paper architecture of Sir John Soane.[16] Whilst *The Percy Histories* described it as 'a work not less pre-eminent amongst the bridges of all ages and counties than the event which it will commemorate as it is unravelled in the annals of ancient or modern history'.[17] The bridge had been under construction before 1815 and was opened for the second anniversary of the victory. Wellington was present at the opening ceremony when the bridge was draped with the flags of all nations and a 202-gun salute represented the number of French cannon taken in the battle. This takes the urban bridge beyond its practical and commemorative function as it becomes a monument. According to Percy's *Histories*, Waterloo Bridge was a popular sight in a city visited by many European luminaries. The sculptor Canova admired the bridge for its Augustan qualities. This sentiment is echoed by Charles Dupin, according to Percy, 'another intelligent foreigner', who thought it 'worthy of the Caesars'.[18]

The monumental possibilities of river crossings had already been recognised, but not realised, by George Dance the younger. His proposal of *c.* 1800 for a double London Bridge, partly to commemorate the Battle of the Nile and the nation in general, responded to the demands of London town planning and the need to upgrade the City. The two stretches of road across the river terminates in grand semi-circular *places* on either bank of the river. The Monument, a symbol of the City's recovery from the Great Fire of 1666, formed the centrepiece of the *place* on the north bank and an obelisk, presumably a reference to the battle of the Nile, was its pendant piece on the south bank. It is a vision of metropolitan modernity equal to any European capital city. The fascination with the commemoration of living and dead heroes was incorporated into the academic tradition in architecture and this can be seen in the display of over forty mausoleum designs at the annual exhibition of the Society of Artists and the Royal Academy between 1768 and 1793.[19] Indeed, bridges and monuments were synonymous in European architectural practice and this certainly featured in architectural education.[20] John Soane won the Royal Academy Schools' Gold Medal competition 1776 with a design for *A Triumphal Bridge*. Soane's design synthesis the complex meaning of a river crossing in a potent image of national glory and architectural magnificence which was perhaps too European for some critics and too expensive for others. Soane was taught by Thomas Sandby who was then Professor of Architecture at the Royal Academy Schools. Sandby's *Bridge of Magnificence*, one of the illustrations to his professorial lectures exhibited at the Academy in 1781, linked Somerset House with the Strand – the line of the later Waterloo Bridge – and comprised Doric colonnades, domed wings and a central Italianate galleria. Sandby's pupil's prize-winning design included similar features but was more ornate and grand and included a pantheon adorned with statues as the central element. Soane's bridge was to be at Westminster and formed a new and grand entrance into London: a fine architectural response to the growing pre-eminence of the West End. Its strikingly modern, classical design which drew on antique Roman prototypes provided a sharp contrast to the ramshackle form of Old London Bridge.

The Thames bridges and the paper architecture relating to them offered the possibility of fusing architectural, political and social ideals. They became signifiers of cultural practices and values. But how did London Bridge and the competition to rebuild it fit into this contextual framework, given the idea of a bridge as a monument to the nation and as representative of the changing social and economic landscape of London as a whole and, in this case, to the City in particular?

LONDON BRIDGE

By the mid-eighteenth century Old London Bridge had undergone many necessary repairs and alterations but had received little in the way of aesthetic attention. By the opening years of the nineteenth century its appearance and its effect on the tides of the Thames caused equal concern earning this description: 'a thick wall, pierced with small uneven holes, through which the water, dammed up by all the clumsy fabric, rushes or rather leaps with a velocity extremely dangerous to boats and barges'.[21] The old houses, which were remnants of the medieval bridge, were removed in 1759 and the centre arch rebuilt by the Corporation of London's architects Robert Taylor and George Dance the elder in the same year. This went some way towards improving the bridge's appearance and reducing the adverse effect on tidal flows, the widened central arch also allowing more river traffic, which improved trade; but these efforts were not enough. The first moves to redevelop the bridge and the surrounding area completely came at the end of the eighteenth century as part of the Port of London improvements.[22] Various new bridge designs were drawn up during the period 1799–1801 including one by Dance the younger. The surveyor Thomas Telford, who had given a negative report on the condition of the old bridge, came up with the proposal that it be replaced by a single-span structure – a celebration of the engineer's rather than the architect's art. This was not realised as there was some uncertainty regarding the technical requirements of producing a cast iron bridge with a span of 600 feet. Yet it remained a potent symbol of modernity, and printed images of Telford's design were in demand for over a decade after its publication. Attention turned again to the state of Old London Bridge in 1821 when John Rennie, another engineer, was also asked for a report on its structural condition. Rennie argued that further repairs and alterations would cost as much as a new structure. The engineer's opinion carried weight as he had already successfully worked on both Waterloo and Southwark Bridges. The Corporation acted on Rennie's advice and sought and Act of Parliament to allow then to replace the bridge.[23]

It was not simply a question of a new structure to provide improved access and a more favourable aesthetic for this enduring symbol of London. London Bridge had since the sixteenth century housed the machinery which pumped the water supply for a large area of London.[24] Although the Old London Bridge Water Works were part of the obstruction to the tides[25] and the river traffic, their role in supplying residents across the city with water was vital. An inquiry into the waterworks revealed that over 216 gallons of water was pumped from the Thames every minute. This was directed across the metropolis and stored in reservoirs and underground tanks. The demand for water was continually increasing as the capital grew in size and population and it was the resources available from the City that helped to meet this need.[26] By 1821 the waterworks had over 10,000 customers and supplied sixty-eight public buildings. The removal of the waterworks was essential for rebuilding the bridge but Parliament would grant permission for this only if the role of the Old London Bridge Water Works was transferred to the New River Company.[27] These terms were embodies in the Act of Parliament in 1823 which granted the Corporation permission to replace the bridge.[28]

In the same year attention turned again to the design for a new London Bridge, but the image of the metropolis it was to form part of and symbolise had changed considerably. London had not only increased dramatically both geographically and demographically but many of the Metropolitan Improvements had been implemented or were under way. Notably here, as we have already seen, Regent Street, Regent's Park and the monumental entrance way into the metropolis from the west at Hyde Park Corner[29] were beginning to transform the image of London (see chapter 5) into a world-class city. These improvements were being orchestrated and overseen by the Offices of Woods and Works – agents of the Crown who were answerable to Parliament and who were largely funded by the public purse. This self-conscious attempt to develop London into a world-class city had implications for the work at London Bridge. Here the responsibility for the work and the initial cost of the entire project fell to the Corporation of London, an autonomous body concerned with the local government of the City. The Act of Parliament which gave the City of London permission to replace London Bridge brought with it some financial support for the project. According to R. L. Jones, a member of the Bridge House Committee which oversaw the work, this was appropriate as the bridge 'was one of great and important public character', and the committee 'might fairly look to the Government for support and assistance'.[30] Despite its financial support, the government did not get involved directly with the design for the new bridge. But there were conditions which aligned the rebuilding of London Bridge to other parts of the Metropolitan Improvements. Like Hyde Park Corner and other projects belonging to the improvements, the width of the road was to be increased, together with the quality of its surface and steepness of its gradient.

Most of the new bridges across the Thames were built by private companies which speculated on the profits from tolls. But government funding was forthcoming for the rebuilding of London Bridge most likely because of the symbiotic nature of the cities of London and Westminster and in recognition of the symbolic potential of London Bridge as an image of a modern metropolis. The government granted £150,000 to be raised by taxes.[31] Chief amongst these was the coal tax levied at 8d. per ton for coal brought to the City for sale by land or through the Port of London. This was one of the principal sources of fuel for the whole of London. This blanket tax was directly towards a building project which was of benefit to a specific group in the City. A second duty on wine at 4d. per ton was also granted. It was estimated that they yield from these two sources of revenue would reach the promised £150,000 by 1858. On its part the Corporation took out a loan of £1,000,000 at 4 per cent from the Bank of England and raised a further £250,000 from private lenders at the lower rate of 3.17 per cent.[32] The estimation of the level of duty required was over-generous and the Corporation's borrowing had been covered by 1852.[33] If the tax continued to its intended date a further £300,000 would be raised, which could be used for other Metropolitan Improvements, but the income potential of these levies came to the attention of the Corporation of London as the new bridge was nearing completion. In 1829 proposals were laid before Parliament for improved London Bridge approaches at an estimated sum of £1,000,000. The monies raised from the coal tax were to be used to defray the cost.[34] There was vigorous opposition from the House of Commons, which objected to the appropriation of its future funds and the House of Lords where coalmine-owning peers such as Lord Durham and Lord Londonderry objected to the potential curtailment of their incomes. Much to the chagrin of his fellow peers, the Duke of Wellington recognised the importance of the City and within it London Bridge to all levels of the capital's infrastructure and stepped in to rescue the scheme for the approaches and secure the funding for it.[35]

THE COMPETITION

The competition to rebuild the bridge was drawn up by the City Committee for the London Bridge Estates (the Bridge House Committee), and several of the entries were exhibited at the Western Exchange, Old Bond Street, in 1823.[36] The Committee was chaired by Mr Montague and had been established early in 1822. The premium offered for the winners were in line with other such competitions: £250, £150 and £100 for first, second and third prizes.[37] The instructions for the competition included that the bridge be faced with granite; that there should be five arches; and that the centre arch should be 23 feet above water level. The new structure should be erected no more than 70 feet west of the present (old) bridge. The note on style reveals much: 'It is desireable [sic] that the bridge should be worthy of the metropolis and the present cultivated state of science, due regard being had at the same time to Economy and convenience of traffic over and under the bridge during the progress and after completion of the works.' But the design should allow 'formation of the necessary approaches as is consistent with the character of so important an entrance to the city of London'. The Offices of Woods and Works refused to have anything to do with the competition or the selection of a winning design. Had it been a government-run project, one of the attached architects of the Office of Works – John Nash, Sir Robert Smirke or Sir John Soane – would have been given the commission. As a result, this prestigious project did not belong to the Metropolitan Improvements in the same way as Regent Street or Smirke's British Museum. Instead the new London Bridge expressed the enduring autonomy of the City and its dislocation from the rest of the metropolis. In recognition of the status of the attached architects, which would add the aura of authority to the competition, the Bridge House Committee employed Nash, Smirke and Soane on a private basis to judge the entries. The competition was, however, entered by architects of the second order. It was won by Charles Fowler with John Boorer and

Charles Bushy coming second and third respectively. The grander competition plans, like the earlier proposal of Dance the younger, all took up valuable space on the north side of the river which could be used for commercial purposes. It was most unlikely that any City merchant would give up profitable real estate in the cause of urban beautification. The Crown had had a similar problem of landowners' reluctance to give up part of their estates for the improvements in the West End, but this had largely been overcome with the use of compulsory purchase. The Corporation, however, had the financial interests of its traders as its primary concern. In the end all the entries were ignored in favour of Rennie's design: a plain, functional structure with few architectural embellishments.

The new London Bridge was executed by John Rennie junior, as his father had died in 1821. This plan proposed that the new bridge be built on the exact site of the old one and elevated at either end to correspond with the level of the old approaches. A temporary timber bridge would be constructed for the duration of the building work. But the narrow approaches by Fish Street Hill were considered most unworthy for the magnificent new bridge and inadequate for the ever-increasing traffic. Rennie's estimate for the new bridge came to £430,000, with a further £20,000 for the construction of the temporary wooden structure. The bridge House Committee recommended that the bridge be moved 180 feet west of the old one, so avoiding the steep hill of Fish Street. The width of the bridge had been increased by 6 feet on Rennie's original scheme in the interest of greater public convenience. The Prime Minister, Lord Liverpool, agreed to the additional expenditure of £42,000 to accommodate the expected increase in traffic. This would, however, render 'new, more commodious, and much more expensive approaches necessary'. But the revised scheme would provide a fitting entrance into the City from the Southwark side of the river. Moreover, as attention turned increasingly to thoroughfares through London, London Bridge was seen as connecting with roads on both sides of the river and creating a continuous route across the city. It was in one sense a stretch of road which crossed water but in another sense monumental approaches offered some commemorative punctuation for this route through the metropolis.

In 1829 the Corporation of London presented designs for the bridge approaches to Parliament. A variety of plans were presented as a supplement to Rennie's original intentions for the approaches and particular attention was paid to the north bank of the Thames where the bridge entered the City.[38] Several drawings exist which relate to the scheme. Rennie junior had hoped that the commission for the design would go his brother-in-law C. R. Cockerell. A drawing by Cockerell held in the British Art Center at Yale suggests

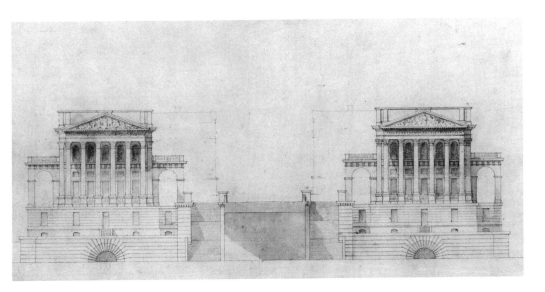

4.3 C. R. Cockerell, *Design for the Approaches to London Bridge*, undated, brown wash over pencil

4.4 Henry Roberts, *Design for Approaches London Bridge – North*, undated, watercolour over graphite

the architect got as far as producing a design (figure 4.3).[39] Another drawing by Henry Roberts, who worked in Smirke's Office from 1825 to 1829, also relates to the scheme and is held in the same collection (figure 4.4).[40] Roberts' connection with the site and the City in general is compelling as in 1832 he won the competition for the Fishmongers' Hall which was adjacent to the new London Bridge on the City side of the river. Both Cockerell's and Roberts' designs provide an adequate response to the urban vision of the Metropolitan Improvements, but the work was given to Robert Smirke, about whom it was remarked, '[Of Smirke's] undoubted purity of taste (we wish we could add fertility of invention) much is to be hoped'.[41] Less generously, Cockerell lamented Smirke's embellishment of the London Bridge approaches, remarking that 'a more unworthy set of buildings was never designed'.

On the other side of the Thames the approach from Southwark now had the Monument – an emblem of the City in view and space would be made for an impressive approach road over 70 feet wide and with a gentle gradient of 1:30. The south side of the river was not forgotten in the plans to embellish the approach to the City. Two anonymous drawings of the London Bridge approaches from the City to the Borough side of the Thames also exist at Yale (figures 4.5 and 4.6). They are undated and represent different iconographic schemes and stylistic detailing. The one might refer to the Battle of the Nile as it has Egyptian-style elements,[42] whilst the other has a more antique Roman feel and may refer to the Augustan image of the Metropolitan Improvements.[43]

Two main themes emerge from this narrative. First, should monuments, as the bridge clearly was, be designed by architects or

4.5 British School C19th, *Design for London Bridge Approach*, undated, pen, ink and wash

4.6 British School C19th, *Design for London Bridge Approach*, undated, pen, ink and wash

engineers? And secondly, if the bridge was a barometer of the general mood of the embellishment of London, how were the tensions revealed between national and civic pride, metropolitan and national systems of government?

ARCHITECT VERSUS ENGINEER

The vigorous reaction by the public to the competition reveals much about the notion of urban identity and the specific role of London Bridge as a symbol within this metropolitan framework. A pamphlet published by I. Andrews in 1823 entitled *London Bridge but no new Taxes*[44] contained a dedication to Nash, Soane and Smirke as the architects attached to the Office of Works. More specifically, the author criticises their role in the London Bridge competition. Their presence may have given the gloss of authority to the contest but the premiums were criticised both by Andrews and anonymously in an open letter to the Member of Parliament George Sumner as being so low as to prevent 'men of adequate talent and reputation' from entering the competition.[45] Moreover the Bridge House Committee rejected the choices of the judges, disqualifying two of them on the grounds that the entrants had not followed instructions.

Pamphlets also appeared pleading the cause of the engineers. These stated that Nash, Soane and Smirke were qualified only to judge the stylistic and not the structural virtues of the new bridge. Andrews is also particularly vociferous on this point and laments the absence of an engineer on the judges' panel. This is endorsed in the open letter to George Sumner MP countering this view – written by 'an architect anon.'. It states that there is a 'mistaken notion prevalent in these times that engineers only are capable of building bridges – but the most beautiful bridges in France and Italy have all been designed by architects. Engineers should only be used for the parts below the water in a great national work of this nature.'[46] There is no doubt that the significance of the bridge as a status symbol of London was recognised by the pamphleteers, and calls for the whole matter to by handed over to a parliamentary committee with public accountability were frequently voiced. This commission would, according to one pamphleteer, '[prevent] Old father Thames being disfigured by a Bridge unworthy of his station among the ruins of Europe' and ensure that the bridge might become 'an ornament to the metropolis'.

The debates about the design and designers of London Bridge show its involvement with and disengagement from the main thrust of the Metropolitan Improvements. It had become part of the image of the modern metropolis, but it remained a fundamental element in the discrete identity of the City of London.

The dynamic between central government and the City was curious. At the heart of it was a complex set of relationships centring on civic pride and the financial autonomy of the City's institutions which covered all manner of trades as well as banking. This was perhaps best typified in the office of the Lord Mayor who had no equivalent elsewhere in London and was second only to the monarch within the confines of the City. But Westminster had begun to overshadow the City. The Metropolitan Improvements which were such a vital part of the creation of a modern metropolis were implemented with all the clout of a government project with state funding. The creation of a rationalised urban environment and not least the construction of an effective road and sewer system were underpinned by the government's ability to raise revenue by taxation. But beyond this there was a more fundamental social and political friction between the cities of London and Westminster in the years directly preceding the 1832 Reform Act. Parliament was made up of only the very upper end of society – the ruling elite. The City, although represented in this body, comprised mainly middle and merchant classes who stood outside the area of national government because of their social caste. During the opening decades of the nineteenth century the metropolis became an instrument of the government system. The rationalisation of street plans and the concerns for the well-being of trade and the populace were hallmarks of this.[47]

The City of London was a discrete entity within the metropolis. It represented the financial and commercial interests of the capital and the country. The Corporation of London administered the business activities and acted as a kind of local government with the Lord Mayor as its principal official. These arrangements were deeply rooted in London's past as, until the middle years of the seventeenth century, the City comprised the largest part of London as a whole and often stood in opposition to both the court and government. Its status was gradually challenged as London grew in size, so diminishing the City's physical dominance of the geography of the metropolis. Moreover, its autonomous local government was overshadowed by the increasing significance and clout of the systems of national government, as expressed through Parliament at Westminster. But the City's sense of civic pride and will to preserve its privileges and rituals did not diminish.

The authority and prestige of the Corporation of London found physical expression in the grand architecture of the Mansion House c. 1740–50 by George Dance the elder.[48] Similarly, the importance of trade and commerce were represented in the rebuilding of the Bank of England by Sir John Soane in the 1790s and the Royal Exchange by Sir William Tite in the 1840s.[49] And, not least, St Paul's Cathedral, perhaps London's most enduring symbol, stands in the City. The size, scale and splendour of these edifices equalled the grand public buildings projects of the West End. There is no doubt that the rebuilding of London Bridge was seen to be as symbolic of the City's status as any of the other large building projects. But here, the part funding of the work by the state threatened the hegemony of the Corporation of London. Yet the built environment is only one signifier of social and political pre-eminence. The roles of place and ritual are equally important.

The City of London and its civic system had long been seen as representative of a kind of republicanism. Expressions of anti-establishment feeling and the wish for egalitarianism became increasingly frequent in the period 1760–1830 and the City was a regular location for these. The City authorities were not always in sympathy with the specific activities of those who demonstrated on their doorstep, even if both parties shared a common concern for the right to vote. But the independent nature of the City and its symbolic identity as a body able to make a stand against national government made it an attractive location for expressions of dissent. John Wilkes is an early case in point. Wilkes campaigned to be Member of Parliament for the City in order to further the case for universal manhood suffrage. His eventual election as MP for Middlesex in 1768 was a victory for the cause. Celebrations by Wilkes's mainly working class supporters took place in the City. The Corporation did not share the mob's enthusiasm, which resulted in the windows of the Mansion House being smashed.[50] The fight for the right to vote became increasingly vocal and vigorous in the post-Napoleonic era. Events in France had demonstrated the potential power of the masses and remained a vivid reminder of the possible consequences both of political egalitarianism or continued repression of electoral freedom. Support for enfranchisement came from the working classes and the politically impotent but increasingly financially predominant urban bourgeoisie. Henry 'Orator' Hunt drew large crowds to his rally for the right to vote at Smithfield in July 1819. In September of that year, spurred on by the Peterloo Massacre, Hunt entered the City followed by a mainly working class crowd. The procession ended at the Mansion House with calls for enfranchisement. The City authorities did not take up the cause of the masses, which was probably as well, but the wealthy merchants and businessmen became increasingly agitated at their lack of political power. The financial and commercial institutions were nationally important and enabled government policy through taxation and loans. They were part of the identity of London and the nation as a whole. By 1830 resentment at the government's failure to widen the franchise had reached a volatile level. As a result, in November of that year William IV declined his traditional invitation to attend the annual Lord Mayor's Banquet. The Prime Minister, Sir Robert Peel, had advised against it as the frequent anti-government riots and demonstrations which were taking place in the City compromised the King's safety.[51] The Cities of Westminster and London were indeed in opposition.

The City was, rather like Charing Cross, a site for the expression of social and political ideals which challenged national systems. But how did it maintain its image of authority and independence as the neighbouring city of Westminster, the home of national government, became increasingly dominant? The isolated grandeur of its key building no doubt helped embellish the authority of the City. But it was the public performance of institutional rituals which underpinned the Corporation of London's local hegemony and the national significance of the City. Most notable amongst these were the annual Lord Mayor's Banquet, where key government ministers were invited to speak on government policy,[52] and the Lord Mayor's Show. The latter remains a piece of street theatre which presents a sort of tradition born out of ritual which fed off the absent presence of the monarchy in eighteenth-century London.[53] The Lord Mayor's official residence, the Mansion House, acted as a kind of court, providing opulent receptions for visiting dignitaries paid for by the Corporation of London. This presented an image of an alternative, more democratic governmental structure.

The ritual and public performance which surrounded the ceremonial laying of a building's foundation stone were used to ensure that London Bridge remained firmly identified with the City. The foundation stone for the new bridge was laid in June 1825 by the Lord Mayor, Alderman John Garrett. The procession for the ceremony began at the Guildhall and the mayor used a ceremonial trowel bearing the arms of the Bridge House Committee and the Corporation of London. 'Ownership' of the project was further expressed as the City Sword and Mace were placed crossways on the foundation stone, and as it was declared laid the Lord Mayor remarked that the bridge 'would reflect credit upon the inhabitants, prove an ornament to the Metropolis and redound [sic] the honour of the Corporation'.[54] The proceedings culminated in a grand banquet in the Egyptian Hall of the Mansion House. The ceremony was witnessed by thousands and performed in the presence of the Duke of York, who took no part in the ritual. The opening of the new London Bridge took place in August 1831 and the old structure was demolished shortly afterwards. By this time fears for royal safety in the City had subsided to the extent that William IV and Queen Adelaide attended the ceremony, but the proceedings and celebratory banquet were confined to the bridge. The procession, led by

William IV, to celebrate this important and highly significant entrance way to the metropolis and the City exited rather entered it. On declaring the bridge open, the King gave credit to the Corporation in his remark that 'it was one of the magnificent improvements for which the City London was renouned [*sic*]'.[55] The Duke of Wellington, who continued to do much to enable the building of the new bridge approaches, declined the invitation to participate in the opening ceremony on the grounds that the opposition expressed to his attendance at the Lord Mayor's Banquet the previous November, which the King did not attend, still stood. Wellington was vigorously opposed to the enfranchisement of the middle classes and had been told that his presence at the banquet would have been 'likely to create a disturbance, for the consequences of which the authorities of the City would not answer'.[56] The bridge's completion before the 1832 Reform Act and Wellington's boycott of the opening ceremony are contradicted by the Duke's vigorous support of the project and the use of the coal tax as a means of funding it. The Duke of Wellington's attitude to the City was complex. Whilst he recognised the rights and privileges of the City and saw it as a valuable part of the constitution of the country, he saw no need for its representatives to have a role in national government either as MPs or through the ballot box. London Bridge provides a focal point for these contradictory attitudes.

A consideration of the symbolic identity of London Bridge for the Regency metropolis reveals some important issues about the social and political landscapes of London and the methods of their production. The dis-location of London Bridge from the emerging architectural identity of the new metropolis – especially its relative isolation from the other Metropolitan Improvements in terms of the urban plan of London – had two main consequences. First, the City and the bridge remained disconnected from the new and emerging road infrastructure of London, and the commemorative and

4.7 *New London Bridge*, engraving by R. Acon from a drawing by T. H. Shepherd, published in T. H. Shepherd, *London and its Environs in the Nineteenth Century*, London, 1829

monumental possibilities of the bridge, although widely discussed and acknowledged, were unrealised. Perhaps this was the result of the insular nature of the City authorities who wished to have no association with the nationalistic iconographies of the Metropolitan Improvements and the erosion of the local autonomy they represented. Secondly, the bridge's role in the economic infrastructure of the City cannot be underestimated. And this identifies it firmly, and perhaps fittingly through its functional engineer-designed structure, with the profit-driven trading heart of the City with its own discrete system of government (figure 4.7).

NOTES

1   A version of this chapter originally appeared as 'London Bridge and its Symbolic Identity in the Regency Metropolis: The Dialectic of Civic and National Pride', *Art History*, 22: (1999), pp. 545–66. Much of the research for this essay was carried out during my tenure as visiting fellow at the Yale Center for British Art. I would like to thank the staff of the Center, especially Elisabeth Fairman and Lori Misura, for their help in locating material. Sir John Soane's Museum also proved to be a valuable source of information and my thanks go to Susan Palmer for her assistance. I must also thank Adrian Rifkin who kindly read and commented on the final draft.

2   The was designed by the engineers Mott, Hay and Anderson with Lord Holford as the architectural adviser, 1967–72.

3   The afterlife of London Bridge is discussed in my essay 'London Bridge Revisited', in D. Arnold and A. Ballantyne (eds), *Architecture in Experience*, London, Routledge, 2004, pp. 261–76.

4   This thematic exploration of London is the basis of my book *Re-presenting the Metropolis*. Here a related methodology is used to examine the specific example of London Bridge. I am following Foucault's ideas about the heterotopic and heterochronic functions of space as expressed in M. Foucault, 'Of Other Spaces (Des Espaces Autres)', *Diacritics* (Spring 1986) trans. J. Miskowiec, pp. 22–7. As such, London Bridge becomes a heterotopia – a counter site which re-enacts, represents and inverts the Utopian mirror image of the metropolis. It enables us to see London in its space–time location through a kaleidoscopic image of spatial oppositions, social rituals and cultural practices.

5   For a fuller discussion of the building of the West End, see Summerson, *Georgian London*.

6   S. and R. Percy, *The Percy Histories or Interesting memories of the rise, progress and presentation of all the capitals of Europe*, 3 vols, London, 1823.

7   Vol. 1, Uv, Port of London Reports 1796–99, 2 vols, London, 1799.

8   Sir Frederick Morton Eden, Bt., *Porto-bello or a Plan for the improvement of the Port and City of London*, London, 1798, p. 41.

9   Ibid., p. 42.

10   Ibid., p. 43.

11   As cited in *The Percy Histories*.

12 Revd Henry Hunter, *The History of London and its Environs*, 2 vols, London, 1811, vol. 1, p. 693.

13 On this point, see my article 'The Arch at Constitution Hill: A New Axis for London', *Apollo*, 138: 379 (Sept. 1993), pp. 129–33.

14 Many of these plans – some of them quite improbable – are outlined in F. Barker and R. Hyde, *London As It Might Have Been*, London, John Murray, 1982.

15 The attempts to commemorate the military achievements of the Duke of Wellington discussed within the paradigm of Bataille's notion of sacrifice forms the basis of my published essay, *The Duke of Wellington and London*, 13th Annual Wellington Lecture, University of Southampton, 2002.

16 I. Andrews, *London Bridge and No New Taxes*, London, 1823.

17 *The Percy Histories*, vol. 2, p. 130.

18 Charles Dupin was a French engineer who made several visits to Britain. His impressions of the engineering and technological achievements of the nation which had defeated Napoleon are recorded in his numerous publications, most notably here: *Voyages dans la Grande Bretagne, Entrepris relatives aux services Publics 1816–19*, Paris, 1824.

19 See D. Stillman, 'Death Defied and Honor Upheld: The Mausoleum in NeoClassical England', *Art Quarterly*, new series, 1:3 (1978), pp. 175–213.

20 This was a pan-European phenomenon. For instance, mausolea were the theme for the French Academy's Prix de Rome in 1762 and similarly the Academie de Dijon in 1780 and in 1791 for the Academy of Parma.

21 Quoted in R. L. Jones, *Reminiscences of the Public Life of Richard Lambert Jones Esq.*, London, privately printed, 1863.

22 The Third Report from the Select Committee upon the Improvements of the Port of London was published in 1801.

23 Rennie's report was submitted on 12 March 1821. The original specification for the new bridge is held in the University of London Library MS 158. Rennie died in October the same year.

24 This dates back to 1581 when Pieter Morice was granted a 500-year lease on one of the arches on London Bridge. The tidal flow was strong enough to turn his patented waterwheel and allow it to pump water up to Cornhill.

25 The waterworks needed a strong tidal flow which was strengthened by the many arches of Old London Bridge. As the number of arches decreased so did the waterwheel's ability to pump adequate supplies of water.

26 For a fuller discussion of London's water supply, see Matthew's *Hydralia: A Historical and Descriptive Account of the Waterworks of London*, London, 1835.

27 These were delicate negotiations as water was a precious commodity. The proprietors of the London Bridge Water Works were paid £10,000, and they were guaranteed 5 per cent of the profits for the term of the 260-year lease, (Jones, *Reminiscences*, p. 10).

28 The Act for the Rebuilding of London Bridge and the Making of Suitable Approaches Thereto received royal assent on 4 July 1823.

29 See Arnold, 'The Arch at Constitution Hill'.

30 Jones, *Reminiscences*.

31 10 Geo. IV, c. 136 and 11 Geo. IV, c. 64.

32 The precise details and forecasts of the financial arrangements between the government and the Corporation are set out in *The First Report of the Select Committee on Metropolitan Improvements*, Parliamentary Papers 1837–8, XVI 418.

33 Ibid.

34 Jones, *Reminiscences*, pp. 32–3.

35 In recognition of his efforts the Duke of Wellington was honoured with an equestrian statue in front of the Royal Exchange. See A. Saunders (ed.), *The Royal Exchange*, London Topographical Society publication no. 152, London, 1997.

36 The catalogue for this exhibition is held at Sir John Soane's Museum, Soane PC 55/2.

37 An exhibition of competition designs for the completion of King's College, Cambridge, which had similar premiums, was exhibited at the same time. The catalogue for this is in Sir John Soane's Museum, Soane PC 55/2.

38 *A professional survey of Old and New London Bridges and their approaches*, 1831, Soane PC 23/4.

39 C. R. Cockerell, *Design for the Approaches to London Bridge*, Yale Center for British Art, Paul Mellon Collection, B1975.2.632.

40 H. Roberts, *Design for the Approaches to London Bridge*, Yale Center for British Art, Paul Mellon Collection, B1975.2.635.

41 *Professional Survey*, Soane PC 23/4, p. 43.

42 British School C19th, Design for London Bridge Approaches, Yale Center for British Art, Paul Mellon Collection, B1975.2.634.

43 British School C19th, Design for London Bridge Approach, Yale Center for British Art, Paul Mellon Collection, B1975.2.633.

44 Soane Museum PC 52/3.

45 *The conduct of the Corporation of the City of London considered in respect of designs submitted to it for the rebuilding of London Bridge in a letter to George Holme Sumner Esq MP by an architect, 1823*. Soane Pamphlets PC 13/2.

46 Ibid.

47 For a fuller discussion of the use of urban space as an instrument of government ideology, see my *Re-presenting the Metropolis*, and my article 'Rationality, Safety and Power'.

48 A thorough account of the building history of the Mansion House appears in S. Jeffery, *The Mansion House*, Corporation of London and Phillimore and Co., Sussex, 1993.

49 There were similar tensions between national and local government in the rebuilding of the Royal Exchange. A detailed history of the Royal Exchange is given in Saunders (ed.), *The Royal Exchange*.

50 This incident and the career and significance of Wilkes to the process of parliamentary reform is discussed in P. Langford, *A Polite People*, Oxford, Oxford University Press, 1989, esp. p. 377.

51 Jones, *Reminiscences*, pp. 47–8.

52 This tradition continues today. The Mansion House speech delivered by the Chancellor of the Exchequer is used by government to outline its financial policies.

53 For a discussion of the role of ritual and the invention of tradition see D. Cannadine, 'The Context, Performance and Meaning of Ritual: The British Monarchy and the "Invention of Tradition", c. 1820–1977', in E. Hobsbawn and P. Ranger (eds), *The Invention of Tradition*, Cambridge, Cambridge University Press, 1983, pp. 101–64.

54 Jones, *Reminiscences*, p.25.

55 *Professional Survey*, Soane PC 23/4, p. 42.

56 Jones, *Reminiscences*, p. 58.

Smoothing and levelling

The grand plans to re-image the western approach to London and to reshape the royal parks of the fashionable West End are not immediately apparent either in the present landscape of the metropolis, or in the paper architecture that might be expected to accompany such an ambitious scheme, which is notably absent. However, a forensic examination of the fragmented evidence in Crown Estate papers and Treasury minute books, held in the National Archives, reveals a coherent attempt to improve the architecture and landscape of this area that was being driven by both George IV and the state. During the early 1820s the area known as Hyde Park Corner at the conjunction of Hyde, St James's and Green Parks underwent substantial development. The site had been the entrance into London from the west, but its absorption into George IV and his ministers' vision of the metropolis as a royal city necessitated the removal of the toll gate that had marked this traditional boundary. The plan for the space included two entrance ways, one into Green Park, then the back garden of Buckingham Palace, and one into Hyde Park, which was becoming an increasingly significant public open space. The iconography of the sculptural decoration of these entrance ways was to reinforce Hyde Park Corner as an urban space dedicated to the celebration of national pride and the nation's heroes, but most importantly the Hanoverian dynasty, as the King sought to enhance both his capital city and his own image. This was a set piece of urban planning, intended to surpass its European counterparts. And it required the levelling of the road to Hyde Park Corner from the west to ensure a smooth approach to this monumental space.

Hyde, St James's and Green Parks surrounded Buckingham Palace, the new royal residence, and formed part of its grounds. As such they collectively constituted the kind of landscape similar to those which surrounded country houses. The landscape of country houses had already been identified as containing a variety of meanings. And although these parks were in an urban setting the landscaping issues surrounding their improvement had resonance with the wider debates about landscape in the early nineteenth century. The use of landscape design principles to shape urban space offered a subtler reading of the cityscape than that presented by the abrupt class consciousness of developments like Regent Street. But this 'smoothing and levelling' of the urban landscape was just as politically charged as that of its rural counterpart. These were not new parks but the spread of the city westwards and increasing awareness of the social and political importance of landscape raised new design questions, and addressed significant ideological issues concerning these urban spaces. The shaping and codifying of the London landscape had begun almost unconsciously with the formation of garden squares as part of the eighteenth-century building boom. Chapter 1 has already demonstrated the importance of Bloomsbury to this kind of urban development. Moreover, the positive reactions to Regent's Park as a public open space show the general appreciation of this caesura in the terraces of houses which were spreading all over London. The royal parks, which converged at Hyde Park Corner, followed on from this. Hyde Park and Green Park bordered, and halted, the development of fashionable west London but they were not part of any speculative development. These lands were owned by the Crown and were designed and laid out to enhance the image of the monarch and the state and to provide effective communication between important public buildings – including Sir John Soane's State Paper Office, one of his last buildings. There were also philanthropic undertones in the concern to provide city dwellers with open spaces and fresh air. The role played by the parks in the shaping of this sensory experience of the city is charted in the final section of the book.

5 Hyde Park Corner

The work at the conjunction of Hyde, St James's and Green Parks at the area known as Hyde Park Corner was central to George IV's and his ministers' vision of London as a royal city fit to rival its European counterparts. The monarch and his chief officials planned to create an urban space dedicated to the celebration of the Hanoverian dynasty, national pride and the nation's heroes. The project, which evolved during the early 1820s, comprised the creation of two entrance ways, one into Green Park,[1] then the back garden of Buckingham Palace, and one into Hyde Park[2] which was becoming an increasingly significant public open space. This required the removal of the toll gate which defined Hyde Park Corner as the traditional entrance into London from the west and the levelling of the approach road to it to make the site more amenable to improvement. The development of Hyde Park Corner in the 1820s shows how it was re-imaged to fit in with George IV's vision for aggrandising London and through this his own reputation. A detailed examination of the work at Hyde Park Corner also allows an exploration of parallel projects that relate to civic and national interests, providing a counterpoint to London Bridge, as well as charting the rise of the public monument as a tool to focus national sentiment through the commemoration of national heroes – in this case the Duke of Wellington. Alongside this we see at Hyde Park Corner how the re-use of antique formulae for urban planning, seen sometimes through the veil of Renaissance or contemporary European models, was another important instrument in determining the re-imaging of London.

A NEW AXIS FOR LONDON

The growth of London westwards had left behind it a trail of once fashionable areas in the east. The city was capped by the New Road at its northern edge, which provided an essential link across the metropolis from east to west. London Bridge served as the principal entrance to the City from the east by river and from the south by road. By contrast, the New Street, later Regent Street, bisected the capital and carved a north–south divide through the city. But the north–south line of Regent Street no longer culminated in its intended focal point of a royal residence, as George IV's move from

Carlton House in 1826 resulted in his former home being demolished soon after its vacation.[3] The royal residence was now Buckingham Palace which was situated at the end of the Mall. The move westwards put the new royal residence on the outer limit of the city and introduced another axial route through London. The Mall ran from the space that is now known as Trafalgar Square (formerly Charing Cross), along St James's Park, to the main entrance of Buckingham Palace which was to be defined by Nash's Marble Arch. The palace was situated in the middle of open land comprised of two parks: St James's to the front and Green Park to the rear. Hyde Park, just to the north of Green Park, also formed part of the large expanse of parkland in this area of London. The place where Hyde and Green Park met was known as Hyde Park Corner – the westernmost edge of the metropolis and the site of a toll gate for those entering the city. The royal move westward redefined the meaning and significance this area from city entrance to a monumental piazza or square dedicated to the Hanoverian monarchy and the nation's military and intellectual prowess.

THE IMPORTANCE OF HYDE PARK CORNER

A monumental gateway at Hyde Park Corner had originally been planned by George III.[4] The idea may have developed out of John Gwynn's proposal in his *London and Westminster Improved*, 1766 for a *place* at Hyde Park Corner from which main avenues radiated. Gwynn felt the area needed improvement as it was so close to royal residences such as Carlton House, Buckingham House and St James's Palace. His idea was developed further in 1778 by Robert Adam who designed a monumental gateway for this site. This plan may well have evolved during the time Adam was designing and building the terrace of brick town houses at Hyde Park Corner in 1771–78. (Apsley House was the most westward of these and had the address No. 1 London.) It comprised an archway flanked on either side by entrances into the two royal parks. The nationalistic overtones of such a monument rendered the plan impractical on financial and ideological grounds – Britain had lost a valuable colony in the expensive American War of Independence. The idea was revived by Jeffery Wyatt who exhibited a scheme at the Royal Academy in 1791. Four years later Sir John Soane, on his appointment as architect to the Office of Woods, provided plans for improvements in the parks including, at the behest of George III, a monumental entrance way to Hyde Park from Piccadilly and an entrance into Green Park. Soane's plans also included a new royal palace in the north-west corner of Green Park. Other architects presented plans for the site, including William Kinnaird who in 1813 published 'View of a

Triumphal Arch, Proposed To Be Erected at Hyde Park Corner, commemorative of the victories achieved by British Arms during the Reign of His Majesty King George the Third'.[5] None of these plans was executed.[6] So Hyde Park Corner already had great significance for the capital and was seen as the gateway into London. The added ingredients in the early nineteenth century were the recent victories over the French at Trafalgar and Waterloo which created the need for adequate commemoration of the nation's war heroes. A fund of £300,000 had been set up by Parliament in 1816 for the erection of commemorative monuments. Perhaps in response to this, in 1817 Soane presented another scheme for Hyde Park Corner which he exhibited at the Royal Academy. This followed Adam's design of an archway running across Piccadilly with decorative sculpture commemorating the two battles.[7] But once again no action was taken.

Two important themes emerge from this: national pride as seen in the plans for a royal London, and the importance placed upon recent military victories and national heroes in the decoration of the monuments in this area. The revival and revision of this long-standing plan in the 1820s was a defining moment in London's history. These new plans for the monumental entrance ways into Hyde and Green Parks were designed not only to evoke nationalist feeling through the celebration of victory over the French and of British cultural achievements, but this triumphalistic iconography was also dovetailed into significant changes in the urban plan of London.

PUBLIC MONUMENTS

The eighteenth century had established a tradition of private monuments for churches, and gardens. The garden monuments drew their inspiration from classical antiquity and helped establish the language of the picturesque, which became an important instrument in the reimaging of urban and rural environments. The inclusion of all'-antica buildings in landscape garden design is evident, for instance, at Stourhead where visitors encountered replicas of buildings such as the Pantheon. Indeed, the narrative function of landscape came sharply into focus here, as Virgil's *Aeneid* was the literary inspiration for the overall design. National sentiments were also expressed through classically inspired monuments, as seen in the Temple of the British Worthies at Stowe or the plethora of columns and obelisks dedicated to to an army of military leaders that peppered the country estates of the elite. As the political map of Europe changed, it became evident that the models of antiquity could aquire new and powerful meaning to encourage public sentiment – particularly nationalistic

feeling within an urban context. An early example of this is John
Flaxman's unrealised giant statue *Britannia Triumphans* (1799)
which was based on Stuart and Revett's reconstruction of the *Athena
Parthenos* which appeared in their *Antiquities of Athens* published
over half a century earlier. Here this image was transformed into a
national monument to the naval victory at the Battle of the Nile and
was intended to dominate the London skyline at Greenwich.

The most popular forms of monuments were temples (national
valhalla), columns, arches and statues as well as miniature urban
plans which presented a complete iconography of celebration. The
most noteworthy of these are the Foro Bonaparte in Milan by the
architect Giannantonio Antolini (1754–1802). This was planned in
the early years of the nineteenth century and intended as a monument to the French victory at the battle of Marengo. It included
piazzas, streets, barracks, warehouses, houses and triumphal arches
and temples, but was never completed and was instead reduced to a
single piazza. It is likely this was based on the Trajan Forum (113 CE),
which was built using the spoils of the Dacian Wars. In its early nineteenth-century manifestation Hyde Park Corner provided an ideal
location or symbolic space for the architectural celebration of nation,
monarch and metropolis based on antique and recent French
precedents, which were in tune with European trends in monumental urban planning and the political language of the English
picturesque.

THE IDEA OF ALIGNMENT AND THE DUKE
OF WELLINGTON

The area around Hyde Park Corner was relatively unencumbered by
buildings and, unlike the Regent Street project, most of the land
belonged to the Crown. Even so there were constraints on the plans.
The most practical and pressing problem was the toll gate situated at
Hyde Park Corner, the lease for which was held by the Pimlico
Turnpike Trust. Its removal was crucial to any development of the
area – especially on the scale that was being planned. Indeed, the
imminent expiry of the lease may have been an added incentive for
the plans to redevelop the area, offering an echo of the impetus for
the Regent's Park project.[8] In the latter case leases on the market
gardens and smallholdings in Marybone Park fell in leaving the land
open for profitable development. The important difference here,
however, is that the work at Hyde Park Corner and in the royal parks
would yield no profit. And, although the improved urban environment could be said to enhance the garden squares in the West End,
these were not owned by the Crown. The bill of £10,000 for funding
the development of Hyde Park Corner, which was put through

Parliament in late 1823, also requested the eradication of the toll gate.[9] The stated reason for this request from George Harrison at the Treasury was that those living west of the toll gates should no longer have to pay to come into London. Moreover, the Office of Woods was expected to speak to the various parties promoting the bill so that the clause to remove the tollgate could be included in it. In March 1824 the Trustees of the roads agreed to this.[10] On the part of the Treasury George Harrison followed up swiftly by also agreeing to the removal of the tollgate.[11]

A second factor in the development of the design of Hyde Park Corner was the Achilles statue 1821–22, dedicated to the Duke of Wellington, which had been paid for by women in gratitude for his victory at Waterloo. The bronze sculpture depicting the Iron Duke as a heroic male nude was situated in the park just behind Apsley House and a short distance from the toll gates at Hyde Park Corner. Shortly after its erection the the poor condition of and vandalism to the fence surrounding the statue became a cause for concern. Edward William Fauquier, the park ranger resident at Hyde Park Lodge, brought this to the attention of George Harrison at the Treasury in a letter of 28 May 1824.[12] Fauquier states that the original intention was to have an iron railing around a stone pedestal and suggests that the design be completed to guard the statue against mischief. The task was taken in hand in a letter from the Office of Woods dated 6 July 1824 stating that railing designs had been solicited from Mr Westmacott.[13]

The siting of the Achilles statue is significant for the layout of Hyde Park Corner as it played an influential role in establishing the axis between the entrances to Hyde and Green Parks, the proposed axis being dependent upon the removal of the toll gate. The idea of linking the statue with the general scheme of improvements was fixed firmly in Charles Arbuthnot's mind by August 1824 as both he and Adams wrote to the Treasury:

> ... with respect to the gates and lodges it has often been suggested to us since the public monument was placed in Hyde Park that it would be a great improvement if the gates of that park and those of Green Park opposite were to be so altered as to make this the principal entrance into Hyde Park directly in front of that monument but as this improvement cannot be effected without removing the turnpike gates to the west of Grosvenor Place which is intended on the renewal of the Trust, now about to expire we defer layout before your Lordships of plans and estimates for this improvement.[14]

It appears that the axis for the Hyde Park Screen and the Green Park Arch (this became known as the Arch at Constitution Hill) was determined by Arbuthnot on the basis of the Achilles statue, and this formed the nucleus of the plan to transform Hyde Park Corner into a *grand place*. Indeed, there had been much talk of a monument to Wellington including an arch at Hyde Park Corner but no firm plans had been made. Moreover, by this time Decimus Burton was established as the architect for the whole project. He had been involved with the original siting of the statue and was then being retained by the Office of Woods to produce designs for the whole of the improvements to the parks.[15] The alignment of the entrances was such a fundamental part of the project that Burton's non-participation would have been surprising. The Wellington statue was included in the plan, as the view of it from Hyde Park Corner was framed by the aligned screen and triumphal arch. The statue also enhanced the iconography of the intended sculptural decoration of the screen and arch at Hyde Park Corner and the new palace (discussed below) which celebrated the nation's military might so providing in part a commemoration of the Duke of Wellington. The Achilles statue was one end of a line which could be traced from Hyde Park to the rear facade of George IV's new palace. As such it was drawn into the iconographical composition through the re-alignment of the roads and entrance ways between the palace and Hyde Park.

The third factor which influenced the siting of the entrance gates to the two parks is the king's decision to move to Buckingham Palace, to which Green Park was the back garden. George IV's architectural ambitions were evident even during his time as Prince Regent. The extravagant redecoration of Carlton House and the Brighton Pavilion are testimony to his eclectic and expensive taste. The lavishly renovated Carlton House had been the focal point of Regent Street, but he tired of each of his many new decorative schemes very quickly and felt that the building was not suitable, particularly in terms of its size, as the residence of the future monarch. On his accession to the throne Parliament took the opportunity to tighten further the purse strings on royal spending – particularly on building projects – but George IV still had considerable latitude and private sums of money and revenues which could be channelled into projects of his choosing.

Since the death of Queen Charlotte in 1818, George IV had had his eye on her former residence, Buckingham House (also called the Queen's Palace). The furore surrounding the funding of the work he wished to carry out on this rather modest house is significant here.[16] As far back as 1818 Lord Liverpool had made it clear that public money would not be forthcoming for any work he undertook on Buckingham House. One year later Parliament granted £150,000 over three years towards the building costs which presented a stark choice between seeking parliamentary authority to sell Crown property to meet any expenditure above £150,000 and 'to complete the whole arrangements (internally and externally) for that sum, without the interference of Parliament'.[17] George IV demanded at least £400,000 and there was stalemate for two years. In the summer of 1821 George IV took Buckingham House out of the control of Sir John Soane (who was overseeing repairs as part of his duties as one of the Attached Architects to the Office of Works) and gave the job to John Nash. By 1822 the King had already made the decision to abandon Carlton House, demolish it and lease the land, and in August of that year Nash submitted plans to the Surveyor General of Works for the conversion of Buckingham House into a royal palace. Work began on 6 June 1825 before either a bill or estimate had been put before Parliament. Moreover, as already noted, the area around the new palace was uncluttered, which avoided many of the problems of land acquisition that had blighted the Regent Street project and which made grander landscaping schemes more feasible. The parks were ready for an overhaul of their landscaping, paths, perimeters and entrances and it may have been brought to the King's attention that the lease of the turnpike trust at Hyde Park Corner was due to expire, so facilitating development in that area. Even so the monarch had rejected a proposal of building a new palace in Hyde Park on the

5.1 Decimus Burton, *Proposed design for the Entrance Gate to the Green Park*, 20 July 1825

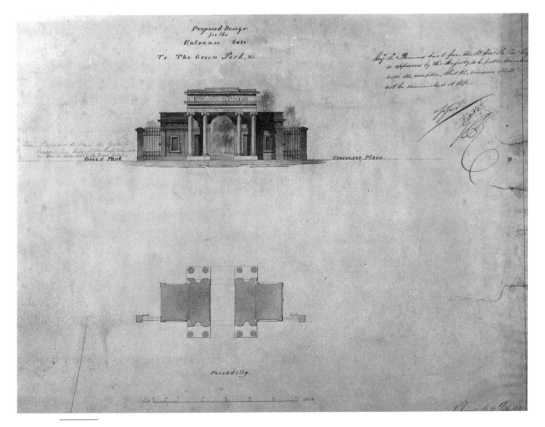

basis that he was too old to see the project through.[18] These developments coincided with the inititative by the Office of Woods to
improve the royal parks that surrounded Buckingham Palace.

Between the time that the work on the royal parks was initiated
and his decision to move, the King must have been aware of the need
for processional routes to his new palace. The Mall was to culminate
in Nash's Marble Arch at the main entrance to the palace. On the
garden side George IV had the Green Park Arch through which he
could proceed into Hyde Park, the site of military exercises and mock
battles, through the Hyde Park Screen. One of the early designs
produced for the Green Park Arch, dated 20 July 1825 (figure 5.1), is
annotated by the architect Decimus Burton '... and that the centre
shall be the Royal Entrance'.[19] But these plans robbed London of the
long awaited monumental entrance way into the city from the west.
The new alignment meant that neither archway was to be placed
astride Piccadilly. Thus the long-standing east–west axis of London
was now subjugated to the new north–south axis leading from Hyde
Park to Buckingham Palace. Those entering London from the west
would pass between the two gateways instead of proceeding through
at least one of them. This is shown in a photograph of a painting by
James Holland showing Hyde Park Corner in 1827 (figure 5.2).[20] This
view includes some of the sculptural decoration which was never
completed.

The missed opportunity of a gateway into London is picked up by
the *Mechanics Magazine* in 1827 which stated that the re-orientation
of the area had robbed London of its best opportunity for a

5.2 *Hyde Park Corner 1827,*
photograph based on a
painting by James Holland,
c. 1875

monumental entrance to the city. Moreover as London was extending at a substantial rate there was now a deficiency in the grandeur of the approaches to the British metropolis. The *Magazine* commented at length on the Hyde Park Screen:

> When the present peace left the English at leisure to turn their attention to internal improvements the erection of a grand triumphal entrance to the metropolis, similar to the Propylaea of Athens, was among the first things contemplated. Several designs were offered to the Government for the purpose; and an understanding came generally to prevail, that such a structure would certainly be erected at Hyde Park Corner. According to the idea which most people formed of the projected building it was to be erected at the summit of the assent from Knightsbridge, and to embrace the whole width of the road, having side entrances to Hyde Park and Green Park, nor can there be a question, that a structure like the Propylaea, erected in such a situation, would have had a most magnificent and imposing effect. To the everlasting discredit, however, of the spirit amid taste which preside over like architectural improvements of this auspicious era, our long talked of 'triumphal entrance' has divided into a mere Park entrance, which, like the Palace, leaves us where we were before without that important addition to the metropolis so fondly anticipated and so much wanted.
>
> ... May I venture to hope that, since Hyde Park Corner has lost the honour designed for it, and since a triumphal entrance into London is a thing still to be accomplished, the claims of Waterloo Bridge to the distinction will yet receive the consideration they merit? [21]

It is interesting to note the elevation of the area to a royal entrance way which celebrated the nation, albeit on a turned axis, was viewed as inferior to the original plans. This criticism did not jaundice the view of the quality of the architecture:

> The Park Entrance, however, considered as an entrance into the Park, must be allowed to reflect great honour on the designer and builder, Mr Decimus Burton ... It will, no doubt, be a source of general regret, that the architect of this gateway (showing, as he has done, a taste decidedly superior to most others) had not the opportunity afforded him of perpetuating his fame by an edifice of a more extended character. Every praise is due to the present structure; it exhibits what we rarely meet with – variety in the midst of uniformity, and a general combination of great chasteness and elegance. The defects complained of in the late beautiful screen before Carlton House have been judiciously avoided; the columns are not raised so high as to exclude a view of the objects beyond them. [22]

The *Mechanics Magazine* also picked up the intended alignment of the arches and the palace:

When the triumphal arch on the opposite side of the road* is complete (the place, in fact, from where the present screen should be viewed), the grouping of the architecture will be altogether extremely novel and striking.

* [footnote] The arch alluded to is a gateway or sort of lodge to the New Palace which is in the course of erection. We shall give a view of it also, in an early number – editor.'[23]

GEORGE IV AND THE ADVENTUS AUGUSTI

There is another factor which may have influenced the proliferation of arches and axes. There is little doubt that George IV was exceptionally fond of triumphal arches. Three existed in his plans for London – the central portion of Hyde Park Screen, the Arch at Constitution Hill (as the Green Park Arch became to be known) and the Marble Arch designed by John Nash as the main entrance into the front of Buckingham Palace. He even had a temporary triumphal arch in the style of a stage set built for his entrance into Dublin![24] But it would underestimate the ambition of Burton and his royal patron to see this scheme only as a series of archways through which the King could process into Hyde Park to watch the military manoeuvres which took place there. It was surely part of the larger plan, of which Hyde Park Corner is one of the most splendid elements, to create a series of monumental spaces, squares and axes in London. The arch had become a monument in its own right during the reign of the Emperor Augustus but the best-known examples are later: the Arch of Septimus Severus 203 CE and the Arch of Constantine 312–15 CE. The public ceremony which accompanied the inauguration of a triumphal arch was know as the 'Adventus Augusti', when the emperor, wearing a laurel wreath, was led in triumph through the city on a chariot. There may have been an element of competition between Britain and France in the use of the triumphal arch. Roman triumphal arches were used widely in the Napoleonic building programmes as they lent themselves well to the promotion of the cult of the personality. In Roman times public buildings and monuments were seen as a manifestation of providentia, and the heavenly authority of the divine sovereign. The tradition of the Adventus Augusti was revived by Napoleon in Venice on 15 August 1806 (his name day), on the inauguration of a bust of the emperor by Eugene Beauharnais in the Venetian Arsenal. Temporary architectural constructions were erected for this event including a triumphal arch by Guisseppe Borsato decorated with Ionic columns and statues (although the Doric order was seen as more appropriate for heroes, according to Vitruvius).[25] In Paris the

Arc du Carrousel (1806–10) by Charles Percier and Pierre Fontaine was constructed as the entrance to the Tuileries Palace. It was based on the arch of Septimus Severus and dedicated to the military heroism of the Grand Armée.

The meaning of these monuments was further enhanced by the use of decorative sculpture. Of particular interest here is the Quadriga – a chariot drawn by four horses. This dates back to ancient Roman times, for example the reign of Augustus when the reverse of the Augustan denarius shows a Parthian arch of Augustus in the Forum Romanun (19 BCE) in which a Quadriga with two figures of victory are clearly visible.[26] François Lemot's design for the Arc du Carrousel had only one figure of victory (at Napoleon's request) and provided the model for John Nash's Marble Arch.

Monuments to the nation's military prowess played an equally important part in the assertion of the power of the state. The victories at Trafalgar and Waterloo afforded ample opportunity for celebration and there were many proposals for commemorative archways, columns and even mausolea to Nelson and Wellington to be placed at strategic points across the city. These would combat the domestic scale of the garden squares surrounded by town houses that comprised the bulk of the urban fabric of the West End and help to augment the status of the city. George IV harnessed the nation's enthusiasm for these into his own service. This can be clearly seen by a consideration of two monuments – the Marble Arch and the Green Park Arch. The triumphal gateways are significant as they are part of the new projected iconography of London created by the King and his architects. Moreover, they show how the desire for a rational street plan was closely connected with the desire of the monarchy to underline its own status and authority.[27] It had been intended that the New Street would terminate at Carlton House. As already discussed, the King's decision in the early 1820s to demolish it and to develop Buckingham House into a new royal palace changed the shape and orientation of the plan for a new London. It created two new axes, one running east–west the other north–south. The Mall ran westwards along St James's Park and terminated at Buckingham Palace. The Green Park Arch provided an entrance to the garden of the new royal residence. It was also aligned with the Hyde Park Screen to provide a fitting, monumental entrance way for the King into Hyde Park, the scene of military parades and mock battles. This meant that the traditional gateway into London from the west at the end of Piccadilly was turned 90 degrees to align with Buckingham Palace (figure 5.3).

This was indeed a grand vision. The planned new system of roads, punctuated with monuments, and impressive public buildings, and culminating in a new royal residence, offered the well-to-do

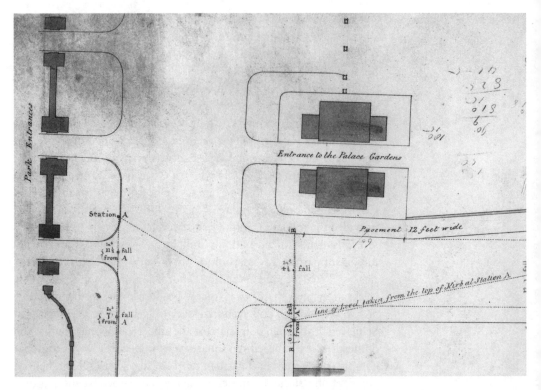

Park Entrances

Station A

Entrance to the Palace Gardens

Pavement 12 feet wide

residents of London a feeling of safety. Both arches were to be decorated with sculptural celebrations of Britain's military victories, intellectual prowess and the Hanoverian dynasty. And every Londoner was invited to celebrate the nation's security, thanks to the King, through the memorials and triumphal archways strategically placed in the royal parks, to which there was public access.

5.3 E. J. Wards, Plan for siting of two arches and alterations to road heights at Hyde Park Corner, undated

THE EVOLUTION OF THE DESIGN OF A ROYAL SQUARE AND PROCESSIONAL ROUTE

The project began on quite an innocuous note with a request from the Treasury on 22 April 1823 to the Office of Woods to report on the state of Hyde Park and St James's and supply some proposals for improvement.[28] That this request went to the Office of Woods might indicate that initially the concern was to carry out basic improvements to the parks such as new drains, improved walkways, rides and fencing, perhaps as a response to the newness and attractive layout and landscaping of Regent's Park. The first written response came from the Office of Woods to the Lords of the Treasury on 28 July 1823.[29] This report on the improvements to be executed in St James's and Hyde Parks concentrated on the current state of the roads, fences and walks and was written by Charles Arbuthnot, N. D. Adams and J. G. Dawkins who had made wide consultations:

and others [measures] had been suggested by different individuals well qualified to offer their opinions upon such matters for the improvement and embellishment of the parks, but not being prepared at present to lay before your Lordships those opinions and suggestions so matured, as to recommend them to be adopted, we propose to limit this report to those objects which appear to us to claim the earliest attention.

The Office of Woods supplied an estimate of £10,000 for the initial works they outlined, proposed that this should be paid for by the Treasury and suggested that it could be repaid to the Treasury by a grant from Parliament:

for which we would suggest that an application should be permitted to be made in the ensuing session, before which time we hope to be able to lay before your Lordships in detail the plan and estimates which have been suggested or occurred to us for the further improvement or embellishment of these parks, and for promoting their enjoyment to the Public.[30]

Writing with reference to this report on 2 September 1823 the Office of Woods requested from the Treasury the sum of £5,000 on account for the repairs they had instructed Mr McAdam to commence on the roads, drives and walkways.[31]

The response came in a letter from George Harrison at the Treasury on 6 October 1823 granting the Office of Woods £5,000 to be repaid out of the money which may be granted by Parliament for work and improvements in the parks.[32] This bill was in passage through Parliament early the following year.[33] Payment was made by the Office of Works to the Office of Woods for any work which would usually have come under their aegis.

The more detailed report was not delivered until 28 September 1825 which included designs and estimates for all the major work. But how did the plan develop, and what was Burton's level of involvement in its evolution? It is important, first of all, to establish how all the work came to be under aegis of the Office of Woods. The level of repair, renewal and development required in the parks was very high and straggled the lines of responsibility drawn between the Office of Woods and the Office of Works, but for the most effective method of executing this work it seemed obvious from an early stage that it should all come under the aegis of one authority. This suggestion was made at the beginning of the scheme by Arbuthnot, Adams and Dawkins who in their report of 28 July 1823 stated that they had 'no wish to undertake duties which belong to other public offices but feel all the works should be under the control and direction of one department subject to the constraint and authority of the Treasury'.[34] This was reinforced in a letter from Arbuthnot and

Adams to the Treasury on 3 August 1824 concerning the proposed
gates and lodges, where they stated: 'we have not required working
drawings or estimates for the new lodge and gates as according to the
established arrangements for works of this description they would be
executed in the Department of the Board of Works'.[35] In his
response to the report and perhaps to the above letter J. C. Herries of
the Treasury wrote on 17 September 1823, '[I] take the point about
the single management',[36] and appointed the Office of Woods to be
in charge as most of the work was under their aegis. Consent was
officially given by the Treasury on 13 September 1824.[37]

This question of single authority had also been a lever to ensure
Burton's involvement with the project. Arbuthnot had presented the
argument that Burton had been chosen on the basis that 'his plans
for the other improvements of the parks [Regent's] have met with so
much approbation'.[38] Arbuthnot's thinking was explained in full in
his evidence to the Parliamentary inquiry of 1828:

> having seen in the Regent's Park, and elsewhere, works which pleased
> my eye, from their architectural beauty and correctness, I made
> inquiries as to the name of their architect, and I was informed that it
> was Mr Decimus Burton. Feeling that it was open for my office to
> employ any architect who, in our opinion, would be likely to perform
> the work entrusted to him satisfactorily for the public, I sent for Mr
> Burton, and desired that he would prepare designs for the erection of
> Lodges at the different entrances into Hyde Park ... Mr Burton showed
> great anxiety to meet the wishes of the Government, and most readily
> undertook to make such alterations as the noblemen and gentlemen,
> to whom they were shown, thought desirable.[39]

Arbuthnot went on to state that he had recommended Burton
because he 'was not one of the established architects of that department [the Office of Woods] there were official difficulties against his
being employed except under our own immediate direction'.[40] This
was not strictly true, however, as Burton was employed to build the
Parliamentary Mews at Storey's Gate in 1825 which fell under the
aegis of the Office of Works.[41]

There are several explanations as to why Arbuthnot was so keen
to use Burton. First, his statements to the 1828 inquiry can be taken
at face value. The Regent's Park project was certainly a model from
which to draw experience for much of the work carried out in the
parks, as discussed below, and there is no doubt that there was
genuine concern as to the state of Hyde, St James's and Green Parks.
Burton had also already been involved with the decision on the siting
of the Achilles statue in Hyde Park.[42] Moreover, George IV may well
have been drawn to Burton for the same reasons as Arbuthnot, but
it is important to view Burton's appointment within the larger

context of all of George IV's architectural projects. The plans for Hyde Park Corner were an essential part of the creation of a royal London. John Nash was to be fully occupied with the improvements to Buckingham Palace as well as the ongoing work at Regent's Park and Regent Street. With Burton's appointment there was a greater chance for both architects to concentrate on their individual responsibilities. Moreover, the cost of the work on Buckingham Palace being carried out by the Office of Works was enormous, estimated at around £200,000. Hitherto untapped sources of funding would be available through the Office of Woods for the work at Hyde Park Corner. The division of work between the two Offices would disguise the total amount being granted by Parliament, as monies would appear to go to each of the recipients for different types of projects.[43]

Although the chosen area for the new gateways was free of most of the restrictions encountered elsewhere in the capital, such as other buildings or obstinate landowners, there was one significant problem: the site was not level. The strong wish to create a homogeneous urban space is evident in the feats of civil engineering undertaken to level off the area of Hyde Park Corner and Knightsbridge. These were expensive engineering works designed to even out the ground and presumably also to increase the visual impact of the work at Hyde Park Corner. They cannot have been made any easier by the fact that as soon as work began on the Hyde Park Screen it was discovered that underground water tanks, which had previously been used to water Piccadilly, were directly beneath the site. The decision was made to strengthen the foundations of the Screen, which was very costly.[44] Moreover, a sub-plinth had to be added to the design because the original plan to lower the road to level off the site completely was modified.[45] An undated drawing in the National Archives shows the alignment of the two arches and the calculations used to alter the road heights (see figure 5.3).[46] Grosvenor Place was to be raised to the level of the plinth of the entrance to Buckingham Palace Gardens and the pavement down Knightsbridge was also to be raised. The original acceptance that expensive engineering works would be necessary to prepare the site and the persistence of Burton in adhering to the intended line and location are significant. They demonstrate the importance of the geographical location and the nature of the project itself.

The engineering works necessary to prepare the site developed alongside the designs for the gateways themselves. The evolution of these designs can be traced through the estimates submitted by the Office of Woods and some surviving drawings. The Office of Woods submitted Decimus Burton's first designs and estimates for lodges and gates on 28 September 1825 for consideration by the Fife House

Committee.[47] The drawings for the Hyde Park Screen and the entrance to Green Park in the collection of the Victoria and Albert Museum give some idea of the evolution of the project. A plan and elevation for the entrance into Green Park at Hyde Park Corner dated 20 July 1825 exists in Burton's hand (see figure 5.1),[48] but this is dated before the presentation of the designs and estimates to the Fife House Committee. It shows an elevation and ground plan of an Ionic triumphal archway. The frieze which, although not detailed, seems to be based on a classical theme (its appearance is not unlike the cast of the Parthenon frieze that was eventually used) stands forward of the rest of the entrance way and is supported by free-standing Ionic columns, two on either side of the arch. There appears to be a plinth over the centre of the arch but no sculptural decoration is indicated. The central arch is flanked by two blind niches, and then small lodges with Egyptian-style windows flanked by Doric pilasters surmounted by a Doric frieze of triglyphs and plain metopes. Although the windows give the impression of there being an interior and logic presumes there would be a lodge here, the shading on the ground plan suggests that this space would have been solid. Gateways are attached to the pilaster on the outer side of the lodge and a freestanding pier. The ground plan indicates that the entrance was to be the same on both facades. The drawing is annotated in pencil on the Green Park side of the entrance: 'It is here Proposed to place the Gates to Constitution Hill – if the King's commands are that the centre shall be the Royal Entrance.' There is an indication of two piers matching those of the lodge on the Green Park side of the entrance. The design received royal approval on 15 August and is annotated: 'Aug 15th Received back from the Rt. Hon. Sir Chas. Long & approved by his Majesty, to be put into execution with the exception, that the windows shall not be diminished at the top.' It was noted as 'apprvd' and initialed 'G R'.

This design is paired with a drawing, of the same date also in the Victoria and Albert Museum, by Burton showing the plan and elevation of the entrance to Hyde Park (the Hyde Park Screen), but notably this is not titled (figure 5.4).[49] The central archway matches that of the Green Park entrance in form and arrangement but there are no lodges behind it. The symmetrical arrangement of the entrance comprises a central arch flanked by two blind niches and a run of five Ionic columns with a blank entablature. These terminate at both ends with a smaller, slightly recessed arch framed by a free-standing Ionic column *in antis* and a Doric pier on either side. Attached to these is a smaller square gateway following the line of the run of Ionic columns framed by Doric pilasters. This scheme was fully approved by the King, also on 15 August. The sources for these initial designs are complex. Just as Nash's Marble Arch was based on

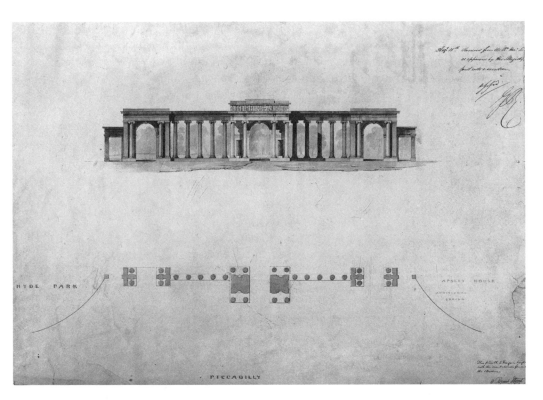

5.4 Decimus Burton,
*Design for the Hyde Park
Screen*, 20 July 1825

the Arch of Constantine, Burton's Green Park Arch was modelled on
the Arch of Titus, both of which were well known through
engravings and veduta paintings and architecture books. The Arch of
Titus had also been the basis of Soane's 1817 design, but the source
for the Hyde Park Screen, or as it was sometimes referred to the
Facade, is less obvious, although Soane's plan of 1817 did include
an Ionic screen running across the entrance to Piccadilly. Screens
were not an unusual architectural feature; they had also been placed
across the facades of Old Montague House (which was in the
process of being transformed into the British Museum) and Carlton
House.

It is likely that Burton was in contact, though probably indirectly,
with the King and that some kind of dialogue between them was
carried on during the time in which the designs for the entrances and
the laying out of the parks and the re-alignment of the roads went
on. These drawings are probably the penultimate versions before the
final designs – which would already have been agreed by the King –
and estimates were submitted to the Fife House Committee for
official royal, Committee and Treasury approval. The Office of
Woods requested authority to proceed and to defray the costs for the
works out of the applicable departmental funds. This permission was
granted by the Treasury on 24 October 1825,[50] but within six months
of receiving approval on 30 March 1826 the Office of Woods

submitted an amended estimate to the Treasury for carrying out the proposed improvement.[51]

The changes meant increased expenditure which was approved by the First Lord of the Treasury, the Chancellor of the Exchequer and the First Commissioner of the Board of Works. Of special interest within these new, extended proposals was the estimated cost of the

entrance into Green Park which increased nearly threefold from £6,858 to £19,291. Despite the huge increase in projected spending, permission was granted for these alterations to the original plan on 5 May 1826.[52] Perhaps Parliament and/or the Treasury had not quite taken on board the magnitude of George IV's vision for the scale of the restructuring and aggrandising of London. Extra funds were found from the Land Revenues Accounts, the Crown's income from its estates. These accounts were submitted to the Commissioners of Woods from 1824.[53] The funds were channelled towards the construction of the gateways.[54] Moreover, a further drawing in the Victoria and Albert Museum shows that this aggrandisement of the scheme may have been in the King's and Burton's minds almost as soon as approval was given for the first scheme.[55] It shows a front and side elevation of the revised design for the Green Park Arch and a ground plan. It is signed and dated by Burton on 5 November 1825 (figure 5.5). The scale of this arch is much larger, in contrast to the harmony of the original design where the two central arches of the gateways into Hyde Park and Green Park would have been the mirror image of each other. Instead, the Green Park Arch dominated the composition through its increased scale and decoration (it was now also larger than the Marble Arch). The basic form of the new design for the arch remains the same, but it is far more decorative and monumental. The order of the new design is Corinthian, including the end pilasters, instead of the Ionic order of the earlier scheme. The design for the continuous frieze which surmounts the freestanding Corinthian columns in the centre of the composition relates to classical relief sculpture and may allude to the Panathenaic procession. There is a plinth but no design for any freestanding sculpture that might surmount the arch, although freestanding figures, directly in line with Corinthian columns, have been added above the architrave. The ground plan shows two separate porter's lodges with doors in the plinth. The drawing bears an initialled note by Burton: 'This design was returned from the Comm. of Woods with their letter dated January 14th 1826 – containing the communication of its being approved by H. Majesty to be executed instead of the original Design I submitted'.

In his evidence to the 1828 inquiry Burton refers to this drawing and the note he made on it. When asked if the King had approved his designs for the Green Park Arch as an entrance to his gardens, Burton responded:

> Certainly I acted with the understanding on making the first design which is set aside. It having been suggested (at one of the meetings before alluded to) by several of the noblemen and gentlemen present it would be more respectful to his Majesty to have this Archway upon a

5.5 Decimus Burton, *Design for the Green Park Arch*, 5 November 1825

141

scale of a character more splendid then that of the Facade Entrance on
the North side of Piccadilly. I was then directed to prepare a second
design which should embrace these objects. This second design
received His Majesty's approval and it is in fact the one now acted
upon.[56]

Burton was then asked if this had been communicated to him in writing. He referred to the memorandum he made at the bottom of the design he was now presenting to the committee (as quoted above).

It is very likely that the King proposed the enlarged scheme himself, especially given the date of the design. It is in keeping with his increasing ambitions for Buckingham Palace, where by the end of 1826 he had certainly planned to move the court.[57] The question here is why, when funds had been so strictly limited for the work on Buckingham Palace, the Treasury was content to sanction the trebling of the expenditure on the entrance into the King's garden and the royal parks. The answer may lie in that little had been achieved in terms of the plans to construct monuments to the victories at Trafalgar and Waterloo and the nation's war heroes. The grander scale of the second design afforded more opportunities for sculptural embellishments. Moreover, the nature of the sculptural decoration did change, as discussed below. The significance of the site, and that designs had been submitted for war memorials to be erected there, make the case even stronger.

THE ICONOGRAPHY OF THE SCHEME

The work at Hyde Park Corner can be compared to the designs for the Marble Arch, which originally stood at the top of the Mall as an entrance into the main front of Buckingham Palace, as they were both for the same patron, George IV. Both the Marble Arch and the Green Park Arch were based on Roman triumphal arches. The Arch of Constantine, the source for Marble Arch, presented an image of a triumphant Christian monarchy. The Arch of Titus, the source for the design of the Green Park Arch (later known as the Arch at Constitution Hill), carried on this theme as it referred to the conquest of Jerusalem.[58] The stylistic and iconographical nature of the proposed sculptural decoration of the Green Park Arch also related to that of Marble Arch in its reference to military and naval victories. Nash had originally approached a leading neo-classical sculptor, John Flaxman, for designs for the Marble Arch and the sculptural decoration of the new palace. These were ready by August 1826, as Nash wrote to Flaxman: 'I shall lay before the King the labours of your pencil and shall be happy to convey to you HM approbation.'[59] Nash also mentions a model which included imagery of 'Lord

Wellington'. This may be the plaster model of the Marble Arch which shows Nash and Flaxman's fusion of architecture and sculpture as a celebration of monarch and state.[60] The artist died in December 1826 shortly after presenting his account for his completed work.[61] Although Flaxman's designs were executed, much of the detail of the work was changed by the executant sculptor Richard Westmacott.[62]

The executed sculptural decoration on the Hyde Park Screen and Green Park Arch was carved by John Henning, one of Burton's regular workforce. The frieze of the Hyde Park Screen was based on the Panathenaic procession which was part of the collection of marble sculpture Lord Elgin had brought back from Greece some years earlier. Henning's father, also called John, had made a cast of the procession on the marbles' arrival in London when they were kept in the forecourt of the Royal Academy.[63] In the Victoria and Albert Museum drawing of the first design for the Green Park Arch the frieze appears to have a Grecian theme, though it is not a replica of the Panathenaic procession. These suggest that the original intention was to create a scheme which was classical in essence, underlining the culture and sophistication of London and/or the monarch. The compositional relationship between the enlarged Green Park Arch (as revised in 1826 and discussed above) and Hyde Park Screen is shown in a perspective drawing in the Royal Institute of British Architects Drawings Collection.[64] This gives a more detailed view of the proposed sculptural embellishments, although they were never executed.

The revised plan of 1826 aggrandised the decorative scheme of the original to include military trophies as well which made reference to the battles of Waterloo and Trafalgar. The Green Park Arch was now to be surmounted by a Quadriga[65] with a figure of Britannia Triumphans and was to include military and naval trophies and free-standing figures (figure 5.6).[66] But the 1828 moratorium on spending imposed by the Duke of Wellington on becoming Prime Minister, due to Nash's excesses at Buckingham Palace, put a stop to all work and in 1830 Burton was ordered to take down the scaffolding.[67] The watercolour gives some indication of the nature of these sculptural embellishments. The scheme for the arch and screen at Hyde Park Corner was to be a celebration of Britain: her military and naval might, the monarchy and the nation's intellectual prowess. The Quadriga with Britannia Triumphans and a freestanding figure surmounts the Green Park Arch. The frieze around the plinth of the statue is Grecian in essence – most notably the inclusion of horsemen in profile wearing Grecian-style helmets. But in the centre, beneath the figure of Britannia and above the centre of the arch, sits a figure wearing British military uniform. The freestanding figures around the plinth are both military – could these relate to Nelson

5.6 *Green Park Arch and Hyde Park Screen*, watercolour, unsigned and undated

and Wellington? Two designs also exist in the Victoria and Albert Museum by John Henning Junior for freestanding female figures representing History and Astronomy.[68] The watercolour also shows some of the sculptural embellishments of the Hyde Park Screen including an equestrian figure of George III above the central archway and military insignia above each of the flanking arches.

The grand scheme for the Hyde Park Screen and Green Park Arch was never completed. Nash's mismanagement of the work at Buckingham Palace led to a moratorium on all building in 1828 and a parliamentary inquiry. Burton's project suffered as a consequence. Despite carrying out his commissions to schedule and to estimate, his designs were never finished.[69] Even so, it is clear Burton's relationship with George IV was significant and that he was treated by the King as one of the executive architects of his nationalistic and imperialistic vision. Indeed, had Burton won the competition for the design of the new St George's Hospital situated on the west side of Hyde Park Corner, which he entered in 1826, he would have had an opportunity to create a new monumental urban space in the first city of empire.[70] But Burton's own vision of how this area of London might have appeared remains enigmatic.

THE CHAIN OF COMMAND

It is important to establish who controlled the improvements in the royal parks, as it sheds light on the nature of the works themselves and the ideology behind them. The chain of command and those who had responsibility and input into the work reveals the similtaneous agendas at work in the re-imaging of London. Foremost here are the parallel concerns of the monarch, George IV, to aggrandise his capital city and therefore his own image, and the governmental institutions which had initiated the Metropolitan Improvements as part of a concerted effort to modernise London and create an urban infrastructure that would support and enhance the political status quo. The architect Decimus Burton was never officially attached to the Office of Works, the main executor of the Metropolitan Improvements, or indeed to the Office of Woods, for whom he acted as architect and arbiter for many of the works and improvements carried out around Knightsbridge, Park Lane and the royal parks. Burton's level of involvement and authority increased rapidly once the projects were begun. He was subject to two chains of command, both of which involved the monarch and one of which had substantially greater powers of veto and amendment. This latter side was headed by Parliament, which granted funds held by the Treasury who in turn granted monies on request to the Office of Woods (or Office of Works when work which would usually have been executed by them was carried out by the Office of Woods). Charles Arbuthnot was the Chief Commissioner of Woods who liaised with the Commissioners and the Treasury. This chain of command took care of and controlled the financial elements of the projects. The other side was mostly concerned with the nature of the projects themselves and their style. This was headed by the monarch, who had ultimate power of veto on the designs. Beneath him was the Fife House Committee which consisted of representatives of the Treasury, Office of Woods and Forests and 'several noblemen and gentlemen interested in the improvements'.[71] Arbuthnot sat on this committee, and he dealt with Burton. Arbuthnot was thus Burton's immediate superior and it was he who first brought Burton in to work on the royal parks. But Burton had to please two masters – the monarch, with the nature and scope of his designs, and the Treasury and, through them, Parliament with the costing and accurate execution of the works.

The King's high level of involvement shows that he was using Burton as his executive architect and designer for a project which took on increasing significance during the first half of the 1820s. In August 1822 John Nash submitted plans to the Surveyor General of Works for the conversion of Buckingham House into a royal palace, but work did not begin until June 1825. Nash's plans were quickly followed in April 1823 by the request for the review of Hyde and Green Parks. The development at Hyde Park Corner ran parallel to the work on the new palace. And the aggrandisement of the scheme,

not least the Green Park Arch as the entrance to the gardens of the
new palace, perhaps received some impetus from work on
Buckingham Palace. There can be no doubt that the King was aware
of both projects and of how they interconnected to create the kind
of rural urban environment he desired through the interaction of
landscape and monumental, classical architecture. But it is perhaps
surprising that Nash was not in control here, or at least involved with
the project in some way. He was, after all, responsible for the
substantial work on Buckingham Palace itself and the adjoining
grounds (part of Green Park) which abutted Hyde Park Corner.
Indeed, Nash claimed to know nothing of how Burton's work at
Hyde Park Corner was to relate to his own designs for the gardens of
Buckingham Palace.[72] This may seem surprising, as both men were
designing separate parts of the same piece of land – Green Park –
which conjoined at Hyde Park Corner, but the veracity of Nash's
claim is not in question. It does suggest, however, that the overall
scheme for Buckingham Palace and its environs was not solely
Nash's. Instead, Nash's work was part of a larger and evolving plan.
This would reinforce the idea that George IV and his officers were
the driving force behind the works in south-west London.[73] Burton
seems to have dealt directly with leading figures in both chains of
command. This was in contrast to his work in Regent's Park where
everything was channelled through Nash or referred to Nash by the
Commissioners of Woods. In the final accounts presented by the
Office of Woods Burton claimed travel expenses to both Stratfield
Saye and Windsor to consult with Mr Arbuthnot (who lived at
Stratfield Saye) and Sir William Knighton the King's Private
Secretary.[74] Burton and Nash were, then, the main executants of
these parallel projects which were intended to enhance the image of
the monarch and the metropolis. Their immediate taskmasters, the
Office of Woods and the Office of Works, indicate the different lines
of funding for each scheme, but the various parties being served by
these large-scale urban improvements suggest that far more complex
sets of interests were in play here. Buckingham Palace and its
grounds, parkland and approaches operated like a country house in
a landscape setting to augment the image of the owner and occupant
– in this case the King. The funding and management of the work at
Hyde Park Corner showed how George IV and his officers were able
to pour money into these substantial improvements to enable the re-
imaging of this part of London. Moreover, the vested interest of
Parliament in the work at Hyde Park Corner is never far from view.
And the large sums made available for the work on the new royal
palace cement the relationship between the two projects as important pieces in the making of a new metropolitan environment. The
redesign of the royal parks is another element in this shared vision

for the West End, and the importance of established practices of landscape design in the country, transported here to the city, is the focus of the final chapter.

Burton's work at Hyde Park Corner is also important as it demonstrates that a substantial public project was carried out at this time without Nash's involvement. This suggest an alternative reading of the role played by Nash in the re-imaging of London, who has previously been presented as being of paramount importance, if not solely responsible for the task.[75] But the point here is not to replace Nash with Burton. Rather it is to show that the work at Hyde Park Corner was a response to a variety of social and political forces whose inter-relationships were complex. Burton was the *agent* through which these found expression in appropriate planning and design of the London landscape.

NOTES

1   This was known as the Green Park Arch, and later the Arch at Constitution Hill. There was not always a clear distinction between Green Park and St James's Park at this time. Moreover, part of Green Park made up the back garden of Buckingham House (later Buckingham Palace). The royal parks are discussed in more detail in chapter 6.

2   This was known as the Hyde Park Screen, or sometimes the Facade.

3   See Arnold, 'The Arch at Constitution Hill'.

4   George III's set of drawings are held at the British Museum, King's Maps xxvii 26 a–c.

5   Copies of this engraving exist in the British Museum, Kings Maps xxvii i and the Bodleian Library (Douce Prints N. 8).

6   See D. Stroud, 'Hyde Park Corner', *Architectural Review*, 106 (1949), pp. 79–97.

7   These plans are illustrated in John Soane, *Designs for Public and Private Buildings*, London, 1828.

8   See p. 53.

9   Cres 8/14 f 334, not dated but between January and March 1824.

10   Cres 8/14 f 348 (27 March 1824).

11   Cres 8/14 f 351 (letter dated 31 March 1824).

12   Cres 8/14 f 414.

13   Cres 8/14 f 414.

14   Cres 8/14 f 454.

15   Work 35/2.

16   For a full discussion of Nash's work at Buckingham Palace see *HKW*, pp. 263 ff.

17   Work 19/3 f 15.

18   Second Report of the Select Committee on Windsor Castle and Buckingham Palace, 1831, p. 271. However, Mrs Arbuthnot recorded on October 1825 that

the King was 'madly eager' for Col. Frederick Trench's plan for a vast palace in Hyde Park, but supposed that his 'd—d Ministers' would not allow it (*The Journal of Mrs Arbuthnot, 1820–1832*, ed. F. Bamford and the Duke of Wellington, 2 vols., London, Macmillan, 1950, vol. 1, p. 420).

19   Victoria and Albert Museum E 2334–1910 A 149 a.

20   Victoria and Albert Museum not accessioned in box no. A149a. A version of the photograph is also in a private collection.

21   *Mechanics Magazine*, 8: 208 (18 August 1827), pp. 65 ff.

22   Ibid.

23   Ibid.

24   Mentioned in C. Maxwell, *Country and Town in Ireland under the Georges*, London, Harrap, 1940.

25   This is discussed by A. Yarrington, *The Commemoration of the Hero 1800–1864: Monuments to the British Victors of the Napoleonic Wars*, New York and London, Garland, 1988, p. 35, note 1.

26   Ibid., p. 36, note 2.

27   The use of ritual and display by monarchs and their governments as a means of asserting authority is recognised by Cannadine, 'The Context, Performance and Meaning of Ritual. This aspect of the work in the royal parks is discussed more fully in chapter 6.

28   Cres 8/14 f 111.

29   Cres 8/14 ff 150–6.

30   Cres 8/14 f 150.

31   Cres 8/14 f 184.

32   As the grant for civil contingencies could not be used for advance funds, the Treasury paid £5,000 out of French Indemnity funds, to be repaid by the Commissioners of Woods when the first monies from the parliamentary grant for works and improvements to the parks were received, (T29/225 f 225, 16 September 1823).

33   Cres 8/14 f 193.

34   Cres 8/14 f 150.

35   Cres 8/14 f 454.

36   Cres 8/14 f 192.

37   Cres 8/14 f 472.

38   Cres 8/16 f 3.

39   1828 Report, p. 123.

40   Ibid., p. 130.

41   The Treasury directed that Burton be appointed architect as he had been employed by the Office of Woods to prepare the original plans (Work 12/63/7 f 5, 7 October 1825).

42   Work 35/2.

43   The financial framework of Burton's payments for his work demonstrates how he stood outside the established systems of renumertaion for attached architects to the Offices of Works. See Appendix A.

44   The work exceeded Burton's original estimate. The main reason given for this by the Office of Woods to the Treasury in a letter of 31 October 1828

was that 'at the outset [it was] necessary to lay additional foundations of considerable substance and to some extent, over a tank which had been used some years since for the watering of Piccadilly. The remains of which were discovered in the immediate line of the intended facade' (Cres 8/16 ff 423–5).

45 Ibid. This was modified as the lowering of the road to the extent originally planned would have greatly inconvenienced local residents.

46 Held in the National Archives PRO, MPE 796, undated, pen and ink by E. J. Wards, 16 Upper Eaton Street, Pimlico.

47 Cres 8/15 f 200. The estimates were: New lodge at Cumberland Gate according to design and estimate No. 1 £2,006 3s. 2d. New Entrance gates at Hyde Park Corner according to design and Estimate No. 2 £9,342 14s. 6d. New Lodge at Hyde Park Corner according to Design and Estimate No. 3 £2,151 1s. 3d. New entrance gates and lodge into Green Park according to Design No. 4 £6,858 3s. 0d. Total £20,358 1s. 11d.

48 Victoria and Albert Museum E 2334–1910 A 149 a.

49 Victoria and Albert Museum D 1299–1907.

50 Cres 8/15 f 211.

51 Cres 8/15 f 281. These were: New entrance gate and lodge into Green Park £1,9291 6s. 0d. Interior post and chain fence by sides of road leading from Cumberland Gate to Hyde Park Corner £4,000 0s. 0d. Bridge over the Serpentine River £3,650 0s. 0d. Total £59,791 6s. 0d.

52 Cres 8/15 f 331.

53 T29/231 f 349, March 1825.

54 This is stated quite clearly in a letter from the Treasury to the Commissioners of Woods dated 19 January 1830, Cres 8/17 f 377: 'no further works at the archway at Constitution Hill can be sanctioned ... [no more charge] for building of this description on the Land Revenues of the crown until the charge upon the revenues for the building of Buckingham Palace shall have ceased.' (In 1828 Wellington, who was then Prime Minister, had ordered the annual diversion £100,000 of the funds of the Office of Woods to help complete Buckingham Palace.)

55 Victoria and Albert Museum, E 2334–1910.

56 Burton's evidence to the 1828 parliamentary inquiry, 1828 Report, 20 May, pp. 444–5.

57 *HKW*, p. 267.

58 My thanks to Professor M. H. Port for drawing my attention to this.

59 British Museum Add. MS 39781 ff 254–5.

60 This is in the collection of the Victoria and Albert Museum; it is considered by H. Clifford Smith in *Country Life* (4 July 1952).

61 Flaxman presented his account on 20 November 1826. This was re-presented by his executrices in July 1828 as Nash had not settled the account (BM Add. MS 39783 f 11).

62 A full discussion of the sculptural decoration of Marble Arch appears in *HKW*, pp. 293–7.

63 The career of John Henning senior and some of John Henning junior's work is discussed in J. Malden, *John Henning (1771–1851)*, Paisley, 1977; see esp the section 'John Henning (1771–1851) "... a very ingenious modeller ..."' (there is no pagination in this booklet).

64 RIBA Drawings Collection XOS/D/5, unsigned, undated watercolour, 24 x 40.5 cm.

65 Yarrington, *The Commeration of the Hero*, pp. 244–5, suggests Burton was thinking of using a design by M. C. Wyatt for a such sculptural group dedicated to George III, and cites various efforts by Wyatt to draw attention to his design. There is no evidence for this. Moreover, the perspective shows that both screen and arch were to be surmounted by a car drawn by horses and accompanying figures.

66 E. H. Baily had agreed to make the statues for £1,600 (Work 4/113).

67 Work 4/1 f 16.

68 Victoria and Albert Museum E 2334–E 2340–1910.

69 By early 1830, despite the fact that Burton's work had not gone excessively beyond his estimates, the Treasury decreed that no further work would be paid for until Buckingham Palace was finished (Cres 8/17 f 377).

70 Burton's entry for the competition is discussed in R. W. Liscombe, *William Wilkins 1778–1839*, Cambridge, Cambridge University Press, 1980, p. 155.

71 Cres 8/17 f 30. In his evidence to the 1828 inquiry Burton named the members of the Fife House Committee as 'Lord Liverpool, Lord Farnborough, Lord Goderich, Mr Peel, Mr Herries and Mr Arbuthnot': at least five of them always attended meetings. 1828 Parliamentary Enquiry, 20 May, pp. 444–5.

72 1828 Report.

73 This is argued throughout the chapters on George IV's building projects in HKW.

74 Burton was paid a total of £10 10s. in travelling expenses in the year 1825 (Cres 8/17 f 206).

75 See for instance Summerson's account of the Metropolitan Improvements in *The Life and Work of John Nash*.

6 The royal parks

The improvements carried out in the royal parks in west London – Hyde, St James's and Green Parks – are perhaps the apogee of the re-imaging of London in the early nineteenth century. The spread of the city westwards, and increasing awareness of the social and political importance of landscape, continue to raise questions about important design issues and address significant ideological issues concerning these urban spaces. The shaping and codifying of the London landscape had begun almost unconsciously with the formation of garden squares as part of the eighteenth-century building boom. Chapter 1 has already demonstrated the important contribution Bloomsbury made to this aspect of urban planning. Moreover, this kind of speculative venture, where architecture and landscape combined to create a distinct community, took on a more up-market image in Regent's Park. The positive reactions to Regent's Park as a public open space, which was the result of the combined efforts of the Crown and a variety of speculative developers and architects, show the general appreciation of this kind of caesura in the terraces of houses that were spreading all over London. Like the royal parks in west London the geographical significance and land value of Regent's Park had improved considerably due to the city's growth. The Regent's Park project was in many ways an attempt to realise fully and to capitalise on this potential. The royal parks follow on from this. Hyde Park and Green Park bordered, and halted, the development of fashionable west London, but they were not part of any speculative development and they offered the possibility of enhancing the environment of the great estates of the West End. Like Regent's Park these Crown lands stood on the periphery of London. Here the focus was principally on the improvement of the landscape for the general augmentation of the area. They were in a poor state of repair and much remedial work and replanting were necessary before any other improvements could be made.

St James's Park was the subject of the most intensive development plans as it was not only its landscape which was the focus of a substantial redesign, but also, rather like in Regent's Park, speculative builders were planning to build new terraces of houses around its perimeter, although not all had been executed. The new terraces were included in John Nash's plans for the development of the area around the site of Carlton House after its demolition in 1826.[1] Nash proposed the construction of Carlton House Terrace (divided by the way leading up to Waterloo Place), and this was realised. He also produced two unexecuted designs for a further terrace on the north side of the park on the site of Marlborough House and a crescent of houses on the south side near Buckingham Gate.[2] St James's Park was to serve as a kind of landscaped garden with a royal focus – Buckingham Palace. The encroaching metropolis changed the relationship of St James's Park to the city as it slowly became surrounded by housing and public buildings and offices. And in Nash's plan it became a kind of extended garden square offering a combination of landscape vista and architecture, which was reminiscent of Regent's Park.[3]

Hyde, St James's and Green Parks surrounded the new royal palace and the latter also formed part of its grounds. As such they collectively constituted the kind of landscape similar to that which surrounded country houses. The landscape of country houses had already been identified as containing a variety of meanings.[4] Although these parks were in an urban setting, the landscaping issues surrounding their improvement had resonance with the wider debates about the landscape in the early nineteenth century. Indeed, the use of landscape design to shape urban space offered a reading of the cityscape that was more nuanced than the class consciousness of developments like Regent Street, which divided rich and poor.

This chapter concentrates on how appropriate landscapes for a city setting were constructed and the aims and ideology behind these designs. In contrast to the state-driven development of London in the early nineteenth century, here the Crown was the landowner and there were no difficult negotiations with perhaps unwilling participants (as seen in the construction of Regent Street).[5] Also, unlike Regent's Park or Regent Street, or indeed Bloomsbury, none of the work depended on the involvement of speculative developers to ensure its execution. These lands were owned by the Crown and, as with a landscape garden, were designed and laid out to enhance the image of the monarch and the state and to provide effective communication between important public buildings. There were also philanthropic undertones in the concern to provide city dwellers with open spaces and fresh air. The shaping of this sensory experience of the city is charted in this study of the improvements carried out in the parks. Together this forms the basis of what is termed here the urban picturesque and allow a continued exploration and expansion of the theme of *rus in urbe* introduced part I of this volume. The notion of the urban picturesque may appear to be a contradiction in terms. Urbanism and urban planning do not at first appear to marry well together with landscape garden design with its bucolic and arcadian associations, but the term is a valid one when used with reference to the landscape parks of the early nineteenth century which were a new kind of urban space.

The eighteenth-century country house and its garden were symbols of the new society – aristocratic, leisured, landed and rich. This did not continue into the nineteenth century without distinct amendments. The city became increasingly important and money was generated by industry creating a new and significant middle class. But the powerful influence of the landscape still had resonance in the nineteenth-century metropolis. Towards the end of the eighteenth century the wars in Europe and the consequent difficulties for foreign travel had encouraged home tourism.[6] This activity had developed to include the appreciation of the landscape in general, rather than just landscape gardens, and advice was on hand as to how to view it.[7] The political significance of the landscape and its ability to engender a sense of nationalism, pleasure and/or well-being in the visitor did not go unnoticed by theorists and Enlightenment thinkers. These principles were used in the urban plan of London to influence the subjective response of the individual to the new urban landscape. The theorists had established the symbolic function of landscape and architecture. Here it was used in the service of monarch, state and nation instead of an individual landowner. The educated population were already accustomed to reading the landscape. Part of the overall plan was that the lower classes too should learn to appreciate these discrete urban spaces.

In positioning the landscaping of the royal parks within the framework of the picturesque it is important to establish how they featured on the urban map and how they determined the reading of it. Leading on from this is the question of how the concepts of the picturesque and its correlative, the beautiful, helped to galvanise monarch, state and nation into an appreciation of this urban plan. The works discussed here can be positioned between two events which signify the changes which took place in the attitudes towards urban landscape during this period – the beginnings of the Regent's Park project and the 1833 Select Committee on Public Walks.[8]

The beginning of the huge development and re-imaging of the urban landscape in the early nineteenth century was heralded, as we have seen, by John Nash's plan for Regent's Park and Regent Street, which was passed in 1813 as 'An act for a more convenient communication from Mary-le-bone Park and the northernmost parts of the metropolis to Charing Cross and for the making of a more convenient sewage for the same'. Nash identified three main objectives: utility to the public, beauty of the metropolis and practicability. The public here were the upper and middle class residents of the West End, and the beauty of the city comprised its architecture and the picturesque landscaping of Regent's Park. But, as demonstrated in chapter 3, this signalled an important development in the idea of the beautification of a city through an overall concern with a city's appearance and the zoning of different classes of residents. There was an important shift in attitude when within twenty years the Committee on Public Walks was set up in 1833. Its report expressed concern about the inequalities caused by the development of all the royal parks in the metropolis. The west and north-west of London were well endowed with public open spaces for the enjoyment of the lower orders whereas elsewhere the intensive building development of the previous fifty years had covered most of the land. These two events frame the bulk of the work in the royal parks and helps elucidate the changing attitudes towards urban landscapes within this twenty-year span. Moreover, an examination of the work in the royal parks reveals the important role landscape design played in the emergence of the modern metropolis.

THE TERM 'PICTURESQUE'

It is important first of all to clarify the meaning of the term 'picturesque' as used here[9] and to examine how it can be useful in a discussion of the royal parks. Although the writings of the Rev. William Gilpin, Uvedale Price and Richard Payne Knight drew together disparate strands of eighteenth-century picturesque theory, these were by no means unified or indeed without their own internal contradictions.[10] But key themes emerge in the work of Gilpin, Price and Payne Knight which shed important light on the definition of the picturesque and its political and/or moral significance. Two strands are significant here: first the definitions of beauty and the picturesque as seen in the works of Gilpin and Price, and secondly the impact Price and Payne Knight had on political readings of the landscape, which featured in debates about the picturesque in the opening decades of the nineteenth century. Both these areas are relevant to the concerns to improve the royal parks in London.

William Gilpin's essay *On Picturesque Beauty* (1792)[11] makes a fundamental distinction between beautiful and picturesque objects and scenes. His version of the picturesque encompasses notions of roughness and ruggedness in an uncultivated landscape where hovels, peasants and ruins have replaced temples and classical gods and goddesses as foci of the picturesque gaze, which was now principally concerned with the aesthetic qualities of the landscape. By contrast, beauty is defined by Gilpin – in 'real objects' (as opposed to pictures) – as being smooth and neat. Significantly, his examples are elegant architecture and improved pleasure grounds. The preference for the rugged in Gilpin's discourse moves the picturesque away from the moral aesthetic prevalent in many earlier writers. This aesthetic allied the use of classical buildings and ruins in a landscape to the 'augustan' virtues of antiquity. But, importantly, the notion of the landscape as having meaning survived.

Gilpin's ideas opened up the debate on defining the picturesque. This theme was taken up by Uvedale Price in his *Essay on the Picturesque* (1794) where he aimed to distinguish the picturesque from the beautiful and the sublime. He argued that it had a separate character 'and [was] not a mere reference to painting'. Price's preference for ruggedness did, as with Gilpin, distance the picturesque from the moral qualities of landscape identified by preceding generations. These concerns were replaced by a more direct emotional response akin to Edmund Burke's sensationist aesthetic[12] which was based on the formal qualities of the landscape. Leading on from this Price also argued for greater freedom in garden design and spoke out against the formality of designers like Capability Brown. Price's criticism of Brown brings out one of the contradictions of picturesque discourse at this time which focused on the denial and recognition of the intrinsic message in the landscape. Although debates about the differentiation between the beautiful and the picturesque might have, on the one hand, moved attention away from reading moral meaning in the landscape, they did not, on the other hand, focus attention on the aesthetic quality of the landscape purely for its own sake. Here, paradoxically, the theorists identified distinct political associations. In his *Essay* Price attacks Brown's 'smoothing and levelling', which he despises in both gardening and political contexts. Indeed Price identifies despotism 'as the most complete leveller'. But the political signals given by Price are not always straightforward. Despite his outburst against despotism Price was not sympathetic to the French Revolution. As a landowner he felt threatened by the political sentiments of the new regime in France. This found expression in his *Thoughts on the Defence of Property* (1797). In his *Essays on the Picturesque* (1794) he aligns good government with naturalism in landscape:[13]

> A good landscape is that in which all the parts are free and unconstrained, but in which, though some are prominent and highly illuminated, and others in shade and retirement; some rough, and others more smooth and polished, yet they are all necessary to the beauty, energy, effect and harmony of the whole. I do not see how good government can be more exactly defined.

In Price's eyes Brown's control of nature in his landscape design and denial of its essential rough and rugged qualities embodied the kind of political principles he despised.

Price's sentiments about Brown were echoed by Richard Payne

Knight who, although sympathetic to the French and American Revolutions, saw no place for such political change in England. But Brown was defended by Humphry Repton,[14] who identified the qualities of the government as being represented in Brown's designs:

> I cannot help seeing great affinity betwixt deducing gardening from the painter's studies of nature, and deducing government from the opinions of man in a savage state. The neatness, simplicity, and elegance of English gardening, have acquired the approbation of the present century, as the happy medium betwixt the wildness of nature and the stiffness of art; in the same manner as the English constitution is the happy medium betwixt the liberty of savages, and the restraint of despotic government; and so long as we enjoy the benefits of these middle degrees betwixt extremes of each, let the experiments of the untried, theoretical improvement be made in some other country.[15]

The implications of these attitudes towards the countryside for the reading of urban landscapes come to the fore when the monarch and his government set about improving the royal parks. The intensity of the debates underscored the sensitivity to the meaning of landscape – its location, whether urban or rural, must surely have been a secondary issue. Indeed the direct association between landscape and politics made by protagonists of both sides of the argument may well have been intensified by the metropolitan context of the royal parks. And it is here that the emergence of *rus in urbe*, a predominant theme in this volume, is complete. We find the monarch – the landowner – reshaping lands and redefining living accommodation as a means of perpetuating and endorsing the Crown's hegemony and prestige. The 'not for profit' ethos of the development of country estates, where aesthetic enhancement was the sole aim, lent itself well to the aims of a royal landowner in an urban context. Not only did the considerable redevelopment of the parks have resonance with debates about reading the landscape but it also corresponded to the thinking of contemporary landscape design theorists, most notable here J. C. Loudon, who was a stout defender of Repton.[16] Although Decimus Burton was chosen as the executive architect, he had not worked on a major landscape project or a country house garden. Instead his expertise had grown out of the increasingly important role of the speculator-developer and the building traditions and planning principles of the garden square. This had been further developed in the designs for Regent's Park villas and his work at Hyde Park Corner where all'antica architecture was married with the demands of modern metropolitan planning. The new demands of the urban fabric meant that country house landscapes, with all their encoded meanings, were now an essential guide in the formation of a new kind of *rus in urbe*. The emphasis on vista and axiality in Burton's work is reminiscent of some of Loudon's comments in his *Encyclopedia of Gardening* (1822).[17] In this text Loudon is critical of too much irregularity which may be mistaken for nature and praises regularity and geometric garden design: 'but forms perfectly regular, and division completely uniform, immediately excite the belief in design, and with this belief, all the admiration which follows the employment of skill and expense'.[18] He recognises that regular forms are found satisfactory as, according to G. W. Leibniz, regularity appeals to reason which acknowledges the cognitive processes involved in reading a landscape.

There is no evidence to suggest Burton was directly influenced by Loudon or indeed any other landscape designer or picturesque theorist. But these ideas were current and the viewing public – those who would experience the new metropolitan environment – as well as the architect himself would have been sensitive to them. Moreover, certain pieces of advice given by landscape design theorists seem very close to Burton's designs, for instance Loudon's advice that 'water in architectural basins, regular canals, or fountains, walks, and woods, of uniform width and perfectly straight, straight walls and hedges, are easily distinguishable from nature's management of these materials, and are highly expressive of the hand of man'.[19]

Burton's work is parallel to the rejection of the pure imitation of nature and the move towards a more obviously constructed landscape with a clear directional force. As such it has resonance with the ideological approach to landscape seen in the work of Repton and before him Brown. This template for the representation of political authority is also connected with the work in the royal parks – especially if landscape design is considered in the context of reactions to the French Revolution. Price and Payne Knight reacted vigorously to the political upheavals across the channel, but their defence of natural landscape, and in the opposing camp Repton's defence of Brown, was that the qualities of the English system of government were embodied within the principles of the design. As discussed in chapter 3, there had already been responses to the French situation in the planning of early nineteenth-century London.[20] The works in the royal parks were part of this continuing response of King and government to the political climate in Britain which found expression in the urban plan of London. Here, the apparent extent of royal lands was redefined and used to underline political authority through its landscaping and relationship to government buildings.

THE RE-IMAGING OF THE ROYAL PARKS

The work in royal parks including the monumental entrance ways and modest lodges for the park keepers, as well as the idea of a public open space, can be examined in the light of the above. But the royal parks can in some ways be seen as a kind of private commission as Burton's terms of engagement were different from those of other major architects who were involved in public works and the King's works at this time. In contrast, John Nash, Sir John Soane and Sir Robert Smirke all enjoyed the status of being an attached Architect to the Office of Works with the attendant national kudos and some-times ridicule. Although Burton's payments were calculated in the same way as for these other architects – payments were made to him on an architect's commission basis of 5 per cent – he remained outside both the Offices of Woods and Works.[21] But this does not appear to have diminished his status as he was frequently used as an arbiter in disputes concerning residents and developers and was one of the 'classical' architects named and shamed in the frontispiece of A. W. N. Pugin's *Contrasts*.

Before the major works began in 1825 the parks were in a rather run-down state with ramshackle buildings for gatekeepers' accom-modation and the housing of farm animals which grazed on the land. The roads and fences were in a poor condition and the largely untended landscape required draining and replanting. Burton's work included the tidying up of the parks by the creation of new roads, fences and plantations; the redesign of the layouts of the grounds, the creation of monumental entrance ways and lodges and the re-orientation of existing roads. Each change might seem to be a minor adjustment or improvement but the cumulative effect was substan-tial. Improvement of the perimeters and entrances to the parks helped to give them definition as discrete and distinctive spaces. New roads, rides and pathways through the parks directed the public through them so ordering their experience of the space and directing them to monuments planned for the parks or buildings at their perimeters.

All work was subject to the King's approval and this is indicative of the hands-on involvement of George IV and, doubtless to the spendthrift monarch's chagrin, Treasury scrutiny. The full plans for the improvements to the parks were presented to the King in an audience granted to the First Commissioner of the Board of the Office of Woods on 16 February 1825.[22] This triangular relationship between monarch, architect and government officials remained throughout period during which the works were being carried out in the parks. The input of all three parties was substantial and the resulting improvements reflected their various concerns. These ranged from the significance of royal parkland in an increasingly urban setting to the conscious reshaping and re-imaging of a modern metropolitan environment. The King even made the suggestion that the land at the back of Piccadilly should be enclosed by an ornamental pleasure ground for which permission was granted by the Treasury on 10 May the same year.[23] The move to renovate and develop the parks came on 22 April 1823[24] when the Treasury asked the Commissioners of Woods for a report on the state of the parks and proposals for improvements. The report was submitted on 28 July that year.[25] This was written by Arbuthnot, Dacres Adams and Dawkins and concerned itself principally with the state of the roads, walks and fences.[26] The majority of the work was overseen by Burton but there were also contributions from other well-known architects and engineers. John McAdam, an important innovator in road-building, began the much needed repairs on the roads in September 1823 at an initial cost of £5,000[27] paid out of parliamentary grant.[28] John Rennie was responsible for the bridge across the Serpentine.[29] Here again we find an experienced engineer involved in the landscaping of London, as Rennie was the son of the designer of Waterloo and Southwark Bridges across the Thames and had posthumously executed his father's design for the rebuilding of London Bridge.

THE SIGNIFICANCE AND HISTORY OF THE AREA

The whole area of the three royal parks was bounded to the north by the Uxbridge Road, to the west by Kensington Palace and Garden, to the east by Park Lane (in the case of Hyde Park) and St James's Palace and Westminster and to the south by Buckingham Palace and Pimlico (figure 6.1). The meeting point of all three parks was Hyde Park Corner. As we have seen, this was already established as a significant gateway into London. Moreover, the geographical scope of these parks shows the essential role they began to play in connecting the vital parts of the metropolis as London moved westwards and more public buildings were constructed around Westminster. One of the principal purposes of the work was to connect the royal parks with the city's existing infrastructure and provide important connective tissue between disparate parts of the urban fabric, both improving communications between parts of the metropolis and directing the gaze and circulatory patterns of visitor and resident.

A brief history of the parks reveals how a largely private royal precinct was transformed into a public open space. Of the parks St James's was the most centrally located and in early times included Green Park, sometimes called Upper St James's. The land had been acquired by Henry VIII to extend the grounds of York Place where he moved from Westminster in 1530. The site was originally part of St James's leper hospital and part marshy fields watered by the Tyburn stream. The hospital was replaced by a hunting lodge and the parkland drained. James I initiated some minor developments

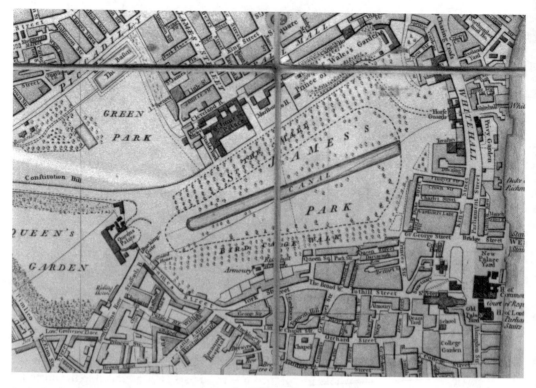

including clearing the undergrowth. His daughter-in-law, Queen Henrietta Maria, first brought the French royal gardener André Mollet to work at St James's when she moved to the palace in 1637.[30] Hunting continued in the park, but it was becoming a place for courtly walks. Even so, it was still a private royal demesne. During the Commonwealth 'James's Park' was exempted from the sale of Crown lands. At the Restoration great works started in the royal parks and Mollet was appointed gardener in chief at St James's Palace.

After the Interregnum St James's Park was embellished with the construction of a canal 100 feet wide and 2,800 feet long aligned to the Whitehall stairs. The canal formed the middle toe of a *patte d'oie*. St James's remained Charles II's favourite park where he paraded French fashion and swam in the canal. There are still reminders of this time: Bird Cage Walk was so called as exotic birds were kept in gilded cages; Pall Mall was where Charles played the French game similar to croquet; Constitution Hill was made for and named after the King's long constitutional walks – not any democratic process!

In the eighteenth century royal interest in the park dwindled. Apart from some odd tinkering by Capability Brown, it was by George III's time only a meadow with the canal providing water for grazing cows. But the public area was still confined to a fenced-off perimeter walk. The park was still seen as private royal land and had been a significant part of court life. In 1814 the Prince Regent (George IV) decided to open St James's Park to the public, on payment of an admission fee, as part of the celebrations for the National Jubilee,[31] which was a premature celebration of victory over the French.[32] But it was an important turning point in the history of the park and in the relationship between city dweller and Crown land. The message was clear: the public was invited to share in the royal gardens at a time of national celebration.[33] It was a clever move, as the sharing of the 'private' space of St James's Park gave the public a feeling of communality with royal land – not unlike that experienced by visitors to country house landscapes. Despite the attention given to St James's Park in 1814 it remained in a poor state of repair until John Nash's relandscaping of the park after the demolition of Carlton House in 1826. This was based in part on a plan drawn up by Capability Brown whilst he was Royal Gardener in 1764[34] and comprised ornamental water, shrubberies, mounds and walks. St James's Park began to play a more important role in the urban fabric in the late 1820s and early 1830s, and in response to this Burton was brought in to do further work.

The history of Hyde Park is closely linked to St James's Park. It was called after the manor of Hyde Park became Crown land, a deer park, during the reign of Henry VIII. Hunts regularly took place there and it was only in 1637 that it was first opened to the public. It was sold off during the Interregnum but was recovered by the restored monarchy. Landscaping began in the early eighteenth century with the laying out of Kensington Palace Garden and later the Serpentine. Rotten Row, the only impressive part of the park remaining in the early nineteenth century, like Pall Mall and Constitution Hill, took its name from royal use. It is derived from 'route du roi', the king's road through the park. By the 1810s the park was used for mock battles and military exercises and so had become a site of spectacle and display with distinctly nationalistic overtones.

THE LANDSCAPE ISSUES

The opening years of the work in the royal parks shows that the plans evolved slowly and were subject to amendment and change. Throughout the redevelopment of the royal parks a distinct landscape aesthetic dominated the planning, with a preference for wide *allées*, vistas, tree-lined roads and monumental entrance ways. Against the background of previous political readings of the landscape the anti-naturalistic landscape of the royal parks, with its rational order, echoed a particular view of the governmental structure of post-Napoleonic Britain. The clear simple lines of his designs for the park were enhanced by screen planting to conceal any anomalies in the landscape and surrounding areas. Decimus Burton also created public pleasure grounds with ornamental planting and waters to enhance the public's experience of these urban spaces, and received some assistance from the Buckingham Palace garden landscapers W. A. Nesfield, Sir William Hooker and William Aiton, all of whom continued to exercise considerable influence on landscape design in Britain for several decades.[35]

As we have seen, the most significant building in the vicinity of the parks was Buckingham Palace, remodelled by John Nash in the latter half of the 1820s, to which the royal parks acted as a kind of landscape garden setting. Originally known as the Queen's Palace, Buckingham Palace had St James's Park to its east facade (main entrance) and Green Park to its north side and rear facade to the south, which was known as the Queen's Garden. Nash was responsible for the architectual work on the new palace and the landscaping of the Queen's Garden, but the relationship between the redesign of the palace and the redesign of the parks is not always clear, nor for that matter the relationship between the two main architects, John Nash and Decimus Burton. In the Regent's Park and Regent Street projects Nash had enjoyed a superior position to Burton, being the offical arbiter of good design. In principle Burton had to defer to Nash, although in reality the latter frequently avoided his responsibilities. Burton's work in the royal parks and at Hyde Park Corner however, as seen earlier, was completely independent of Nash. It was controlled by the Office of Woods, not the Office of Works, and had a different chains of command and financial structures.

Park Lane was one of the most significant borders of the parks. It ran along the eastern edge of Hyde Park and marked a stopping place for the spread of the fashionable West End. Moreover, it was a wide straight road with distinct possibilities for enhancement. The Office of Woods stepped in here when in August 1824 Arbuthnot and Adams wrote to the Treasury suggesting that the new lodges and gates be built opposite Stanhope and Chesterfield Streets and that a new lodge and gates be constructed at the Grosvenor Gate.[36] Not everyone saw this as an improvement: the tenants of the Earl Grosvenor living at 345 Park Lane, Lieutenant-General W. Thornton, Captain Brenton and Mr Fitzgerald, objected to the siting of gates opposite the house, stating that they should be directly at the end of Grosvenor Street with carriage gates at either side of the lodge. Moreover, they stated that part of their rent included a contribution to the upkeep of the park.[37] The connection between the park and the city was reinforced by a request from Arbuthnot and Dawkins in June 1826 to alter the line of the road from Hyde Park to Grosvenor Square to create a neater entrance and improved alignment between the two.[38] Although Burton had produced the designs and estimates for the Stanhope and Grosvenor lodges in September 1824, it was not until January 1829 that he was instructed to produce working drawings.[39] Despite an overspend of nearly £5,000[40] the works in Park Lane, and Burton's involvement with them, did not cease, as in May of the same year he was requested by the Commissioners to estimate the cost of raising the road at the north entrance into Grosvenor Place and to determine how much of this should be paid for by the Crown.[41] The work on Park Lane is indicative of the way in which the urban topography was reshaped – smoothed and levelled – in an attempt to harmonise the cityscape through easier connections and improved vistas. This was to ensure that the developments at Hyde Park Corner married well with the rest of the road layout at this juncture. The Office of Woods was also keen to profit from any existing improvements – especially if they did not have to pay for them. In a letter to the Treasury Arbuthnot and Adams remarked that the fences on the east side of Park Lane had been maintained by the owners of the houses at their own cost.[42] They had replaced brick walls with iron fences and this work should be continued and the design kept consistent. On the east side the line between park and city should be defined by a continuous post and chain fence running from Cumberland Gate to Hyde Park Corner.[43]

HYDE PARK

As in the case of Hyde Park Corner, the Office of Woods emerges once more as a driving force in the redevelopment of Hyde Park. The initial report signed by Arbuthnot, Dacres Adams and Dawkins in 1823 concerned itself principally with the state of the roads, walks and fences in Hyde Park.[44] This concern with infrastructures echoed the preoccupations of rural landowners who were in the process of upgrading their estates with turnpike roads and better drainage. In both cases the new technologies that facilitated improved transport systems and land use also achieved a more pleasing aesthetic, which in turn enhanced the image of the landowner. The Commissioners stressed that they had sought many opinions and the most urgent work required was drainage (figure 6.2). They also stated that the roads needed to be repaired and resurfaced and they had commissioned a report from McAdam about this. Their suggestions regarding the roads included the widening of the roads leading from Hyde Park Corner to Cumberland Gate, too narrow at 30 feet wide, and near the Magazine, which was only 24 feet wide. Conversely, Rotten Row was too wide and needed narrowing to 70 feet. The following year Arbuthnot and Adams suggested the east wall of Kensington Gardens be extended and the road and footpath from Cumberland Gate to Kensington Gardens improved, including a new

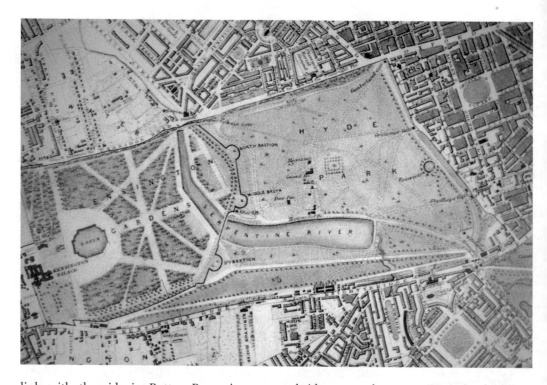

link with the ride in Rotten Row via a stone bridge over the Serpentine.[45] A drawing also exists dated 23 May 1823 showing the plans for widened carriageways, a section of the road on the north side of the park, a section of the roof plan for a lodge for Hyde Park and the position of the Hyde Park Screen and Arch at Constitution Hill.[46] Final plans and proposals produced by Burton at the behest of Charles Arbuthnot were submitted on 28 September 1825.[47] Hyde Park was indeed in need of many basic repairs to its fabric and perimeter fences but the improvements went well beyond this. The letter from Arbuthnot and Adams to the Treasury dated 3 August 1824, which shows the connection between the Achilles statue and the laying out of Hyde Park Corner, also gives an idea of the improvements the Commissioners had in mind: 'With respect to the Gates and lodges it has often been suggested to us since the Public monument was placed in Hyde Park [the Achilles statue], that it would be a great improvement if the gates of that park and those of Green park opposite were to be altered as to make this the principal entrance into Hyde Park.'[48] As we have seen, Burton responded to this with his designs for the Hyde Park Screen and the Green Park Arch. At the same time he also produced designs for a new lodge at Cumberland Gate.[49]

Hyde Park was, like most other urban developments in London, the result of collaboration between a range of bodies. Once again there is some parity between urban and rural patterns of

6.2 Society for the Diffusion of Useful Knowledge (SDUK), map of London, 1843, detail showing the layout of Hyde Park

6.3 Decimus Burton,
*Design for Bayswater
Lodge*, *Hyde Park*,
transverse section,
July 1827

6.4 Decimus Burton,
*Design for Bayswater
Lodge*, *Hyde Park*, ground
plan, July 1827

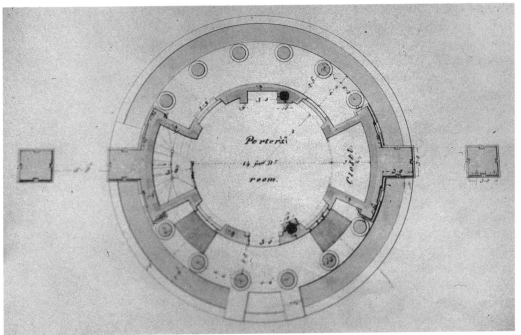

development. Here the Crown replaced the aristocratic landowner, the Office of Woods his steward, and Burton the architect in charge of fabricating the appropriate landscape image and urban sensory experience. The patchy nature of the documentary evidence gives little scope for establishing the overall vision for the park. Moreover, the various chains of command and the lively interest in the works taken by local residents clearly influenced the direction of the improvements. But the unrealised designs for the Bayswater Road lodge (1827) give some further idea of the way in which Burton intended to punctuate the perimeter of the park with monumental entrance ways (figures 6.3 and 6.4).[50] The circular structure with a colonnaded facade and imposing entrance gates would have greatly enhanced the park and complemented the work at Hyde Park Corner. Together with Burton's design for the Bath Gate and Chelsea Water Company Fountain, also of 1827 (see below), this indicates that Burton's vision for the parks was ambitious. These individual set pieces, together with the Hyde Park Screen and Arch at Constitution Hill, would not have looked out of place in the most prestigious landscaped garden. But the 1828 moratorium halted work, ensuring that the grand re-imaging would never be completed.[51]

Shortly after work was halted a further entrance to Hyde Park was proposed by local residents to the north of the park wanting better access to the area to the south of it. In 1829 an entrance from the Uxbridge Road was proposed by Messrs Capps and Oldfield.[52] They also wished to replace the wall outside their house with an iron railing. The Office of Woods reported to the Treasury on this application[53] and permission was granted to take down the wall 'subject to our architect's [Burton's] approval' and to put up an iron fence. The application for a road into the park could not yet be recommended.

GREEN PARK

The Commissioners' report on the improvements to the royal parks says little about the intentions for Green Park. This was perhaps because the park formed part of the back garden to Buckingham Palace, plans for this area were ongoing and Nash appeared to have been less than co-operative with the work to improve the parks (figure 6.1). The area was sometimes also included in the discussion of the plans for St James's Park. Burton's efforts had focused principally on the entrance to the park from Hyde Park Corner, but the local residents also exerted some influence on the development of the landscape.

The waterworks in this area of London had already caused problems with the foundations of Hyde Park Screen. The Chelsea

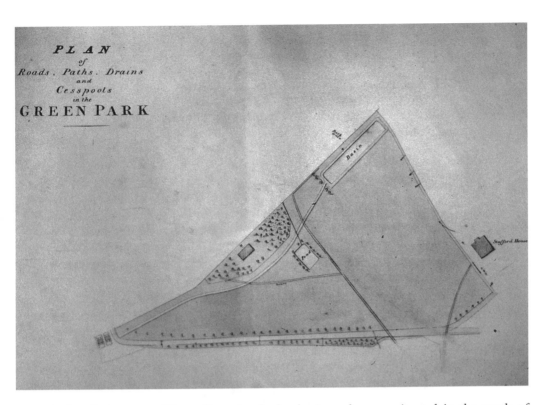

PLAN
of
Roads . Paths . Drains
and
Cesspools
in the
GREEN PARK

6.5 Decimus Burton, *Survey Drawing of the Roads, Parks and Drains in Green Park*, 1829

Water Company had a basin and pump situated in the north of Green Park near the Bath Gate entrance which fronted Piccadilly. In 1827 complaints from the residents of Piccadilly and Arlington Street, directly opposite the entrance, about the unsightly nature of the gate and pump and of the ugly appearance of the present iron main or waste pipe at the west end of the basin prompted a review of the landscaping of this area (figure 6.5).[54] In August of the same year the Commissioners of Woods passed on the residents' complaints to the Treasury with the suggestion that the area could be made ornamental. Burton had already been asked to supply designs and estimates for improved entrance at Bath Gate. He was also required to render the basin and the flow of water from the iron main as ornamental as possible in unison with what had already been executed by him in part of the general plans of improvement.[55]

Burton prepared a drawing for a new monumental entrance way and an appropriate lodge in lieu of the existing unsightly building (figures 6.6, 6.7, 6.8),[56] remarking that the site was conspicuous as it was in view not only of Piccadilly but also of the new palace, and therefore it should be of superior character.[57] He was concerned with how the design would appear from both inside and outside the park as seen in figure 6.6. He planned a handsome new balustrade fence around the basin and proposed to remove the present stand pipe from its position in the centre of the basin and construct a fountain of marble and artificial stone upon a base of granite and Yorkshire stone. The drawing implies a loose reference to the Four Rivers Fountain in Rome. According to Burton the design would be 'practical and functional and ornamental' [58] – the hallmark of much of Burton's work in the royal parks. This scheme provided another entrance way into the royal parks – this time from Piccadilly. Burton's presentation drawing shows the impressive view of the

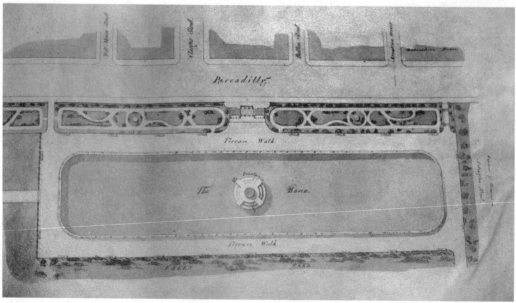

entrance gate from Piccadilly. Like the other entrances to the parks this was based on classical prototypes, here a Greek Doric temple facade. The view from the park is also shown, but this is of the fountain and water basin which was to be aligned with the entrance way, this axiality strengthened the composition. To increase the public's enjoyment, the surrounding area was to be landscaped into a pleasure ground. It is also possible that another symbolic monument was considered as part of the scheme. A letter from Burton to his friend J. W. Croker records:[59]

> I have consulted Mr Simpson the Engineer of the Chelsea Water Works Company respecting the substitution of the Pillar for the Obelisk in the Reservoir and the correct sum he estimates as the *extra* which would be occasioned by this, and the Square Pedestal Tank, in lieu of the circular one , would be £300 ...
>
> Unless, therefore, you are of the opinion of the Obelisk will be an unhandsome object I would be inclined to request that the endeavour to obtain favour to the Treasury the additional grant should not be made, as I understand much difficulty would be made – but on this point I beg your opinion.

It is not clear what, if anything, Croker had to do with the scheme.[60] He was certainly interested in monuments and had an active interest in Burton's career. It is likely that Burton was either following up an idea of Croker's or using him as a sounding board for his own

left 6.6 Decimus Burton, *Design for the Chelsea Water Co., Green Park*, detail of monumental entrance way from Piccadilly, plan and elevation, March 1827

6.7 Decimus Burton, *Design for the Chelsea Water Co., Green Park*, detail of plan for fountain and basin, March 1827

below 6.8 Decimus Burton, *Design for the Chelsea Water Co., Green Park*, detail of elevation of fountain March 1827

thoughts. The design was approved and Burton was asked to supply an estimate for the fountain. The specified materials and cost indicate that this was a significant part of the landscaping and general improvements of this area (see Appendix B).[61]

But the plans were put on hold until more funds were available. The cost of the works in the royal parks, especially the entrance ways at Hyde Park Corner, had escalated considerably, but were totally eclipsed by the expenditure on the new palace.[62] A letter from the Treasury to the Office of Woods in August 1827[63] stated that the improvements were desirable, but deferred detailed consideration of the proposal until both the Office's funds and the work already in hand were in a fit state to allow the new work to be undertaken.

The 1828 moratorium on all works in the parks left much unfinished. Some projects were taken up again as seen, for instance, in the Stanhope and Grosvenor lodges and entrances above. Perhaps the most curious element in the evolution of the design of Green Park comes after the death of George IV. Chapter 5 outlined the disputed role the Green Park Arch played in the landscaping of Buckingham Palace. But the documentation concerning the design of the arch and the evidence given to the 1828 inquiry made no mention of the construction of a road leading through the arch away from Hyde Park Corner. It appears a road was intended to lead from the arch to the garden facade of the palace but this was blocked by Nash's reservoir in the gardens, so when work was halted in 1828 the arch led nowhere. A survey by Burton of the road patterns, drains and cesspools of the park, dated 1829, shows the dislocated position of the arch (figure 6.5).[64] This must have appeared like a rather destitute symbol of George IV's extravagance. But the importance of the geographical location and of the park itself remained.

Shortly after his accession to the throne William IV recognised this and in a second phase of work in the parks began, with Burton still as the leading figure. This involved making better connections between Green and St James's Parks and the surrounding buildings – in particular the new State Paper Office, designed by Sir John Soane, and the Palace of Westminster where Soane had also designed a monumental entrance for George IV. In some of the documentation the two parks are elided and this reinforces the approach to these parks in the early 1830s as a homogeneous entity. In April 1831 Duncannon and Dacres Adams wrote to the Treasury with a report on making an entrance to Green Park through the archway at Constitution Hill. They stated that the King (now William IV) had indicated that the archway should be made available as an entrance into the park and was willing to give up a small portion of the ground from the new palace in St James's Park (actually Green Park) to enable the construction of a road.[65] Decimus Burton had been asked to provide a plan and estimate to carry out the King's intention.[66] Burton produced three alternatives and estimates which the Commissioners included with their report. The three designs offered the cheapest solution, 'the handsomest' and most expensive, and a middle way (see Appendix C).[67]

Burton discussed his plans in a reported conversation with the First Commissioner regarding the adaptation of the archway according to the King's wishes which he appended to his plans. He had been hopeful that Nash's reservoir would be removed and in another letter to Croker in January 1831 stated: 'a report I hear has been made by an Engineer I think it is likely the reservoir there will be declared to be unnecessary'.[68] But in all three alternatives the line of the road was to be south rather than north of the reservoir in the palace grounds. This would give better space for the turn in the road and the approach to the arch would be less abrupt. It was to replace the present line of Constitution Hill which according to Burton formed an acute and unsightly angle at its junction with the arch. The Commissioners recommended design A as it was not so different from the rest, but was the cheapest and quickest to execute to fulfil the King's wishes, and it did not preclude adoption of the more expensive designs B and C at a later date.

In October 1831 design A for an archway as a public entrance into Green Park was approved by the King, albeit with some of his alterations which increased the expenditure, and the work was authorised on 25 October 1831.[69] In December that year Burton requested iron railings be placed on the south side of Constitution Hill and the enclosed ground and around the reservoir 'late in Buckingham Palace Garden'.[70] He argued that better fencing would improve the look of the area and prevent (unspecified) nuisances taking place there. The cost of improving the fence could be mitigated to some extent by retaining the reservoir in Green Park, which used to be in the gardens of Buckingham Palace to water those gardens, and the roads in St James's Park when necessary. This would save money then being paid to the Chelsea Water Company.

Burton's preference for a new straight road from the reservoir to the Mall reflects his enduring vision for the landscape of the royal parks, that they should provide areas for public recreation, convenient connections between important areas of the city and strong directional axes along which the visitor could experience the new urban landscape. The turning over of the King's private land to public enjoyment was politically symbolic and signified a new relationship between the monarch and the city.

It is perhaps surprising, after the attention paid to St James's Park by Nash, that Burton was brought in to carry out further improvements during the reign of William IV. Like his previous works these ranged from improvements for greater public convenience to the redevelopment of landscape features and the creation of new entrances and lodges. The park connected the governmental buildings of Westminster – especially Sir John Soane's new State Paper Office[71] – with Buckingham Palace and the Mall. Burton's work in St James's Park began after his laying out of the road to connect the park to the Arch at Constitution Hill and his brief was to enhance this network of connections. This was especially significant as Buckingham Palace was an unpopular, expensive white elephant at this time, being hurriedly finished by Edward Blore.[72] William IV did not want to live in it but, probably because of its excessive cost, a new significant use was being sought for it – including the idea that it serve as the new Palace of Westminster after the fire of 1834. Indeed, by the mid 1830s the royal emphasis of the parks was diminishing in favour of their benefit to the population at large and as providers of routes through the western portion of the metropolis. The King took only a passing interest in the final stages of the works on St James's Park, and the design schemes were more a result of the dialogue between the Commissioners of Woods and Decimus Burton. But there was an increasing awareness of public opinion and convenience and the important role local residents could play in the enabling and execution of these improvements.

Despite the extensive works carried out by Nash many areas of the park were still quite run down. This was particularly the case with the perimeter and entrances on the south side of the park which were hardly appropriate for an area of increasing national significance. Moreover, the landscaping of St James's Park did not lend itself to providing good communications across the park. As the role of the royal parks in the infrastructure of London developed, so they were required to give appropriate access to significant sites and buildings in the urban landscape. This had not always been wanted by the local residents, for instance in 1830 when strong objections were made to Nash's plan to form an opening from Waterloo Place to St James's Park between the two wings of Carlton House Terrace.[73]

By March 1832 Burton was involved in constructing a new lodge and gates into the park at Pimlico, also referred to as the Buckingham Gate.[74] The new buildings were to create a more impressive gateway into the park adjacent to the palace itself.[75] The lodge was to be constructed of Portland stone and Bath ashlar facing.[76] Alongside replacing the ramshackle existing entrance

Burton also remodelled the general approach to the park. He re-aligned the railings of the park and widened and improved the adjoining parts of St James's Street.[77] He also recommended that the old enclosure walls of the yard used by soldiers south of the guard-house should be removed and the space levelled and paved to complete the approach to the new gates.[78]

These works are important in their own right as they create a prestigious entrance into the developing precinct with royal and state significance. While Nash had concentrated on creating a public pleasure ground and reworking the interior of the park, Burton re-defined the perimeter of the park to create a grander context, created better and more impressive communication across and around the park and constructed fewer but more imposing entrance ways. This gave clearer definition to the park and guided the visitor's experience of the park through the new roads and walkways which gave directional force to the overall plan of the area. The work became more significant when in December 1832 Burton drew up plans to connect Buckingham Gate with the Mall and ultimately the Arch at Constitution Hill. The line of the fence to the east of the new entrance was altered and the old gates from Constitution Hill were to be used to provide access for those on foot, and occasionally carriages, between the Mall and Bird Cage Walk. These individually minor but collectively significant works also included the improvement of the approach to the Arch at Constitution Hill.[79]

The redefining of the perimeter of St James's Park continued with the presentation of a memorial from the occupiers of houses fronting Bird Cage Walk between Storey's Gate and the new barracks in March 1834.[80] This had been a private road but in the summer of 1833 the King granted permission for a new road passing through the park on the south side leading from Great George Street to Pimlico which was to remain open till late at night during parliamentary sessions.[81] It had been necessary to extend the railings enclosing the pleasure grounds on the north side of Bird Cage Walk and to make foot and carriage gates. This had meant the construction of new railings from Storey's Gate to the enclosure in July of that year.[82]

The impetus to improve the area came from the memorialists' complaints and that the roads and walkways formed an important link between Storey's Gate and Soane's State Paper Office which was nearing completion. Burton was reminded of the significance of the area when the designs were requested from him. Not only was Bird Cage Walk now open to the public, but its importance was increased as it provided a link between the new palace and the splendid build-ings in Grosvenor Place and the Houses of Parliament. His designs were to be 'ornamental as well as useful' and he was to bear in mind the embellishments recently carried out north of the park and in the other parks in the metropolis.[83] Burton also wished to improve the general appearance of the area. The irregular step of ground had become an annoyance and the broken line of wall belonging to houses abutting the park needed to be concealed by planting and the provision of a small area in front of the houses towards the park. He submitted his plans and estimates for embellishment and improvement of the area in early 1834,[84] and the general design was submitted to the King by the First Commissioner and approved by March. Burton's designs were in accordance with the other improvements carried out for the Crown, but the whole work was considered too expensive to be done at once. Therefore only certain portions were to be executed immediately. So like the plans for the road connecting the Mall to the Arch at Constitution Hill this work was part of a larger scheme. These plans and estimates give a clear indication of the nature of the works and the costs [85] (see Appendix D).

The Commissioners were delighted with the scheme as the most essential parts of the design would meet the requirements of the memorialists.[86] Moreover it would provide 'a most handsome line of approach and communication between the new palace and Splendid Buildings before alluded to and the Houses of Parliament and Public Departments in Westminster [that is the new State Paper Office]'.[87] It is clear that the improvements in the park were meant to play a significant part in the re-imaging of London and to create a feeling of connectivity between key areas, whilst acknowledging the importance of vista in the urban landscape.

The significance of the royal parks within the city and the connections they provided is underlined by a letter from Burton to Alexander Milne in November 1834. This letter gives a clear idea of the architect's aims and how the scheme had developed during the course of 1834:

> I beg to acknowledge your letter of the 21st September. communicating the commands of the Commissioners of HM's Woods &c that I should consider & report to them as to my opinion on the best mode of laying out and improving so much of the Bird Cage Walk in St James's Park, as extends from the Barracks to Storey's Gate, and so much of the Malls immediately connected therewith as extend from Storey's Gate to the new State Paper Office, explaining that a principal object of the Board in suggesting any Improvements on the Southern side of the Park would be to exclude from view the broken and unsightly line of Wall belonging to the Houses in that Quarter, and that the Board conceive this might be effected by the erection of an iron railing at such a distance from those houses as would give to the respective occupiers the use and all the advantages of a small planted area in front of the same so in the event of such plan being adopted, The Board wish me to state the regulations under which these Inclosures should be

occupied, and the proportion in which the respective parties should contribute to the expense, and whether such contribution should be by an annual acknowledgement, or by payment in 'one Sum'.[88]

Burton had given these matters careful consideration and was submitting two alternative plans:

In preparing these Plans I have borne in mind the increasing import-ance of the Bird Cage Walk as a Road of great traffic since it has been thrown open to the Public for most descriptions of Carriages, and being a line of communication constantly thronged with foot passengers. This circumstance induces me to recommend that a foot-path should be added on the North side of the Road, and that the present railing should be set back for the purpose.

This line of Road must continue to rise in importance as forming the direct communication between the new Palace as well as the numerous and splendid buildings near Grosvenor Place, and the Houses of Parliament – Attention therefore should be paid to the ornamental as well as the useful, so as to accord with the other sides of the Park particularly the Mall Road and Facade on the north side; – As well as widening the Road by the additional footpath, means should be adopted for concealing the deformities referred to in your Letter. The line of Road should be altered at the East end so as to blend better with that of Great George Street; and it will be observed, that by the latter line being thus continued into the Park, a space will be obtained for a Shrubbery or Lawn with a low facade wall to screen the back yard walls of the unsightly projecting Houses in Princes Court, the only course perhaps under the circumstances to be adopted in regard to the houses, – whilst however the most desirable one would be to remove them altogether, or, if this cannot be effected to stucco and embellish them – the shabby Lodge and Cowhouses near Princes Court should be entirely removed, and a lodge erected in a more convenient situation for the Public.

Burton went on to discuss both plans, pointing out that the railing already erected in front of the Barracks should be continued to Storey's Gate. The two landscape alternatives he supplied show different appropriations of land between the park and the backyards of the houses.[89] Plan No. 1 shows the widening and straightening of the road and enclosure of the land in front of the houses on the south side of Bird Cage Walk.[90] Plan No. 2 shows the land to be laid out as gardens for the houses in Duke Street.[91] Plan No. 1 showed the whole of the space given over to the householders, but this would leave an important corner of the park in the hands of private owners who might not all upkeep their new gardens adequately. Moreover, Burton was concerned that the unsightly backs of these houses would not be properly concealed by shrubbery. Plan No. 2 was that a new

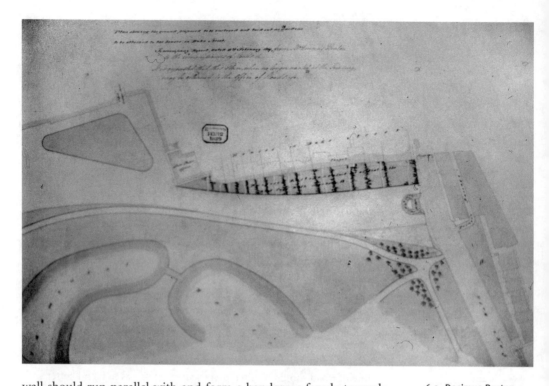

wall should run parallel with and form a handsome facade towards the road, leaving a 15-foot border or shrubbery to be maintained by the Commissioners' gardeners (figure 6.9). The 8-foot-high wall and the space behind could be sold to the house owners on the proviso that no structure was to be built over this height. In this way the same plantations and facade could be continued in front of the barrack yard. Burton remarked that 'The continuity of such a line of plantation and facade from Storey's Gate to Buckingham Gate would have a striking effect and with these on one side and the beautiful gardens of St James's Park on the other, the Bird Cage walk would become a handsome and convenient Avenue worthy of the use for which it is destined.'

His plans for restructuring and redefining the park continue with a proposal for a royal entrance:

The Piers and railings of Storeys Gate should be removed, a handsome Gateway of an appropriate character placed there forming a Royal Entrance to the Park & Buckingham Palace from the Houses of Parliament, Westminster – the Brighton Palace &c the effect of this would, exclusive of its general utility, be extremely good, viewed from the Park, but more especially on entering Town from Westminster Bridge. I beg to submit herewith a Design for a Gateway in this situation.

Burton's design for the new Parliamentary Mews in Westminster

6.9 Decimus Burton, *Design for the Landscaping around Storey's Gate St James's Park*, detail of Plan No. 2, 11 February 1839

(1825–26) (figure 6.10) had already made a contribution to upgrading the aesthetic of this area. Here we see how the parks, as well as being vehicles for the spectacle of royalty, were envisaged as part of the metropolis as a whole and the increasing importance of the image of the city both to those within it and to those approaching it.

The plan also included a reduction in the number of the entrances to the park from the south and proposed to widen and improve the remaining ones as the intended work at Storey's Gate rendered the entrance from Princes Court superfluous. The entrance by Dartmouth House was unsatisfactory and needed improvement. This prompted the suggestion that part of the Irish Office be taken down, or the vacant ground belonging to Christ's Hospital to the west of Dartmouth House be used to accommodate a superior design and better approaches. Burton was also involved with the improvements to the Mall which he went on to discuss:

> [In] regard to the improvement to the Mall, extending thence towards the State Paper Office. I beg to observe the Plan now submitted agrees in principle, with that which I had the honor to lay before the Commis[sioner]s in August last year, which obtained the approval of His Majesty.
>
> In both instances it is proposed to enclose a space of Ground for Shrubberies or lawns against the back yard Walls of the Duke Street Houses. But my late Surveys made in consequence of the wider field which I am called on to take in my present Report have led me to suggest the propriety of altering the line of Railing which encloses the interior of St James's Park, extending from the Bird Cage Walk to a point opposite the House Guards – By which means the approach to Storey's Gate from the Northward will be opened and improved. The

6.10 Thomas Shepherd, *London in the Nineteenth Century*, London, 1829, view of the Parliamentary Mews designed by Decimus Burton

new State Paper Office will be exposed to more advantage, the fence in question will take an easier line, and opportunity will be given for planting or turfing a border between the Garden wall and the public Mall where at present the space only allows of their being parted by the iron railing.[92]

The exceptionally complicated estimate, even by Burton's finicky standards, that accompanied his report (see Appendix E) was to allow easy apportionment of the costs of the works. All the sums quoted included architect's commission and clerk of work's salary, and could be reduced if competition amongst tradesmen 'be resorted to'. Here, however, we can see how the local residents were included in the plan as it was rightly assumed they would be interested in improving their property, its amenities and therefore their financial investment and social prestige. Both estimates assume that the division and railing of the land given over to the householders would be paid for at least in part by them and that they would agree to pay reasonable rents. The whole space of ground enclosed by the facade wall was around 25,000 feet, a rent of 1.5d. per foot would yield an annual rent of £150 5s. per house. This provided up to 5 per cent of the cost of the facade wall and railing required to enclose the ground that was proposed to be granted to the householders. The same arrangement could be made with the land behind the Duke Street houses, but the irregular shape of some of the plots would vary the rents between 6d. and 2d. per foot. The vision was certainly ambitious but the Treasury could not sanction such an expense, insisting instead on the preservation of the existing line of the road from Storey's to Pimlico Gate and the existing fence around the park.[93]

The matter was taken up again by the Office of Woods in August 1836 who wrote to the Treasury including Burton's 1834 plan for enclosing with an iron railing and laying out as ornamental pleasure gardens, the ground to the passage leading to Queen Square and from the east side of the passage to the passage leading to the Dartmouth Steps and from this passage to the lodge near Princes Court.[94] Alongside the estimate of £3,195 18s. Burton also proposed an arrangement which would help to fund the works, which would again involve local residents. Treasury approval was sought for Burton to enter into agreements with the owners of property in Queen Square, Park Street and Great Queen Street, Westminster to secure to the Crown in respect of the improvements and to occupy plots of ground in front of their houses a rent of 0.5d. per foot, approximately £75 per annum, which would yield 5 per cent on the cost of the railings, garden or other works connected with the improvements.

The principal elements of the proposed enclosure of Bird Cage

Walk dated 12 August 1836 included 6 foot high wrought iron railings, stone curbing and a fence, together with a newly laid out and planted pleasure ground and new paths and drains.[95] The total cost of the works including labour and architect's fees (5 per cent) was £3,195 18s. Burton had already approached the residents with the plan and all were satisfied with it and wished the Commissioners and the Treasury to know this. The Treasury granted permission for the work on 6 October 1836, provided the estimate was not exceeded.[96] In February of the following year Burton produced a design for a gatekeeper's lodge at Storey's Gate at the request of the Commissioners of Woods.[97] They argued in a letter to the Treasury that the present lodge was ill placed and was not in keeping with the improved state of the park.[98] The Treasury authorised the construction of the lodges in May of the same year and Burton's work on this part of the park drew to a close.[99]

The decision in the early 1820s to improve the royal parks grew out of the desire to underline the authority of monarch and government through the improvement of the urban fabric of London. Previous chapters have demonstrated how this was achieved, or at least attempted, in other parts of the metropolis through the construction of new roads across and entrances into the city. In the royal parks the principles of design used elsewhere in London were applied to these landscapes. The political message encoded in the rational order of the layouts could be read by a public already sensitive to the symbolic nature of landscape as discussed by the picturesque theorists.

The question remains why these works were undertaken as, compared to Regent Street or Hyde Park Corner, they made a less obvious physical intervention in the cityscape and offered little opportunity for profitable speculative development. But if it is remembered that great attention had been paid to the creation of a ceremonial entrance way at Hyde Park Corner two points emerge. First, the question of circulation must be considered. The plans for the royal parks included a road leading from the entrance at Hyde Park Corner towards Westminster. The plans for St James's Park included the embellishment of Bird Cage Walk, the creation of a royal entrance at Storey's Gate and better communication between the Mall and other routes through the park. The aim was to create a new network of connections between monuments to the monarch and nation, which comprised the entrances at Hyde Park Corner and Buckingham Palace, to the important governmental buildings which fringed the parks. The effect of this plan was to underline the importance to the general public of these elements of the cityscape through the landscape. The public's enjoyment of these spaces was enhanced further by improved access and the creation of pleasure grounds.

Secondly, this network of roads and rides created a possible processional route for the King to travel in a dignified way through the city. This aspect of the works in London has already been noted in the discussion of Hyde Park Corner. The improvement of the royal parks is a continuation of this grand vision. The dislocation of this newly developed area of London from the rest of the city may offer some explanation for this aim, but there is a deeper symbolism in this kind of road network. George IV was highly unpopular monarch and his successor, William IV, did not enjoy the public's admiration for long. The establishing of ritual, the appearance of tradition and the underlining of authority have been identified as ways in which the British monarchy defended its position.[100] A processional route contextualised within a landscape that underscored the nature of the government and the presence of traditional institutions can be viewed as an attempt to emphasise the King's authority.

These ideas were also expressed by architects other than Burton, for instance Sir John Soane presented numerous plans at the Royal Academy exhibitions and in his *Designs for Public and Private Buildings* which relate to the improvement of this area of London and the establishing of a route from Buckingham Palace to Whitehall via a planned monument to the Duke of York.[101] Burton's interventions in the landscape were more subtle than Soane's ambitious and ultimately unrealisable paper architecture. He gave directional focus to the parks through the re-aligning of the roads and walkways. The redefining of perimeters emphasised the parks' place in the urban fabric. The monumental entrance ways made them appear to be special precincts through which the visitor's experience was shaped by the restructuring of the roads and walks. The parks were also a complement to the new buildings which stood in or around them – especially the state offices and the new royal palace.

Although the royal parks did little to enhance the image of George IV or his successor, the advantages they gave to the general population was noted. The improved public open spaces of the royal parks had succeded in providing enjoyment and pleasure to visitors of all classes. The importance of public open spaces was investigated by the Select Committee on Public Walks of 1833. The report summarised many of the changes which had taken place in the London landscape in the previous fifty years. First, the population of the city had increased dramatically in 1750, 676,250; in 1800, 900,000 and in 1833, 1,500,000 – this figure included the ever-expanding suburbs. Secondly, the report confirmed that over the preceding fifty years there had been a building boom and increase in property values that had led to many open spaces being enclosed. It also summarised the aims and achievements of the development of the royal parks and their status within the urban fabric:

St James's Park, Green Park and Hyde Park ... afford to the inhabitants of this Western portion of the Metropolis inestimable advantages as Public Walks. The two latter Parks are open to all classes. St James's Park has lately been planted and improved with great taste, and the interior is now opened, as well as Kensington gardens, to all persons well-behaved and properly dressed. Your Committee remark with pleasure the advantage they afford to the Public, as also the great facility of approach to this beautiful Park, caused by opening a handsome stone footway from the bottom of Regent-street: for this accommodation it is understood the Public are indebted to His present Majesty.[102]

But the emphasis on the significance of urban landscapes had subtly changed. Public access to these open spaces remained of paramount importance. The links between open land, fresh air and health came to the fore whilst the 'royal emphasis' diminished.

The beneficial effects of a feeling of well-being experienced by the populace through the parks should, according to the Committee, be spread more evenly across London. Land owned either by the Crown or the Duchy of Cornwall was sought for public open spaces across London and other large cities. The benefits of these landscapes and the feeling of state generosity and national pride they engendered in the populace were considered a useful tool.[103] As well as public walks the committee recommended places for exercise and recreation for the humbler classes. Without this 'facillity for regulated amusement ... great mischief must arise'. It was felt that open places reserved for amusement would wean the humbler classes from drink, dog fights and boxing, and that relaxation for both rich and poor must be a spring to industry. A small admission charge to such areas was even suggested, to defray costs, perhaps in recognition of the huge amount of public funds that had been spent on the works in the royal parks.

In many ways the debates around public open spaces in the metropolis have come full circle to the views expressed about the Foundling Hospital in chapter 1. Here Decimus was able to galvanise those living on the borders of the parks to contribute to their improvements. It was almost as if the parks were considered as a variation of the garden square by these residents. The royal parks also demonstrate the subtle fine tuning of the urban landscape to connect with or to emphasise buildings or monuments of national significance. The self-conscious way in which this was achieved through dialogue between the architect, the Office of Woods and the public indicates a growing awareness of the potency of the urban landscape and the resulting rural urbanism made a substantial impact on the re-imaging of London. The political 'smoothing and levelling' of the landscape had taken on a new significance.

1 George IV had decided to vacate Carlton House in favour of Buckingham Palace in 1825. The Act of Parliament authorising the demolition of Carlton House and placing the redevelopment of the site and surrounding area in the hands of the Commissioners of Woods was passed in 1826 (3 Geo. IV, c. 7).

2 See Summerson, *The Life and Work of John Nash*, pp. 166–9.

3 There were strong similarties between Nash's plan for St James's and the original Regent's Park project which included plans for a royal palace as a focal point for the design.

4 At the end of the eighteenth century the interpretation and meaning of landscape was discussed at length by the Rev. William Gilpin, Uvedale Price and Richard Payne Knight. Some of their works are considered later in this chapter.

5 This had been the case during the construction of Regent Street (see chapter 3).

6 This phenomenon is discussed in L. Colley, *Britons: Forging the Nation, 1707–1837*, New Haven and London, Yale University Press, 1992.

7 For a fuller discussion of the ways in which the middle and upper classes were taught to view the landscape see M. Andrews, 'A Picturesque Template: The Tourists and their Guidebooks', in Arnold (ed.), *The Picturesque in Late Georgian England*, pp. 3–10.

8 1833 Report (448) xv.

9 A discussion of changing attitudes towards the meaning of the term 'picturesque' can be found in the editors' introduction, S. Copley and P. Garside (eds), *The Politics of the Picturesque*, Cambridge, Cambridge University Press, 1994, pp. 1–12.

10 On this point see W. Hipple, *The Beautiful, the Sublime and the Picturesque in Eighteenth-Century British Aesthetic Theory*, Carbondale, Ill., Southern Illinois University Press, 1957, Section 2, esp. pp. 185–284.

11 W. Gilpin, *Three Essays: On Picturesque Beauty; On Picturesque Travel; and, On Sketching Landscape: to which is added a Poem on Landscape Painting*, London, 1792.

12 See E. Burke, *An Analytical Enquiry into the Origin of our Ideas of the Sublime and the Beautiful*, London, 1757, esp. parts 2 and 3.

13 Price published follow-on volumes to his *Essay on the Picturesque*, (1792) as *Essays on the Picturesque*, London, 1794. This quotation appears in vol. 1, p. 39.

14 The controversy between Price, Payne Knight and Repton over Capability Brown and other issues concerning the picturesque is discussed in Hipple, *The Beautiful, the Sublime and the Picturesque*, esp. chs 15, 16 and 17.

15 Letter of 1794 from Repton to Uvedale Price Esq. London, in J. C. Loudon, *The Landscape Gardening and Landscape Architecture of the late Humphry Repton Esq. being his entire works on these subjects*, London, 1840, p. 106.

16 This is evident in Loudon, *The Landscape Gardening and Landscape Architecture of the late Humphry Repton Esq.*

17 J. C. Loudon, *Encyclopaedia of Gardening*, 1822, book 4, chs 1–5, 'On the

Principles of Landscape Gardening', pp. 1150–98.

18 Ibid., p. 1151.

19 Ibid.

20 This is seen in the added security afforded to Londoners in the development of what became Trafalgar Square and the construction of Regent Street (see chapter 3). For a fuller discussion see also D. Arnold, 'Rationality, Safety and Power: The Street Planning of Later Georgian London', *The Georgian Group Journal*, London, 1995, pp. 37–50, 132–3.

21 See, for example, Appendix B.

22 Cres 8/15.

23 Ibid.

24 Cres 8/14 f 111.

25 Cres 8/14 ff 150–6.

26 Cres 8/14 ff 150–6.

27 Cres 8/14 f 184.

28 Cres 8/14 f 193.

29 Cres 8/14 f 150.

30 Mollet later wrote *Le Jardin de Plaisir*, Paris, 1651.

31 Reference is made to the opening of the park to the public to celebrate the National Jubilee in 1814 in T29/222.

32 The Treaty of Paris was signed on 30 May 1814, and it was believed Napoleon had been defeated.

33 There were many lavish events, some organised by George IV, to celebrate the National Jubilee. Nash was involved in the arrangements for the very extravagant private celebrations at Carlton House, and he designed a Chinese bridge and pagoda for St James's Park which stood until the 1820s. Nash's work is discussed in Summerson, *John Nash*, pp. 97–9. The celebrations for the National Jubilee are outlined in C. Fox (ed.), *London – World City 1800–1840*, New Haven and London, Yale University Press, 1992, pp. 247–8.

34 Summerson, *The Life and Work of John Nash*, p. 169.

35 Cres 8/20 and Cres 8/24. Burton worked with all three later in his career: Nesfield at Grimstone, Hooker at Kew 1843/4 and Aiton at the Botanic Gardens.

36 Cres 8/14 ff 454–455.

37 Cres 8/15 f 44 (30 December 1824). This was agreed on 16 February the following year.

38 Cres 8/15 f 343. The estimated cost was £1,082 12s. 10½d.

39 By then the costs were calculated at: Lodges £6,366 10s. 4d., Architect £366 10s. 10d., Clerk of Works £88 1s. 6d., giving a total of £6,821 2s. 8d. Cottam and Williams were the contractors for erecting the gates. On 29 January 1829 the Treasury asked Burton to account for the overspend (Cres 8/17 f 7).

40 Arbuthnot and Adams had originally suggested a figure of around £2,000 (Cres 8/14 ff 454–455).

41 Cres 8/17 f 19.

42 Cres 8/14 ff 454–455.

43 Cres 8/17 f 30.

44 Cres 8/14 ff 150–156.

45 Cres 8/14 f 150, 26 July 1824; estimate from McAdam, £3,412 7s.

46 Cres 2/637.

47 Cres 8/15 f 200.

48 Cres 8/14 ff 454–455.

49 PRO, MPE 754. The designs for the Hyde Park Screen and Green Park Arch are in the Victoria and Albert Museum, D1299–1907 and E2334–1910 149a respectively. All three designs are dated 20 July 1825.

50 PRO, MPE 794, July 1827, comprises a book of designs and specifications for the Bayswater Road entrance lodge.

51 In 1828 the Duke of Wellington, on becoming Prime Minister, put a moratorium on all Crown building projects. This was largely a reaction to the huge sums being spent on Buckingham Palace but other developments were also halted. See *HKW*, pp. 157–78.

52 Cres 8/17 f 52, 16 February 1829.

53 Cres 8/17 f 63, 27 February 1829.

54 Cres 8/16 f 69.

55 Ibid.

56 PRO, MPE 1250, Design for a Fountain in Green Park, March 1827.

57 Cres 8/16 f 71.

58 Ibid.

59 BUD/1/1/1.

60 Croker was MP for Yarmouth Isle of Wight and a close friend of Burton who did much to promote his career. He had been involved with the erection of monuments to Nelson in Norfolk and Dublin. He was part of the George IV–Marquess of Hertford set and may have secured Burton commissions through these connections. He was one of the founders of the Athenaeum Club, designed by Burton 1827–30.

61 Cres 8/16 f 71. See Appendix B.

62 This is outlined in *HKW*, pp. 268–71, 273–5.

63 Cres 8/16 f 73, 28 August 1827.

64 PRO, MPE 769.

65 Cres 8/18 f 271.

66 BUD/1/1/5.

67 Cres 8/18 f 271. See Appendix.

68 BUD/1/1/15, 13 January 1831.

69 Expenditure rose from £1,394 3s. 1d. to £2,037 13s. 1d. (Cres 8/18 f 271).

70 This was at a cost of £1,027 (Cres 8/18 f 443).

71 Soane's New State Paper Office was constructed on Duke Street 1830–34. See *HKW*, pp. 567–70.

72 According to H. Colvin, *A Biographical Dictionary of Architects*, 3rd edn, London and New Haven, Yale University Press, 1995, p. 130, Blore's reputation as 'the cheap architect' secured him the commission to finish off Nash's work between 1832 and 1837.

73 Cres 2/534.

74 Cres 8/19 f 92.

75 BUD/1/1/5, 13 January 1831. Burton stated that he had already been called upon to provide a design for the new entrance with one gate to Bird Cage Walk and one to the park.

76 Cres 8/19 f 92.

77 Ibid.

78 Ibid. The old gates and lodge were to be taken down and the materials sold to help fund the work.

79 Cres 8/19 ff 319–20.

80 Cres 8/20 ff 259–61.

81 Cres 8/20 f 35.

82 Ibid.

83 Cres 8/20 ff 259–60.

84 Ibid.

85 Cres 8/20 f 261.

86 Cres 8/20 f 263. Burton was to act as arbiter in deciding how the respective parties should contribute to the works.

87 Cres 8/20 f 261.

88 Cres 8/20 ff 263–6.

89 The two plans by Burton relate to this project but are dated after the other documentary evidence.

90 PRO, MPE 958, 6 June 1838.

91 PRO, MPE 809, 12 February 1839.

92 Cres 8/20 f 266. See Appendix E.

93 Cres 8/20 f 364.

94 Cres 8/20 f 358.

95 Cres 8/21 f 360 (12 August 1836): 1,346 feet of wrought iron railings at a cost of £874 18s.; 1,400 feet of stone curb at £350; Division fence including stone plinth at a cost of £514 10s. £480 was estimated for laying out and planting the pleasure ground and forming new paths and drains.

96 Cres 8/21 f 383.

97 As usual, alternatives of varying cost and complexity were provided. Design No. 3 was chosen at a total cost of £861.

98 Cres 8/21 f 423.

99 Cres 8/22 f 12.

100 On this point see Cannadine, 'The Context, Performance and Meaning of Ritual', pp. 101–64.

101 See Soane, *Designs for Public and Private Buildings*.

102 1833 Report, p. 5.

103 Ibid., p. 8.

Appendices

The financial framework of Burton's payments

Payments to Burton do not appear to have followed the system in operation at the Office of Works of a commission of usually 3 or 5 per cent as seen in Burton's construction of a new Parliamentary Mews.[1] Instead a more complicated system was in operation as outlined in a letter to the Treasury from Lowther, Dacres Adams and Dawkins in the Office of Woods of 25 July 1829 giving the total expenditure for the work in Hyde, St James's and Green Parks, and in a letter to the Treasury from Lowther and Dawkins on 26 November of that year stating the sundry payments made in 1828. The payments to Burton are as follows:

Roads

1825

Plan for laying out Roads in Hyde Park – a Plan of the whole Park shewing the Improvements – 4 drawings of the line of the Road between Grosvenor Street, and Hyde Park Corner, and other explanatory Drawings &tc £100

Travelling Expenses to Windsor and Strathfieldsay to consult with Mr Arbuthnot and Sir William Knighton on the same £10 10s.

Fencing

1826

Commission £3 6s. 6d.[2]

Lodges and Gates at Cumberland, Grosvenor and Stanhope Streets

1825

Commission for Designing and Superintending the erection of the above Lodges and Gates £366 10s. 10d.

1826

Two separate payments of £61 6s. 2d., and £118 10s. 6d. were made for 'Professional Services'

Burton was also paid commission of 6s. 6d. on work carried out by Messrs Bennet and Hunt amounting to £6 12s. 8d.

1828

Professional Services 7s. 10d.

Facade and Lodge at Hyde Park Corner, with Ornamental Gates, Iron Railing &tc

1826
> Professional Services £280 16s.

1828
> Professional Services £24 17s.

Lighting

1826
> Burton was paid commission of £3 5s. 6d. on James Deirlle's work on the lighting at Cumberland Gate amounting to £65 10s. 10d.

Lodges and Gateways at the Entrance into the Green Park, at the top of Constitution Hill

1826
> For professional Services relating to these Lodges and Gateways, and the Facade Entrance into Hyde Park (part of £1,078 6s. 8d.) £515 18s.

1827
> For professional Services relating to these (works cited as paid for that year) and other Works £1,185 2s. 7d.

1828
> For professional Services £215 14s. 2d.

The statement of accounts is concluded by

> Architects Commission on Bills remaining unpaid £319 7s. 4d.[3]

Burton is the only architect mentioned in the accounts and correspondence concerning the works in the parks.[4] Through the nature of the payments he can be attributed with overall responsibility for the designs, for overseeing the construction of the new gates and lodges and for the changes in the layout of the parks and their alignment at Hyde Park Corner. Burton benefited from two separate methods of payment. The method established in the Office of Works of an architect charging commission for works carried out by workmen under his supervision. Here Burton charged the higher rate of 5 per cent. The payments for 'Professional Services' are less conventional and considerably higher in value than the usual architect's commission. The payments to Burton in 1826 for the lodges and gateway (that is, Green Park Arch) into Green Park and the Facade Entrance into Hyde Park (that is, Hyde Park Screen) were around 10 per cent of the cost of works executed (that is, £5,011 15s.). In the following year payments made for the same were of a similar proportion (that is, the total sum of works executed was £12,615 1s. 3¼d.). These are substantial sums of money and they underline the importance of Burton's role in the whole of the works on the royal parks. More significantly, these large payments in relation to the development of Hyde Park Corner show Burton to be a very important contributor to the King's overall development of a royal London and enjoying a level of privilege in his renumeration and status which was akin to that experienced by John Nash. Moreover, the autonomy enjoyed by Burton in the design and execution of his project was greater than that of Nash in the work at Regent's Park and Regent Street which relied on private money and the ability or willingness of the builders and speculative developers to invest in and adhere to his approved designs. In contrast to Nash, Burton had a steady flow of funding and was out of the scrutinising gaze of the Treasury, being responsible only to the Fife House Committee and ultimately to the monarch for his designs.

NOTES

1   Cres 8/15 f 390 cites Burton as architect receiving a commission of 3 per cent.

2   This was on the repair work carried out that year which amounted to nearly £464 (Cres 8/17 f 209). This level of commission is derisory. But the ledger is ambiguous and the sum may refer only to commission on painting work carried out on the fences by Messrs Bennett and Hunt, Burton's usual firm of builders, which amounted to £66 7s. 6d. which would imply the usual 5 per cent commission for work overseen by an architect.

3   Cres 8/17 ff 200–17 and ff 324–7.

4   The only exception to this is Mr Rennie who received the commission to build the bridge over the Serpentine. He was selected by the Treasury as he was 'a very competent person for the undertaking' (1828 Report, p 25).

B   Cres 8/16 f 71

Fountain constructed in marble and artificial
   stone or terracotta   £2,100

Base of steps and lower basin of granite including
   brickwork and foundation of Yorkshire
   stone landing   £2,800

For removal and refixing of cast iron stand pipe –
   including every expense in removing and
   relaying main pipes &tc   £350

                                    £5,250

Incidentals 10 per cent

                                    £525

                         Total   £5,775

Cres 8/18 f 271

Design and Estimate marked A

for alteration of the road near the archway only as is necessary
to form the intended entrance at the top of Constitution Hill,
including the expense of altering the iron railing and so much of
the king's garden wall as must be taken down and replaced
amounting to

£1,394 3s. 1d.

Design and Estimate B

including the whole of the works comprized in the plan A and
extension of that design – removing the present road which is
very close to the intended private apartments of the palace, to
give more space to premises on that side and avoid noise, dust
&tc

£1,993 15s. 4d.

Design and Estimate C

A & B and the formation of an entire new line of road from the
archway to the Mall by which Mr Burton is of the opinion the
handsomest effect would be produced

£2,681 7s. 10d.

D   Cres 8/20 f 261

Estimates according to plan No 1

New railing foot gates and foundation on
    south side of Bird Cage Walk from
    Storey's Gate to barrack ground
    1,300 linear feet   £1,390 8s. 0d.

Taking up and setting back present railing
    and foundations on north side of Bird
    Cage Walk to new line from Buckingham
    Gate to proposed new building
    2,316 linear feet   £853 6s. 6d.

New footpath and altering line of road
    lamps &tc   £794 13s.

                                  £3,038 7s. 6d.

New lodge according to design No. 2   £900

Piers, iron gates to garden &tc   £370

                                £1,270 7s. 6d.

                  Total   £4,308

Cres 8/20 f 266

E

Burton's plans and estimates were:

Plan No 1

new railing, foot gates and foundations
to south side of Bird Cage Walk from
Storeys Gate to the Barrack Grounds   £1,390 8s. 0d.

1,300 linear feet

Taking and setting back present railing
foundations on the north side of Bird
cage Walk to the new line from
Buckingham Gate to proposed new lodge   £855 6s. 6d.

12,316 linear feet

£2,245 14s. 6d.

Trenching and planting border 15 feet wide   £165

new footpath and altering the line of the
road lamps   £794 13s.

Improving the Dartmouth Steps or obtaining
and forming new entrance west of Dartmouth
house   £330

£3,533 7s. 6d.

Estimate according to plan No. 2

Amount from No. 1   £3,533 7s. 6d.

Facade wall with Bath Stone cornice, blocking
and pier caps   £1,485

if above formed with stucco and not stone
(i.e. details) price reduced by   £350

£5,018 7s. 6d.

New Lodge according to the design submitted
August 1833   £1,200

for piers and iron gates &tc to garden   £350

£1,570

or

lodge according to second design gates as before   £900

£370

£1,270

New lamps gates railings across the avenue to
 horseguards   £250

Refixing present railing of park garden to the
 new line from opposite Horse guards to the
 new lodge   £396 11s.

Altering road, making good turf &c   £100

£746 11s.

500 feet of railing (some new) to enclose
 shrubbery at the back of Duke Street houses   £497 4s.

New gateway at Storey's Gate according to enclosed
 design including ornamental iron gate railings
 and lamps   £750

Select bibliography

CONTEMPORARY SOURCES

Andrews, I., *London Bridge and No New Taxes*, London, 1823

Anon., *The Ambulator*, London, 1811

Burke, E., *An Analytical Enquiry into the Origin of our Ideas of the Sublime and the Beautiful*, London, 1757

Colman, H., *European Life and Manners in Familiar Letters to Friends*, 2 vols, Boston and London, 1850

Dobie, R., *The History of the United Parishes of St Giles in the Fields and St George Bloomsbury*, London, 1829

Eden, F. M. (Sir), *Porto-bello or a Plan for the improvement of the Port and City of London*, London, 1798

Gilpin, W., *Three Essays: On Picturesque Beauty; On Picturesque Travel; and On Sketching Landscape: to which is added a Poem on Landscape Painting*, London, 1792

Hunter, H. (Revd), *The History of London and its Environs*, 2 vols, London, 1811

Jones, R. L., *Reminiscences of the Public Life of Richard Lambert Jones Esq.*, London, privately printed, 1863

Loudon, J. C., *Encyclopaedia of Gardening*, London, 1822

Loudon, J. C., *The Landscape Gardening and Landscape Architecture of the late Humphry Repton Esq. being his entire works on these subjects*, London, 1840

Percy, S. and R. Percy, *The Percy Histories or Interesting memories of the rise, progress and presentation of all the capitals of Europe*, 3 vols, London, 1823

Repton, H., *The Picture of London*, 3rd edn, London, 1815

Robinson, H. C., *Diary*, ed. T. Sadler, London, 1872

Silliman, B., *A Journal of Travels in England, Holland and Scotland and of two passages over the Atlantic in the years 1805–1806*, 3 vols., New Haven, The Trustees of Yale College, 1820

Smollett, T., *The Expedition of Humphry Clinker*, London, 1771

Soane, J., *Designs for Public and Private Buildings*, London, 1828

Young, A., *A Six Weeks Tour through the Southern Counties of England and Wales*, London, 1768

SECONDARY SOURCES

Books

Andrews, M., *The Search for the Picturesque*, Aldershot, Scolar Press, 1989

Arnold, D., *Belov'd by Ev'ry Muse: Richard Boyle 3rd Earl of Burlington and 4th Earl of Cork (1694–1753)*, London, Georgian Group, 1994

Arnold, D. (ed.), *The Picturesque in Late Georgian England*, Papers given at the Georgian Group Symposium 1994, London, Georgian Group, 1995

Arnold, D., *Re-presenting the Metropolis: Architecture, Urban Experience and Social Life in London 1800–1840*, Aldershot, Ashgate, 2000

Arnold, D., *The Georgian Country House: Architecture, Landscape and Society*, 2nd edn, Stroud, Sutton, 2003

Arnold, D. (ed.), *Cultural Identities and the Aesthetics of Britishness*, Manchester, Manchester University Press, 2004

Arnold, D. and A. Ballantyne (eds), *Architecture in Experience*, London, Routledge, 2004

Ballantyne, A., *Architecture, Landscape and Liberty: Richard Payne-Knight and the Picturesque*, Cambridge, Cambridge University Press, 1997

Barker, F. and R. Hyde, *London As It Might Have Been*, London, John Murray, 1982

Beckett, J. V., *The Aristocracy in England 1660–1914*, Oxford, Clarendon Press, 1986

de Beer, E. S. (ed.), *John Evelyn: London Revived*, Oxford, Clarendon Press, 1938

Colley, L., *Britons: Forging the Nation, 1707–1837*, New Haven and London, Yale University Press, 1992

Copley, S. and Garside P. (eds), *The Politics of the Picturesque*, Cambridge, Cambridge University Press, 1994

Daniels, S. and D. Cosgrove, *The Iconography of Landscape*, Cambridge, Cambridge University Press, 1988

Davis, M. T. (ed.), *The London Corresponding Society 1792–1799*, 6 vols, London, Pickering and Chatto, 2002

Davis, T., *John Nash: The Prince Regent's Architect*, London, Studio, 1966

Foucault, M., *Discipline and Punish: The Birth of the Prison*, trans. Alan Sheridan (1977), Harmondsworth, Penguin, 1991

Fox, C. (ed.), *London – World City 1800–1840*, New Haven and London, Yale University Press, 1992

Habakkuk, H. A., *Marriage, Debt and the Estate System: English Landownership 1650–1950*, Oxford, Clarendon Press, 1994

Hipple, W., *The Beautiful, the Sublime and the Picturesque in Eighteenth-Century British Aesthetic Theory*, Carbondale, Ill., Southern Illinois University Press, 1957

Hobhouse, H., *A History of Regent Street*, London, Macdonald and Jane's in association with Queen Anne Press, 1975

Hobsbawn, E. and P. Ranger (eds), *The Invention of Tradition*, Cambridge, Cambridge University Press, 1983

Jeffery, S., *The Mansion House*, Sussex ,Corporation of London and Phillimore and Co., 1993

Langford, P., *A Polite People*, Oxford, Oxford University Press, 1989

Liscombe, R. W., *William Wilkins 1778–1839*, Cambridge, Cambridge University Press, 1980

McKellar, E., *The Birth of Modern London*, Manchester, Manchester University Press, 1999

Mace, R., *Trafalgar Square: Emblem of Empire*, London, Lawrence and Wishart, 1976

Mingay, G. E., *English Landed Society in the Eighteenth Century*, London, Routledge, 1963

Olsen, D. J., *Town Planning in London: The Eighteenth and Nineteenth Centuries*, 2nd edn, New Haven and London, Yale University Press, 1964

Picon, A., *French Architects and Engineers in the Age of Enlightenment*, Cambridge, Cambridge University Press, 1992

du Prey, P. de la R., *Sir John Soane the Making of an Architect*, Chicago and London, University of Chicago Press, 1982

Rasmussen, S. E., *London, the Unique City*, Cambridge, Mass., MIT, 1982

Samuel, E. C., *The Villas in Regent's Park and their Residents*, London, Bedford College, 1959

Saunders, A., *Regent's Park from 1086 to the Present Day*, 2nd edn, London, Bedford College, 1981

Saunders, A. (ed.), *The Royal Exchange*, London Topographical Society publication no. 152, London, 1997

Scherren, H., *The Zoological Society of London*, London, 1905

Summerson, J., *Georgian London*, Harmondsworth, Peregrine, 1947

Summerson, J., *John Nash: Architect to King George IV*, 2nd edn, London, Allen and Unwin, 1949

Summerson, J., *The Life and Work of John Nash Architect*, London and Cambridge, Mass., MIT Press, 1980

Thompson, F. M. L., *English Landed Society in the Nineteenth Century*, London, Routledge, 1963

Tinniswood, A., *A History of Country House Visiting*, Oxford and London, Blackwell and the National Trust, 1989

Williamson, T., *Polite Landscapes: Gardens and Society in Eighteenth-Century England*, Stroud, Sutton, 1995

Yarrington, A., *The Commemoration of the Hero 1800–1864: Monuments to the British Victors of the Napoleonic Wars*, New York and London, Garland, 1988

Articles

Arnold, D., 'The Arch at Constitution Hill: A New Axis for London', *Apollo*, 138 (379) (Sept. 1993), pp. 129–33

Arnold, D., 'Rationality, Safety and Power: The Street Planning of Later Georgian London', *Georgian Group Journal* (1995), pp. 37–50

Arnold, D., 'London Bridge and its Symbolic Identity in the Regency Metropolis: The dialectic of Civic and National Pride', *Art History*, 22: (1999), pp. 545–66

Cannadine, D., 'The Landowner as Millionaire: The Finances of the Dukes of Devonshire, c. 1800 – c. 1926', *Agricultural History Review*, (1997), pp. 77–97

Cooper, N., 'The Myth of Cottage Life', *Country Life*, 141 (1967), pp. 1290–3

Crook, J. M., 'The Villas in Regent's Park', pts 1 and 2, *Country Life*, 143 (1968), pp. 22–5; 84–7

Fussell, G. E. and C. Goodman, 'The Housing of the Rural Population in the Eighteenth Century', *Economic History Review*, 2 (1930–33), pp. 63–90

Honour, H., 'The Regent's Park Colosseum', *Country Life*, 2nd Jan. 1953

Meynell, G., 'The Royal Botanic Society's Gardens, Regent's Park', *London Journal*, 6:2 (1980)

Stevenson, J., 'The London "Crimp" Riots of 1774', *International Review of Social History*, 16 (1971), pp. 40–58

Stillman, D., 'Death Defied and Honor Upheld: The Mausoleum in Neo-Classical England', *Art Quarterly*, new series, 1:3 (1978), pp. 175–213

Stroud, D., 'Hyde Park Corner', *Architectural Review*, 106 (1949), pp. 79–97

Index